D0833445

Thresholds between Philosophy and Psychoanalysis

The Philadelphia Association is always linked with the name of R.D. Laing, one of its founders, but very little is known about its unorthodox contribution to the development of psychoanalysis. Founded in 1965, it took as its aim the relief of mental illness of all descriptions, in particular schizophrenia. At its inception it was a focus for people, with a diversity of backgrounds and interests, concerned with 'mental illness' and how society defines it. Its members – who included psychoanalysts, psychiatrists and artists – developed a philosophical critique of psychoanalysis grounded in phenomenology, and an 'anti-psychiatry' critique of the institutional treatment of the mentally ill. They favoured the setting up of therapeutic community households of which the best known was Kingsley Hall. The PA was then very much part of the counter culture – it staged, for example, the famous Dialectics of Liberation Congress at London's Roundhouse in1967. The psychotherapists who currently belong to the Philadelphia Association continue to work with community households and to offer a psychotherapy training.

Here the authors share their innovative and distinctive approach on a number of interrelated themes: the therapeutic community and different ways it can be understood; work with deeply regressed patients; the concept of identity in a social context; the debate between Lacan and Derrida on Poe's 'The Purloined Letter'; the phenomenology of knowledge and transference and authority. Together, they offer a cogent critique of many psychiatric and psychoanalytic assumptions.

The contributors are Robin Cooper, Joseph Friedman, Steven Gans, John Heaton, Chris Oakley, Haya Oakley and Paul Zeal. They are all psychotherapists and members of the Philadelphia Association.

Thresholds between Philosophy and Psychoanalysis

Papers from the Philadelphia Association

ROBIN COOPER
JOSEPH FRIEDMAN
STEVEN GANS
J.M. HEATON
CHRIS OAKLEY
HAYA OAKLEY
PAUL ZEAL

'an association in which the free development of each
is the condition of the free development of all'

Free Association Books / London / 1989

First published in Great Britain 1989 by
Free Association Books
26 Freegrove Road
London N7 9RQ

British Library Cataloguing in Publication Data

Cooper, Robin
  Thresholds between philosophy and
  psychoanalysis: papers from the Philadelphia
  Association
  1. Psychoanalysis
  I. Title   II. Philadelphia Association
  150.19'5

  ISBN 1-85343-041-2

Typeset by MC Typeset Ltd, Gillingham, Kent.

Printed and bound in Great Britain by
Short Run Press Ltd, Exeter

CONTENTS

PREFACE

This book consists of contributions from some of the current members of the Philadelphia Association. It appears in its final form with inevitable compromises, but without having strayed too far from our original intention.

Robin Cooper co-ordinated the production of the book. He would like to extend his thanks, on behalf of all the contributors, to Ann Scott of Free Association Books, for her championing of the project from the start, for her editorial acumen, and particularly for her contribution to the historical introduction 'Beginnings', for it was with her help that a patchwork became a coherent chapter.

We should also like to take this opportunity to express our deep indebtedness to the Golden Gate Foundation, whose generosity in supporting our work has helped open up the next chapter of our story. Thanks finally are due to Dr Leon Redler for his provocative criticism, to associate members and students, and to our wider network, who over the years have contributed in many different ways to the conviviality out of which this book has arisen.

Introducing an incomplete project

CHRIS OAKLEY

ONE OF THE functions of an introduction is to show how one might proceed; to suggest a compelling line of approach. Thinking about the Philadelphia Association, however, one comes up against a persistent indirectness. What unfolds is a lattice-work of complicated intersections that quite purposefully avoids the presentation of a coherent whole, a fixity of identity, or a finished product. Right at the outset, then, is a positioning of a warning sign, for if what is longed for is a firm conceptual model, disappointment is guaranteed.

The Philadelphia Association is what? A concept? A practice? A phase? A style? What are its forms, its effects, indeed where does it stand? What follows is hardly a conventional means of presenting a psychoanalytic organization, although the Philadelphia Association is undeniably, although not exclusively, one. It is neither an account of our history, nor is it an attempt to set out a consistent, unified account of our principles and practices. The institution of psychoanalysis is divided into numerous and often conflicting national and international organizations, and is a complex conglomerate of schools, societies, schisms and splinter groups. Indeed like many others we have our offices, policies, traditions, mode of administration, methods of training and graduation, and no doubt an analytic style if not technique. It would be possible, as with other psychoanalytic organizations, to become enmeshed in the 'vieux jeu' of struggling for superiority over the dogmatic ownership of 'true psychoanalysis'. Such struggles are habitually carried out either by an adherence to a somewhat spurious Freudian legacy, or by an attempt to advance or improve Freud's ideas in the direction that it is assumed he would have taken were he to have lived longer. That is, one can take up the position of a specific way station in the 'Freudian beyond'. Alternatively we could involve

1

ourselves in the traditional psychoanalytic method of designating our position through affiliation or discipleship, such as Kleinian or Lacanian. There is the attendant problematic of authority resting on such officializing representational conceit, and of the difficulties of thinking for oneself.

Difficulties are inherent in speaking of the psychoanalytic movement or tradition. There is the specific difficulty of homogenization, of glossing over the differences that are at play within the field; even this term, the field, suggests enclosure and appropriation. Clearly, though, it is possible to distinguish an intellectual tradition that prevails in much of Europe in contrast to that in the British Isles. For example, whilst it has recently been entirely appropriate to speak of a 'world of French psychoanalytic culture' (Turkle, 1979), this has hardly been the case here in England. In France and Italy, for example, an interest in the arts and the intellectual, which would be unthinkable without an interest in psychoanalysis, has an automatic proximity to the subversive and the avant-garde.

What appears to have happened in Britain is that much of the subversive edge of psychoanalysis has become diluted. Initially Freud and psychoanalysis were seen as marginal, quite beyond any coincidence with good sense. But what was once excessive, outrageous, scandalous even, has become commonplace. Further, it is generally assumed that there is an association of psychoanalysis with the establishment, as represented by the Institute of Psycho-Analysis and the International Psychoanalytical Association. Indeed there is the somewhat stagnant convention that the monopoly on the name psychoanalysis belongs to them, and is justified in the name of policies on training. Far from the original dream of psychoanalysis combating the forces of false normativity, of conformity and its concern with respectability, we are witness to the upwelling of microsocieties within and outside establishment psychoanalysis, with their insistence on preservation of the species via segregation and subordination. Precisely because of this, we have no desire to be incorporated into the established institution and thus risk being drawn into its potentially restrictive and doctrinaire obligations. Equally we have no wish to be excluded by any who would seek to subdue or subordinate a sensitivity to difference without a collapse into oppositionality. Rather our desire is to

2

maintain a scepticism in the face of autonomous spheres or separate fields of expertise. Either incorporation or exclusion would give rise to the repression of our discourse. So whilst being neither inside nor outside 'proper' psychoanalysis, we make no claim to a position of transcendence. We merely seek to disclose the increasingly fertile ferment that plays both within and across the boundaries of each of the disciplines of philosophy and psychoanalysis.

The papers that comprise this book stem from a collaboration between a number of colleagues within the Philadelphia Association. Whilst 'Beginnings' does deal with our history, the book deliberately attempts not to synthesize or summarize the work of our small organization. Indeed we seek to endorse a critique of representation, whilst acknowledging that one can never be entirely outside it.

One can never be entirely outside representation because we are subjected to it as one of the basic principles of the cultural imperative of our age. Culture, a structure of the unconscious that forms and gives shape to our lives, demands that we identify ourselves as this rather than that. The lure of identity and of being able to identify is generated by the implicit system of evaluation in language, to which we are all subject. This 'code' or system of arrangement, which begins with the *Fort/Da* does not operate neutrally. (*Fort/Da* refers to Freud's account, in *Beyond the Pleasure Principle* (1920), of watching his grandson playing with a cotton-reel toy. This was alternately thrown away, accompanied by a sound approximating to *fort*: gone, and then pulled back with the sound *da*: there. It is taken to be an account of our birth into language, as instanced by the capacity to symbolize presence and absence, and marks the passage to a more complex relation to the world.) There is always a plus or minus play of opposition: presence is good, absence is bad (or vice versa). It is in this way that what is principally an arrangement has the appearance of a founding value. Consequently, if we fail to comply by not re-presenting ourselves in the form of a sealed identity we risk the accusation, latent within our culture, of disingenuousness, of not playing the game, of 'bad form'.

Also set within the prevailing discourse is the issue of logocentrism: the idea of a fixed, identifiable point of reference around which all else will converge. Psychoanalysis is habitually approached, both by its practitioners and as a discursive order, as focusing or centring on an individual. It is from his or her viewpoint that all relationships will be constructed or reconstructed. Our aim would be to decentre this by evoking the place of the between, thus dissolving the logic of inner and outer. It is a function of human beings' alienation, of our subordination to the cultural hegemony of dividing and disconnecting and simultaneously creating imaginary unities, that there arises the fallacy of such 'inner structures'. To say this is not to dismiss psychoanalytic accounts of psychic realities as irrelevant, but rather to situate these as interpersonal rather than as intrapsychic. As an illustration, we would understand 'defence mechanisms' as occurring in what goes on between us, in language, rather than inside one or other or both. Equally, it would be fallacious to understand the unconscious as an entity located inside us; rather, we are in unconsciousness. But even the use of the term 'in' is crudely problematic, since there is neither an inside nor an outside to language. Considerable difficulties stem from the assumption of an outside, an unmoved being, a locus of absolute truth. It is this assumption that reinstalls a system of enclosure, habitually taking the form of a circle, with the inevitable centre in the middle. It is this idea of the centre which dominates discourse.

The fundamental human relation (I/Thou) cannot be reduced to two centres exchanging signals or communications with each other, for there is something 'other' than this. The relation, structured by language, can never form an uninterrupted circle (the fiction of the unity of presence). In an imaginary sense it can be drawn around 'us' (I/Thou); can be that which ties or binds us together (as in the family circle); and that which distinguishes us, as speaking beings, from the rest. There will always be a supplement, however, a remainder: that which fails to be completely enclosed by any account or signification. Any 'sphere' or body of knowledge – indeed any institution – is informed by this metaphor of the circle, with the inherent complication of a centre and periphery, of boundaries, of inside and outside. They incline inexorably towards the cul-de-sac of enclosure, the closed totalizing system.

It is true that the practice of psychoanalysis involves allowing one's attention to float, and being satisfied with a partial understanding; nevertheless at the core of psychoanalytic thinking a tendency towards privileging systematic explanations can be discerned. Anything that cannot be woven into a universalizable system – any irreducible otherness – will tend to be discarded in order to preserve a manifest consistency. One could be drawn into following the logic of the dialectic, that is, by taking up an antithetical stance. But this would potentially result in being stuck on the pin of the counterpoint, thus caught up in an imaginary (egotistical or adversarial) duality. The history of our organization has indeed been suffused with vestiges of revolt and reaction, of which the term 'anti-psychiatry' is probably the most well known. However, despite the attractions of anarchy and the avant-garde (which tend to sustain the ultimately Utopian falsehood of 'pure presence': the fiction that one could arrive, having pared away all defences, at a position of transcendence), it is precisely this counterpoint that ensnares one in a form of simplistic negation from which no genuine emancipation can emerge.

The machinery of the dialectic is ultimately totalizing, in that all will be subject to synthesis: for every concept there can be an anti-concept, so, following Derrida (1987; p.xxv: '*pli* means fold . . . The expression *ne pas faire pli* (literally, not to make a fold) means to be of no consequence'), we propose that our motif be that of the fold, where the supplement or remainder is tucked into the process of representation. But crucial to this motif is the idea that the supplement is unrepresentable. The fold can be seen as a deviation or as an interruption, a critical intervention thus decentring the dialectic so that one is left with no centre, nor any final destination or goal.

All the authors within this book have moved away from a classical Freudian frame of reference, but this is not to be equated with becoming unpsychoanalytic. Our project would be difficult to conceive without Continental theory, particularly existentialism, phenomenology, structuralism and their aftermath. But here there is the possibility of coming up against the problem of plurality and the tendency towards relativism: a position that all positions within the psychoanalytic community are now declared open and equal. We would recognize this view that 'Everything works' or, as some might put it, 'It's all up for grabs', as the inversion of a fatalistic belief, widely denied, that nothing really works, and ultimately only an instance of a despairing acquiescence in the face of the realization that the psychoanalytic establishment is dominant but dead. Dead in that psychoanalysis becomes a depository of faith, elaborated on occasions by pious scholasticism, congealing into absolute knowledge. Either such relativism or such wearisome dogmatism would be a distortion of our desire. It is not that we wish to give philosophy a privileged place, as that which defines other fields; but by returning it to the midst of psychoanalysis the promise of a revitalization of psychoanalysis emerges. The aim would be to make implicit assumptions as clear and as explicit as possible. After all, this has an extraordinary proximity to the thrust of psychoanalytic practice itself.

But why such emphasis on phenomenology? In an early stage of his career, Freud attended a series of lectures by the nineteenth-century philosopher, Brentano. Brentano's reformed philosophy gave psychology a central role and it was from Brentano that phenomenology received the decisive impulse for its emphasis on description rather than explanation. In the same audience was another student, Edmund Husserl, who was to become a seminal figure in the phenomenological movement. It is from such synchronicities that the trajectories of phenomenology and psychoanalysis have unfolded. Both share similar concerns or latencies: to have no other objective than to elucidate what is, to describe without the addition of judgements or imperatives, no more, no less. Of course, with psychoanalysis it is in the pursuit of this practice (which may involve the paradox that such value-free judgement is unrealizable) that healing occurs. 'Phenomenology brings to psychoanalysis categories and means of expression which it needs in order to be completely itself', whilst psychoanalysis 'brings material which provides substance to what phenomenology has said in general about the relations of man with the world and the interhuman bond' (Merleau-Ponty, 1969).

Sadly the prevalent tradition within psychoanalytic orthodoxy has been one of resistance towards philosophy. There has been a tendency within Anglo-American psychoanalysis to relegate philosophical concerns to the status of defence; or to the illusory search for systems underpinned by an assumption of final unity, seen as a betrayal of the Freudian enterprise. Of course, there are important exceptions to this: Bion's application of Plato and Kant to psychoanalysis is particularly prominent among them. However, as evidence of the scanty regard given to philosophical concerns let us take, as an illustration of tokenism, the almost legendary status of a comparatively short paper by the psychoanalyst Jim Home (1966), which suggested ways in which psychoanalysis was a theory of meaning rather than cause. The significance of this is not that the content of the paper is so exceptional, but rather that the paper itself constitutes an exception.

Of course a suspicion of philosophy hardly rests with psychoanalysis alone, for it is far more widespread than that. But our thesis is that to repress philosophy is merely to enable implicit assumptions to dominate, often accompanied by vestiges of dogmatism, and without being seriously interrogated. It would be wrong to claim uniqueness, but it remains a prevailing characteristic of the way of the Philadelphia Association, a way through phenomenology to thought, that we wish to open up a thoughtfulness about the interplay of difference. It is there that an exciting and productive intercourse occurs.

The themes in these essays are knotted around the erotic, community, institutions, identity, responsibility, knowledge, transference and authority. They allow neither for a satisfactory combination, nor for an easy separation. Whilst there is no standardized format, and it would be impossible to reduce the differences to a bland homogeneity, there is a sharing of basic concerns within a network of ideas. Perhaps it should be noted that none of this explicitly deals with truth, yet, as with psychoanalysis itself, that is precisely what we are after.

Psychoanalysis is frequently misunderstood as a causal theory, which explains psychological phenomena as a result of prior events, rather than placing emphasis on it as a theory of meaning (Rycroft, 1966). Now meaning is inexorably caught up in language, in discourse, and psychoanalysis is repeatedly referred to as 'the talking cure'. However, when a distillation of truth is based on language, we are obliged to acknowledge that truth cannot be contained by what we say. First, because, whatever we say, language will say what it wants. For the phenomenological conception of language sees language as a path rather than as a technique, or an 'instrument' for communication. Words transcend the people who 'use' them, so that in order to understand language (and indeed ourselves) we have to submit to it, and let 'it' speak. Second, because what is conveyed as truth, within the context of the human sciences, is ultimately opinion, stories amongst stories. These then are inevitably set in the context of prevailing social values, which are continuously framing and shaping the truth claims of any knowledge. 'Everything is literature' (Flower Mac-Cannell, 1986) and psychoanalysis appears to recognize as much with its convention of referring precisely 'to the literature'.

Chapter 1 of this book gives a short account of our history; inevitably partial, but one revealing the various concerns that inform our way. It is always difficult to deal adequately with what were crucial and often stormy separations, and it could be said that such situations are analogous to a multilayered cake. Any bite into it will taste simultaneously of a mixture of the personal, political, and theoretical. Bearing this in mind, there is no wish to play out the game of personal denunciation, but to underline the special and central role (see how difficult it is to avoid this term!) that R.D. Laing had in the unfolding of a small but significant subculture in Britain.

The idea of a post-war subculture characterized by 'pop, protest, art, "sick" (psychiatry/psychoanalysis), and poetry' coming together as 'the underground' has been chronicled by Jeff Nuttall (1968).

One crucial theme in this subculture went beyond a straightforward recognition of psychiatry's interference with individual liberty, or a dismantling of the fiction of medical neutrality, which could merely veil forms of political oppression. The direction was towards a more global social critique, via the motif of the schizophrenic's position in our society. This was exemplified in two ways: in Laing's polemic of the mad as the sane in an insane world; and in the idea that the psychotic experience was spiritually privileged. Despite repeated attempts to disalign himself from any claim that madness was superior to true sanity, Laing has persistently been represented as involved with a potentially harmful identification with the mad (a word etymologically linked to 'hurt'). This conferring of mythological status on both Laing and schizophrenia is linked with a tendency towards dissociation from the sadness, isolation and sheer tedium that characterize so many schizophrenic lives.

However, whilst being sympathetic to some of the anti-psychiatric position – for we cannot do justice to an understanding of man's being without reference to madness – what is in danger of being lost in dreams of an apocalyptic overthrow of psychiatric power is the critique of psychiatry's fundamental assumptions. This critique posits psychiatric theory as primarily based on the pejorative concept of madness as a lack: of integration, or of rationality, rather than recognizing it as a particular form of articulation in the world, albeit very different or 'other', and often notoriously difficult to understand. The aim of anti-psychiatry always was, and we are inheritors of this tradition, to purge all such normative, or psychiatric, values from psychoanalysis, and indeed from all our ways of dealing with people. Nothing prevents one from underlining the persistent likelihood of falling back on or collapsing into a framework of social norms.

A close examination of our history will reveal that, following Laing's inspiration, a primacy in the organization's endeavours has been the provision of asylum in the shape of community households. Thus it is no accident that the opening chapters are concerned with this practice. In chapter 2, Robin Cooper's delicate incorporation of Heideggerian phenomenology, with its emphasis on dwelling as what crucially distinguishes human being, opens up our relation to the tradition of the therapeutic communities. We begin in dwelling and where we stand will be limited to what we can or cannot stand; whilst what we can understand will inform how we hold, and what holds together, what we are able to be in touch with, and what is touched upon. However, the house-hold must stand, before any of this can become understandable, and for such projects to have any standing. A common misunderstanding in relation to these communities is to regard them as alternatives to mental hospitals, thus creating imaginary oppositionality. We are sympathetic to a critique of much of psychiatric practice, and wish that hospitals were indeed more hospitable, but it would be misleading to suggest that we are 'against' psychiatry any more than we are 'for' it. Rather we wish to raise questions about its philosophy.

In Chapter 3 Joe Friedman repudiates the modern myth of progress and mastery by a return to Greek philosophy, in order to show the phenomenological understanding inherent in the Homeric epics. The conviction that development in arts, technology or knowledge of any variety will inevitably lead to an improvement for mankind as a whole is being held with less confidence. This is hardly surprising when increased developments and discoveries within the techno-sciences (a term coined by the post-modernist Jean-François Lyotard (1986)) appear to be more of an aid (sic) than a hindrance to disease. (Take the destabilization of individuals and, on occasion, societies which can occur via the spread and development of antibiotics, as exemplified by the damaging intrusion into the tribal areas of the headwaters of the Amazon.) Friedman dismantles the privileged place given to technological rationality and the work ethic. With particular reference to the 'work' of our households in which no service is provided other than the principle of encouraging people to live their lives, he shows that this understanding of work is quite distinct from prevailing assumptions.

Within the psychiatric field, work is habitually thought to be that which can be done on something in somebody. We either do it for someone or do it to someone. One can recognize the aggressiveness that lurks in the activity of philanthropy; such work is quite distinct from an attentiveness to the things themselves. It is this attentiveness that is the hallmark of the sacred play space of therapy, whether individual or community. All therapy is crucially determined by structures of play, and its means are those of speech. 'Free association', or the wildness of intimacy, is what is potentially at play between the participants, but this is not to say that this is what is necessarily going on.

Chapter 4, Steven Gans's paper on the Lacan–Derrida debate, concerning Edgar Allan Poe's story, 'The Purloined Letter', is a prime illustration of the cross-fertilization that occurs when the boundaries of philosophy, psychoanalysis and literature are loosened. Lacan placed his seminar on 'The Purloined Letter' in pole position in the French edition of *Écrits*, and his reading of it designated the detective story as a parable for psychoanalysis. The story demonstrates that what is constitutive for the subject is the symbolic order, with particular reference to the social tie. It exemplifies the decisive orientation that we receive from the itinerary of the signifier. If we stick strictly to the letter, around which the Poe story turns, language is never a set of fixed, identical meanings. Any concept of the psyche as being the centre of man's truth is thus irretrievably dislodged. It is from this launching pad that Gans takes off into what he terms 'the vortex of Derridean deconstruction (hesitation)' to raise fundamental questions about psychoanalysis and philosophy. Such an essay may require several readings.

Interestingly enough, it was also Lacan who claimed that Plato's *Symposium* was one of the profoundest of all works on the transference. John Heaton's scholarly exposition, in Chapter 5, of the comparisons between Freud and Plato brings into question, by emphasizing the roots of psychotherapy in Greek philosophy, any priority that Freud or psychoanalysis might lay claim to in relation to matters erotic. The Socratic tradition is a prime illustration of this. Here any idea of desire as being a mental property lodged in the psyche is explicitly repudiated. For Plato the between is the erotic, and this can never be excluded from any discourse. This 'between' can never be formalized: knowledge of it cannot be possessed like facts or formulae, for the fact is that it possesses us. What this 'between' refers to is the surplus of enjoyment (a term that Lacan used in quite another context) which remains in the shadow of the transference. Here a distinction is to be made concerning the desire of the analyst. One may be ensnared between the desire to be the analyst, with its implicit trajectory of identity, repetition and stagnation – of trying to imitate an impossible ideal – and the desire which is the desire of enjoyment. Neurosis is the refusal of this desire, a desire not to desire. Such concerns will clearly affect the very heart of therapeutic free association.

At this point I must say a little about what link, if any, the Philadelphia Association has with Lacanian teaching, given that Lacan is cited in four of the essays. During the 1960s, when Lacan was establishing himself within French culture, indeed as legend, he was virtually ignored in England and in America. The place of controversy and subversion in these two countries was taken up by R.D. Laing, who was, in fact, aware of Lacan's work at an early

11

stage. Now a careful reading of our history and some of the small print of Laing's publications, as well as those of his colleagues, will show references to 'studies in Existentialism and Phenomenology' and 'The Institute of Phenomenological Studies', pointing towards the philosophical underpinnings of the enterprise.

In fact this institute was little more than a mailing address used around the time of the congress on the Dialectics of Liberation (July 1967), but the phenomenology was more substantial. I have already mentioned the resistance to Continental philosophy amongst the psychoanalytic community, a resistance which our organization has persistently opposed. Not surprisingly, we found some affinity with a teaching which is informed, as Lacan's was, by the writing of Hegel, Heidegger, Merleau-Ponty and Jean Paul Sartre, among others. 'To be sure', wrote William Richardson in his essay on 'Psychoanalysis and the being question', 'there were other philosophical influences on him [Lacan] besides Heidegger and Hegel . . . but it was these two Germans in particular who marked him most deeply, and indeed the influence remained even after he had ceased to refer to them' (1983). How ironic, then, that Lacan claimed, in 1972, that 'mathematical formalism is our aim, our ideal' and wanted a 'rupture' with anything that smacked of philosophy. And in many ways it would be delightful to extrude the late Lacan, as he himself appeared to do with the late Freud (Lacan claimed that the innovative core ran from 1900 and *The Interpretation of Dreams* until 1915). One would thus retain the phenomenological thrust of Lacan's earlier work. But things are never so simple. So whilst there may be affinities and proximities we are not 'Lacanians', and would have no wish to be constrained by any formal filiations. 'Togetherness' is always predicated on difference.

My own chapter attempts, via a reference to Lacanian psychoanalysis, the 'casual' phenomenology of Roland Barthes, and the unrelenting rigour of Emmanuel Levinas, to raise questions regarding the concept of the self. I am arguing that within the metaphor of the centre persists the Cartesian *moi* or me, and that this exemplary term of identification is quite unequivocally self-centred. In any attempt to decentre consciousness, the 'cogito', as the focus or centre of knowing, is the project of a critique of the privilege of ontology. There can be the misguided ideal of a self-sufficiency of being. As we strive to persevere in our own being, egoism is our unavoidable fate, for we appear to desire to enforce and increase it, often being only too deaf to the suffering of others and indeed ourselves. In emphasizing the responsibility of self, which is primarily located in the between of the face-to-face, there is a proposal to turn from ontology to ethics, the natural condition of our life.

To counter any prejudice that philosophy leads to a preponderance of theoretical or textual encounters, Haya Oakley's more clinical contribution in Chapter 7 illustrates the point that such concerns are neither mere abstractions nor a narrow application of specific tenets, but crucially inform a description of the work, which is in a tradition of working with psychotic or deeply regressed patients.

Paul Zeal also illustrates the effacing of boundaries between various genres by his mixture of the literary and conceptual modes. In Chapter 8 he cuts an erratic path through the philosophical and psychoanalytic undergrowth to open out a discourse on desire. The importance of this is linked to the hazardous nature of this, and indeed our organization's enterprise. If all our ways of defining and describing human beings, whether they be scientific, anthropological or philosophical, are fundamentally anchored in the ego-sphere of the discourse of the (subjective) centre, then perhaps only a more rhetorical or literary style offers a glimmer of an alternative. Here there is no intention to blur specific identities, or the languages or idioms of specific disciplines, for we claim an interest in the poetics of language which remains irreducibly idiomatic.

So maybe it is not accidental that it is to Michel Foucault and his compelling account of Velázquez's painting of the Spanish royal family, *Las Meninas*, that we turn in order to present some final nuances of our style of self-portrait. For Foucault is one of the intellectual figures of our age to evade categorization. How are we to name his work? Philosophy? Political history? Social science? More recently he has been situated in 'anti-ocular discourse' (Jay, 1986), a discourse in which the privileging of vision and of the traditional humanist subject centred on the possibility of enlightenment, the illusions of imagistic representation, and the dependence of the 'I' on the totalizing gaze of the 'eye' – all have been put under scrutiny, thereby placing in question vision's previous

position of primacy. One might say that it has indeed been sup-
planted by a growing opacity, although the linking of the view of
the world and the (w)hole of the eye persists. We literally go round,
looking at the world, in circles; this no doubt informs the hierarchical ordering, the logo- or ocular-centrism of prevailing
discourse.

Velázquez's painting is no orthodox portrait of the royal family.
Those familiar with the painting (and those not will find it in
Foucault's *The Order of Things*) will know that what appears on
the canvas is an unfolding of the perceptual field of the King and
Queen; the object of the gaze is not them but the objective of their
desire illustrated via their regard, incorporated within which is a
distant but distinct reflection of themselves. Through this the
spectator's appetite is aroused and inexorably comes up against the
frustration of the frame, epitomized by the tantalizing back of
Velázquez's own canvas. One is drawn to want to see further and
move freely without any fixed point of reference. As with the
psychoanalytic relationship the purpose is to move, to evoke, to
arouse and to open up closed systems, rather than to foreclose the
potentiality of the other by presenting themselves to themselves as
complete, unified and sealed within their own image.

Indubitably we have difficulty in relinquishing an attachment to
the subversive, despite acknowledging the inevitable difficulties
inherent in this. Against all the odds we wish to shake received
assumptions by proposing this cross-disciplinary interweave, thus
effecting a critical intervention, the site of the fold, in the terrain of
established and establishment psychoanalysis. Our desire is to
open its somewhat closed systems, to rethink its universalizing
tendencies, and to raise a challenge in the face of master narratives
under the guise of the 'discourse of others', or another discourse.
No single introduction could encompass or enclose such a terrain,
nor would seek to close off any of the borders.

1
Beginnings

ROBIN COOPER, with STEVEN GANS,
J.M. HEATON, HAYA OAKLEY
and PAUL ZEAL

. . . I have set before thee an open door, and no
man can shut it.
– Revelation 3:8

It is our concern that [the] households be
asylums, sanctuaries, and places of hospitality.
– Philadelphia Association leaflet, *c.* 1976

THE PHILADELPHIA ASSOCIATION, founded in 1965 as a charity, took as its objective the relief of mental illness of all descriptions, in particular schizophrenia. Its first Report, however, four years later, emphasized that these aims had been set out in terms appropriate to the association's formal existence as a charity, and outside these constraints it became possible to state a more radical intention: 'We aim to change the way the "facts" of "mental health" and "mental illness" are seen.'

The original members of the Philadelphia Association were a diverse group of forward-looking individuals, all with some organic connection to one another, and all with strong feelings about mental-health issues. One could almost speak of a yeast formation. Some were radical intellectuals or writers, some from the helping professions, some artists. There was Raymond Blake, a psychotherapist and group analyst; Sidney Briskin, a social worker; Joan Cunnold, an artist; Clancy Sigal, the expatriate American writer and political radical; the psychiatrists David Cooper and Aaron Esterson; and the psychiatrist and psychoanalyst R. D. Laing.

Then there was a formal group of advisers, made up of people already prominent in their own field, who included Dr Maxwell Jones and Dr Tom Main, both significant figures within the emerging 'therapeutic community' movement; Dr Jock Sutherland, Medical Director of the Tavistock Clinic; Marie Jahoda, later to be Professor of Sociology at Sussex University; and Professor Eric Trist, a founder member of the Tavistock Institute of Human Relations. Undeniably, however, the two people most central to the founding of the Philadelphia Association were R. D. Laing and the late David Cooper. And of these it is the name of R. D. Laing with which the Philadelphia Association is most indissolubly linked.

R. D. Laing was born in Glasgow in 1928, and subsequently took his medical degree there. Artaud, Hegel, Husserl, Sartre, Merleau-Ponty and Heidegger were then, as they would be today, unusual reading for a medical student; at any rate they were powerfully to influence, from the beginning, his development as a psychiatrist. Following graduation and subsequent psychiatric experience, first in the British Army and then in a Glasgow hospital, Laing moved to London where he trained at the Institute of Psycho-Analysis:

> When I left Glasgow to take up a job at the Tavistock Clinic and to undergo four years of training at the Institute of Psycho-Analysis, it was becoming clearer to me where my interest lay. It had to do with mental misery. What were the necessary or sufficient conditions to occasion mental misery of any kind? . . . The psychiatrist–patient rift across the sane–mad line seemed to play a part in some of the misery and disorder occurring within the field of psychiatry, Maybe this loss of human camaraderie was the most important thing. Maybe its restoration was the *sine qua non* of 'treatment' . . . Could an understanding of communication, miscommunication, noncommunication and excommunication contribute to the problems of Western psychiatry? (Laing, 1985, pp. 145–6)

Laing was on the staff of the Tavistock Clinic between 1957 and 1967, conducting research into the families of schizophrenics with the Tavistock Institute of Human Relations. This proved to be a period of extraordinarily fruitful co-operation between Laing and his colleagues, both inside and outside the Tavistock, and led to the publication of *Sanity, Madness and the Family* (Laing and Esterson, 1964), and *Interpersonal Perception* (Laing, Phillipson and Lee, 1966). At the same time, the first of a number of books which were soon to bring Laing considerable fame in the intellectual and popular culture as a whole had already been published. What was widely recognized about *The Divided Self* (1960) was Laing's originality in bringing together two fields hitherto thought by the Anglo-Saxon mind to be equally unintelligible – schizophrenic expression and existential writing – and awakening a more widespread understanding of both.

David Cooper was a South African psychiatrist who had come to England in the late 1950s. Courageously and uncompromisingly critical of institutional psychiatric violence, he started Villa 21 at Shenley Hospital, in London's northern green belt, in 1962. In this ward for young male schizophrenics, hierarchical differences between patients and staff were eliminated to a considerable degree. This departure from tradition gave rise to much controversy both within and without the hospital, and the 'experiment' was stopped in 1966. But its work, which went far beyond the then innovative institutional 'therapeutic community' model, became widely known through Cooper's first book, *Psychiatry and Antipsychiatry* (1967).

Cooper, like Laing, was profoundly influenced by phenomenology and existentialism (especially the writings of Sartre), and by Marxism: the two men jointly wrote a presentation of Sartre's major (and then untranslated) work of the fifties, published as *Reason and Violence* (Laing and Cooper, 1964). Like Laing, Cooper was to become a successful and controversial writer, addressing himself particularly to the politics of psychiatry: psychiatry seen in a broader context, embracing, for example, family life and its vicissitudes.

If the visionary passion of Laing and Cooper was inspirational in the founding of the Philadelphia Association, there were other figures who remained more in the background, but were also of importance during the early years. One such person was Dr E. Graham Howe. Howe – whom Laing was later to refer to as a 'master psychologist' – was a distinctly original voice within psychotherapy and psychiatry, who had for many years been making

17

clear and bold statements about the nature of 'schizophrenia' which were very close to Laing's own views.

Howe began his career as a psychotherapist as a member of the original Tavistock Clinic in 1928. He worked with Krishnamurti in the thirties and after the war studied Buddhism in Sri Lanka with Nyanoponika Mahathera for a year. The author of nine books, of which the best known is probably *Cure or Heal?* (1965), his work is distinguished by a blending of psychoanalytic psychology with authoritative readings of Eastern and Christian texts. His writings are the subject of a study by Henry Miller, and he was also an influence upon Alan Watts, the popularizer of Eastern philosophy. In some ways simplistic, but written in the voice of plain common sense spiced with a dash of Gurdjieff, the idea that psychiatry had more to learn from the schizophrenic than the schizophrenic from psychiatry was representative of Howe's thought; his interest in religion was to be a great influence on Laing.

Laing met Howe in 1960, when Howe was Chairman of the Langham Clinic in London. The Langham offered low-fee psychotherapy and trained psychotherapists, with teachers from both Freudian and Jungian schools. Two future members of the Philadelphia Association, Raymond Blake and John Heaton, had already trained there, and Laing was invited to become chairman of the clinic in 1962.

These first years of the Philadelphia Association, especially between 1965 and 1967, were characterized by regular informal discussions amongst a small group of psychotherapists and psychoanalysts interested in philosophy, including Laing, Aaron Esterson and John Heaton. The evening gatherings were held at the Hampstead home of the psychoanalyst Paul Senft, now probably best known as founder and editor of *The Human Context*. This book-length journal, published in London every four months between 1968 and 1974, was of bold scope, if somewhat uneven quality; its aims were 'to explore the conceptual and methodological links between the sciences of man . . . in their implicit philosophical assumptions . . . from a mainly European vantage point'. Paul Senft provided academic rigour, an atmosphere of being kept on one's toes intellectually. This was especially important in the case of Laing, whose understanding of phenomenology is recalled, by one member of the early group, as wayward.

Senft had studied phenomenology in Prague with Edmund Husserl, the founder of phenomenology. Husserl had a profound influence on thinkers like Heidegger, Sartre and Merleau-Ponty, as well as psychiatrists such as Freud's friend Binswanger, Medard Boss and, later on, Jacques Lacan. But it was perhaps Merleau-Ponty who addressed most clearly and explicitly the relation between phenomenology and psychoanalysis. In an article whose first English publication was in Senft's journal (Merleau-Ponty, 1970), Merleau-Ponty spoke of the two disciplines, despite their different idioms, as 'both tending towards the same latency'. In phenomenology this latency – or potential, or generative source – was opened up in terms of language and intersubjectivity, embodiment, incarnation in the lived world. For Merleau-Ponty, phenomenology thus offered a powerful corrective to the prevailing psychologism of psychoanalysis, whose latency (the unconscious) was understood more restrictively, in terms of inner drives or object representations.

Both Graham Howe and Paul Senft were to break with Laing within a few years. One of the issues which came between Laing and Howe – and culminated in Graham Howe asking Laing to resign from the Langham Clinic – concerned the therapeutic use of psychedelic drugs, into which Laing was 'conducting research'. Although Laing did not take up the view that psychedelics *should* be used in psychiatry, Howe believed that LSD could be dangerous, even a cheap con, and that Laing's interest in it was misplaced. Paul Senft, on the other hand, disagreed with Laing more over his understanding of phenomenology and its interpretation within psychoanalytic discourse. Senft thought that Laing was not prepared seriously to think through his rather populist blending of phenomenology and psychoanalysis – nor to acknowledge the implications of phenomenology's critique of psychoanalytic psychologism, with its stress on 'interiority'.

In the beginning, in fact, the dialogue which the Philadelphia Association opened up from this phenomenological perspective was more with psychiatry than with psychoanalysis. The works already mentioned – as well as the later work of Esterson, *The Leaves of Spring* (1970), which goes in more detail into one of the families described in *Sanity, Madness and the Family* – were important contributions to that dialogue. *The Self and Others* (Laing, 1961), however, directly questions some of the assumptions within psychoanalysis, and rethinks intra-psychic defences and unconscious phantasy, for example, in terms more appreciative of their interpersonal nature. Laing's critique of Susan Isaacs's classic paper 'The nature and function of phantasy' (Isaacs, 1952) illustrates this disinclination to use the term unconscious experience, 'because I cannot resolve satisfactorily in my mind the contradiction between the two words' (Laing, 1961, p. 30).

> One source of confusion is the particular dichotomous schema in which the whole theory is cast . . . [entailing] a distinction between 'the inner world of the mind', on the one hand, and 'the external world of the subject's bodily development and behaviour, and hence of other people's minds and bodies', on the other . . . A person may experience himself in terms of this set of distinctions . . . However, it is quite another matter to take such a form of self-division as one's theoretical starting point. (Laing, 1961, pp. 23, 24)

Indeed, running through the Philadelphia Association's history is the attempt to respect the person against all odds, against invalidatory, pejorative psychiatric diagnoses, or psychoanalytic reductions of the patient's problems to a conflict of their inner world. This has made for awkward kinships being claimed in various quarters: in, for example, the movement of anti-psychiatry, a term which David Cooper proposed and Laing rejected (ineffectually, to the extent that Laing continued to be associated in the public mind with it); in the various patients-against-psychiatry projects that blossomed in the seventies; and from some of the new Gestalt, humanistic and encounter psychologies and psychotherapies, not least those which invoked the terms 'existential' or 'phenomenology' in their self-descriptions. These kinships were made awkward, not because there were no patches of common ground, but because conceptual, ideological and stylistic differences all but ruled out their cultivation. Again, under 'awkward kinships' one might mention Laing's adoption as darling of the New Left, bound, as it was, to culminate in the sorts of misunderstandings and

disillusionments which are vehemently described in Peter Sedgwick's critique of conservatism in anti-psychiatry, *Psycho Politics*
(1982, pp. 69, 73, 89, 94–5).

The story of the Philadelphia Association remains, in large part,
the story of its household communities. These communities
started from a recognition of the need for places of sanctuary,
asylum, refuge, or dwelling, felt by some people who find themselves in extreme mental distress. The very first Philadelphia
Association households, set up in private houses in the late sixties,
made clear this distinction between hospitalization and hospitality. One, in Granville Road, Finchley, in a house owned by R. D.
Laing, was looked after by Ben Churchill, a psychotherapist;
another was in the home of Sidney Briskin. But the one which set
the course for a controversial future was Kingsley Hall.

Kingsley Hall was built in the 1920s by the philanthropic socia-
lists Muriel and Doris Lester, to serve the local community of
Bromley-by-Bow in the East End of London. It was a large building
and, although well known for Gandhi's stay there during his nego-
tiations with the British Government in 1931, by 1964 it was
under-used. In that year the Kingsley Hall Trustees, encouraged by
Muriel Lester, were prepared to lease it to the Philadelphia Association for a peppercorn rent. It was a building eminently suited to
its new purpose. Kinglsey Hall was to be a place where people
could live together, and where behaviour that would be intolerable
in most places might be feasible. The ground floor included a
games room with ropes from the ceiling and a full-sized snooker
table and table-tennis table; on the second floor there was a parapet
open to the sky around a number of cells or bedrooms. The basement was a large cavern, in which Mary Barnes lived for a while in
a tin trunk.

Amongst those who have ventured their opinion about Kingsley
Hall – and there has been no shortage – Mary Barnes is one who
speaks for herself. This former nursing tutor who had been hospitalized, and had the typically poor prognosis of a chronic schizophrenic liable to psychotic episodes, gave her own account of her
'journey through madness' in a celebrated book which included her

21

therapist Joseph Berke's account of it too (Barnes and Berke, 1971). Dr Berke had arrived from New York to work under Laing's supervision in 1965, bringing to bear some of the wilder ambitions of the New York counter-culture (see Berke, 1969). He was soon followed by three other colleagues, also from Albert Einstein Medical College, including Dr Leon Redler (later to become a member of the Philadelphia Association) and Dr Morton Schatzman.

The success of *Mary Barnes: Two Accounts of a Journey through Madness*, and of the play *Mary Barnes* which David Edgar adapted from her story – with their evident interest for so many people almost as a 'model' of how to go mad – have given Mary Barnes an incontestable place within the psychotherapeutic Hall of Fame. Kingsley Hall itself – with its reputation for psychedelic and literary happenings – was one of the crucibles of the 1960s. It seemed, to many people, to appear in the guise of 'Meditation Manor' in Clancy Sigal's novel *Zone of the Interior* (1976).

Kingsley Hall was not to everyone's taste, whether they were personally involved or not. Gilles Deleuze and Félix Guattari, for instance, criticized Kingsley Hall for what they took to be its latent structures of bourgeois, oedipalized family life, 'familialism' (1972). At the end of the day, they believed Kingsley Hall was far from radical: deeply conservative, it embodied all the conventional hierarchies of power. Guattari returned to the theme in an article in *Le Nouvel Observateur* in 1973. 'No one', he wrote of Kingsley Hall,

> could escape the simplistic reduction of all things to the same old triangle (father, mother and child) that confines all situations that exceed what are considered the bounds of normality within the mould of oedipal psychoanalysis . . . Familialism means magically denying the social reality, avoiding all connection with real fluxes. All that remains possible is dreaming . . . or even, in moments of intense crisis, a little urine-soaked corner to retreat to, alone. (Guattari, 1973, pp. 52, 54)

How ironic that David Cooper, writing *The Death of the Family* at around that time (Cooper 1971), should equally have been criticized precisely for his undermining of conventional family structures!

22

Thomas Szasz – rather surprisingly, in view of his concern to privilege the autonomy of the individual – saw the Philadelphia Association's interest in the regressions, which (to him) epitomized the households, as evidence of a perpetuation of a mystifying 'myth of mental illness'. If there was no such thing as mental illness, Szasz's view went, why was Kingsley Hall 'treating' people in a community set up for a therapeutic purpose? To him there was a contradiction in the idea of an anti-therapeutic therapeutic community.

The ensuing debate, polarized around Szasz and anti-psychiatry, centred upon Kingsley Hall and was conducted in a literary magazine some years after the event. There were contributions at considerable length from Szasz and the psychiatrist and broadcaster Anthony Clare; and from Aaron Esterson and Joe Berke (Berke having now left to start the Arbours Housing Association). From the Philadelphia Association there were Leon Redler and another American, Steven Gans. The debate was described in the *Observer* of 10 April 1977:

> For months now an astonishing debate about the uses and abuses of psychiatry has dominated the pages of the literary magazine *The New Review*. In its way the acrimonious attack on the unorthodox views of R. D. Laing by his fellow psychiatrist, the American Dr Thomas S. Szasz, is as important to psychiatry as the famous Leavis–Snow debate of the 1960s was to literature.

At the height of Kingsley Hall's vitality, in the summer of 1967, an unusual gathering took place in the Roundhouse, London (at that time a primary venue for the counter-culture). For two hot July weeks the Congress of the Dialectics of Liberation, convened by the Institute of Phenomenological Studies under the aegis of the Philadelphia Association, drew together some of the threads of the peculiar PA weave. Looking at the jacket of the book, which compiled some of the principal addresses (see Cooper, 1968), one is reminded that the Dialectics of Liberation was 'a unique expression of the politics of modern dissent, in which existential psychiatrists, Marxist intellectuals, anarchists and political leaders met to discuss – and to constitute – the key social issues of the next decade'.

At any rate, it was an extraordinary experience to hear, within a fortnight, R. D. Laing on 'The obvious' ('To state the obvious is to share with you what (in your view) my misconceptions might be', in Cooper, 1968, pp. 13–14); Stokeley Carmichael on Black Power; Herbert Marcuse on 'Liberation from the affluent society'; and Gregory Bateson on 'Conscious purpose versus nature'. There were talks by the sociologist and anthropologist Jules Henry on preparation for warfare, the philosopher John Gerassi on imperialism and revolution, and the economist Paul Sweezy on the future of capitalism – and by David Cooper, 'Beyond words'. All the while, other sorts of gatherings would take place around the likes of Allen Ginsberg, Emmet Grogan of the San Francisco Diggers, and Vietnamese monks. The experience was memorably described by Sheila Rowbotham in the autobiographical part of her early essay on contemporary feminism, *Woman's Consciousness, Man's World*:

> It was a peculiar collection of the incompatible and reluctant forces of liberation. The revolutionary left – or bits of it – encountered the mind-blowers . . . It was more of a two-week-long trauma than a conference. I experienced a severe sense of dislocation throughout . . . [but] the idea of taking hold of your own definitions stuck. So did the tortured delicacy of Laing. (Rowbotham, 1973, pp. 22–3)

Kingsley Hall, the Dialectics of Liberation and the establishing and flourishing of the Philadelphia Association became the backdrop to R. D. Laing's rise to fame. With the phenomenal success of *The Politics of Experience and the Bird of Paradise* (1967), and following two American tours, he had became an internationally acclaimed and controversial figure. Then in 1970, and at the height of this success, he left to spend a year in India, to meditate with the masters of the Hinayana Buddhist tradition (one of them that same Nyanoponika Mahathera with whom Graham Howe had meditated many years before). On returning he packed London's largest meeting halls and regaled audiences with accounts of his personal odyssey to resolve the epistemological splits of the Western world.

The desire for continuity beyond the Dialectics of Liberation Congress – not hard to understand – led initially to the Anti-University of London, which took place in Old Street and provided an energetic forum for discussion of radical issues. In due course, the Anti-University gave way to the PA's study programme, which now runs each year as a three-term course, 'Introduction to Social Phenomenology'.

Meanwhile, its lease having expired in May 1970, Kingsley Hall was given back to its trustees. The same weekend, the Archway Community was started by Dr Leon Redler, Paul Zeal and Michael Yokum, in short-life housing by arrangement with a housing association. It was there that the documentary film *Asylum* was made, directed by Peter Robinson with hand-held cameras and minimal intrusion by the film crew. *Asylum* brought vividly to light the issues raised by David Mercer's earlier work, *Family Life*. Mercer's drama, initially a stage play and later adapted for television, followed the deterioration in the mind of a fictional nineteen-year-old girl whose parents subject her to a series of contradictory messages and double-binds. Eventually hospitalized, she is wheeled on for medical students as a 'case' of catatonic withdrawal. *Asylum*, by contrast, gives us a series of vignettes of community life, this time concentrating on the responses of the parents who visit their sons or daughters in the household.

Over several years, the Archway Community extended to eight houses in neighbouring streets, all derelict and due for demolition. In 1973 the first long-term home for the community was set up in Tollington Park by Paul Zeal and Haya Oakley, therapists to the Archway Community during its last five years. But of all the houses stretching from Archway to Crouch End, only one remains, The Grove. It is actually owned by the Philadelphia Association, thanks to the energetic fund-raising labours of Sid Briskin and the actress, Suzy Kendall (the down payment for the mortgage was raised at a cabaret with many rising stars, including the actor, Michael Caine). During that time there was also a brief revival of our presence in the East End of London in the shape of the community in De Beauvoir Square, set up by Chris Oakley between 1974 and 1978.

Other forms of change were inevitable in a small organization. Joe Berke and Morton Schatzman, without having become members of the PA, left to found the Arbours Housing Association, also based in London. Arbours was without doubt inspired by aspects of the PA's work and culture, for example its concern with

25

psychoanalysis, critique of psychiatry, and the Kingsley Hall experience. It did not, however, take up the deeper questions raised by phenomenology.

In these early years of the Philadelphia Association, formal training in psychotherapy or community training was to become a contentious issue. It was one of the issues over which David Cooper decided to part company, despite mutul feelings of fondness and kinship. He, whose brilliance and compassion had inspired the Villa 21 project in Shenley Hospital, in which patients had unprecedented say in their affairs, felt that institutionalization of training should be resisted for political reasons. He was concerned to 'undermine the bourgeois state' rather than to produce more of the same.

Training programmes had nevertheless begun, by 1969, and were on increasingly traditional lines for psychoanalytically oriented courses, involving personal analysis, supervision of training cases and study of the classic texts. The reading list for students, however, compared with those of other organizations was, and remains, distinctive. Along with the usual psychoanalytic texts were works of phenomenology and existentialism. Anthropology was on the curriculum and there was also a keen interest in the relevance of Buddhist and Zen meditation, and Hatha yoga. Central to this combination of practices was the view that the psychoanalytic tradition could be seen as a kind of meditative tradition, or, as Heidegger put it, that meditative thinking was a *form* of thinking. In the study courses the emphasis was a philosophical one – on the texts themselves, and on knowing how to read them. There were no 'basic' texts followed by 'specialized' texts. As a way of encouraging students to develop skill in a critical interpretative practice, this was in keeping with the PA's understanding that in a training there is no beginning and no end.

Another phase in the PA's evolution began with Dr Hugh Crawford's return to the United Kingdom in 1968, after twenty years working as a psychiatrist in Canada and the United States. Hugh Crawford had known Ronald Laing since their days as medical students at Glasgow, and the Philadelphia Association was a first port of call. Crawford, now in his early forties, was straining on a leash. While in North America he had made a solitary excursion

26

into phenomenology, having found his American psychiatric experience a lonely one. The two men were very different: Crawford's charisma was that of the sailor, a little reminiscent of Hemingway. Laing's was more that of the arabesque, the fashionably chic. At any rate, within a few months of his arrival Crawford was elected a member of the Philadelphia Association, had started his psychotherapy practice, and had become closely involved with the concerns of the Association.

Two years later Crawford secured a property and founded a new PA community household in Portland Road, a shabby but newly fashionable street in Holland Park, London. This house had spawned three offshoots by the time that it closed in 1980, one of them a smallholding in the Oxfordshire countryside. Portland Road was to fulfil a vision which Crawford had been nurturing in isolation and frustration during his years in orthodox psychiatry, and it was to occupy a position of considerable importance until his death in 1980. The house closed soon after, already weakened by prolonged legal battles with the Royal Borough of Kensington and Chelsea, over issues of planning and use.

Portland Road's importance derived from Hugh Crawford's original conception of principles and practice, which helped revitalize the initiative the households had already been taking. This revitalization was not only inspired by his uncompromising presence, but informed by his searching reading of the phenomenologists – in particular Merleau-Ponty and Bachelard – and Freud. What was distinctive about Hugh Crawford's approach to the households was his ability to show – in ordinary but memorable language – the issues that emerged around hospitality, conviviality, being at home, and their central importance to any sort of well-being. For Crawford the dimension of *dwelling* represented the next step for psychoanalysis to take, to move beyond a conception of the therapeutic 'hour', and think more deeply about the roots of the therapeutic.

The sense of Portland Road as simultaneously an ordinary household, a 'therapeutic community' and a place of learning was enhanced when the study programme in social phenomenology found its home in the basement, alongside the Philadelphia Association offices. Then there were the visits from students, trainees,

27

academics, prospective members of the household and those occasional roving spirits who might only a few years before have been drawn to the Dialectics of Liberation.

Although it is true that the reputation of the Philadelphia Association households may rest upon their ways of approaching psychotic episodes – such as Mary Barnes's experience – it would be quite misleading to suppose that the whole focus of the Association is upon psychosis; or that their capacity to contain these episodes is the sole *raison d'être* of the households. Far from it. People have always come, and will no doubt continue to come, to the households for a multiplicity of reasons. It is true that, from the first, Kingsley Hall, the households had an interest in offering asylum to individuals who were acutely psychotic. And indeed, during the time of Portland Road a number of highly disturbed individuals were seen, to varying extents, through their acute episodes or, as they were called, 'freak-outs'. This was not because of some ideology which privileged psychotic experience. The concern for asylum has to be understood, first of all, in the context of available alternatives. Laing, Cooper and later Crawford approached the households from their experience of working in mental institutions, and having emphatic reactions to this experience: they felt there *had* to be some other way.

Yet if these households started off as 'reactions', as alternatives, they did not remain so. The discipline became honed; there was time, too, for those whose unfinished business took the form of the long hard slog. By the time of Portland Road, it was very much the significance of the ordinariness of dwelling which was opened up, illuminated, sometimes very starkly and hellishly, by those more extraordinary occasions of acute psychosis.

Portland Road and its offshoot houses had always been associated with one powerful individual, and the uncertainty and sense of loss that emerged during Hugh Crawford's long illness culminated in grief and confusion following his death. This loss, felt throughout the whole network, was of more than the man: it was the end of an era. Hugh Crawford's presence in the Philadelphia Association did have a holding function, accommodating and mediating Laing's sometimes extravagant position intellectually as well as emotionally. With Hugh gone, the balance was disturbed, and what had been a healthy tension collapsed. It became increasingly difficult to work with Laing in any committee structure, for he no longer seemed answerable to the company. Laing became more and more the absent chairman, appearing to have lost interest in either doing the work of the organization or enabling others to do it. The Philadelphia Association could no longer grow or develop its ideas in this atmosphere.

Laing resigned his membership of the Philadelphia Association in 1981. It was a sad loss of a long partnership, conceived and inspired throughout by his ideas. Most of them – especially the idea of the intelligibility of madness, and the importance of asylum and hospitality – are still very much at the heart of the Philadelphia Association's work, and inform some – though not all – of the pieces in this collection.

The break with Laing reverberated throughout the Philadelphia Association and its immediate network. Allegiances of social, intellectual and transferential natures were questioned, and people whose primary attachment was to the charisma of Laing felt they had to leave. This was also the occasion for the Philadelphia Association to part company with some of the network whose concerns were more to do with yoga and natural childbirth than with phenomenology or psychoanalysis.

One major parting of the ways that was already in motion concerned Laing's continuing flirtation with humanistic therapies, which had begun in the 1970s with his rediscovery of the writer and therapist Francis Mott. Mott's work on the notion of, and clinical evidence for, pre-natal consciousness (1949, 1959) informed Laing's *The Facts of Life* (1976), and was being widely taken up within the organization. This was adding an exciting new dimension to the analytic work in the network, for it seemed to contribute to the intelligibility of certain pathological structures, particularly when working analytically with psychosis. Some therapists were finding that there were patients for whom the idiom or metaphors of intra-uterine life proved to be the most mutative and powerful.

At this time too, however, an interest in birth and pre-birth experience was spreading throughout the humanistic movement, and 'rebirthing' workshops, where various techniques were practised to release unresolved birth traumas, mushroomed throughout Europe and North America. Whilst Laing appeared captivated and inspired by this, the idea of 'rebirthing' 200 people at the Inn on the Park on a Sunday afternoon seemed to many to be a negation of the psychoanalytic, phenomenological, and even common-sense understanding of what it is to come into the world. Tensions as fundamental as these could not be resolved.

When Laing left, the PA chose not to replace him with a new chairman, a decision which has remained part of the culture of the Association. Those who stayed on, now the senior tier, found a renewed strength in a structure less dominated by personality. The training for psychotherapists and community therapists continued, new Philadelphia Association households opened just as others closed. Most notably, with Laing and Crawford's sometimes justified and sometimes unfounded fear of 'others' now removed, a greater exchange of ideas between the Association and other organizations began to take place. It is not our desire to present a united front, and our differences are exemplified by the chapters in this book. We meet where psychoanalysis and philosophy cross paths. It is where this book begins.

2
Dwelling and the 'therapeutic community'

ROBIN COOPER

T HE PHILADELPHIA ASSOCIATION is probably best known for its work in the founding of therapeutic-community households. The first of these, Kingsley Hall, was set up in 1965; since then there have been a further eighteen. A recent publication of the association claims that 'the experience of the past twenty years has demonstrated that episodes of personal crisis, of seemingly inescapable distress and confusion, and of stark madness, may for many people best be negotiated in the context of such dwellings'. In this paper I ask: what is a dwelling? And what might the nature of dwelling tell us about the way in which our households lay claim to be therapeutic?

THE PLIGHT OF DWELLING

The phenomenological movement, whose central themes are so much to do with origins, with first things, arrives with Bachelard, Heidegger and Levinas in quite explicit discussion of dwelling. Of these thinkers, it is Heidegger who most obviously demands serious attention from those whose field of practice is psychotherapeutic. As a point of departure for our discussion here, we may consider some of the concluding remarks from Heidegger's essay, 'Building dwelling thinking'.

> We are attempting to trace in thought the nature of dwelling. The next step on this path would be the question: what is the state of dwelling in our precarious age? On all sides we hear talk about the housing shortage, and with good reason. Nor is there just talk: there is action too. We try to fill the need by providing houses, by promoting the building of houses, planning the

whole architectural enterprise. However hard and bitter, however hampering and threatening the lack of houses remains, the *real plight of dwelling* does not merely lie in lack of houses. The real plight of dwelling lies in this, that mortals ever search anew for the nature of dwelling, that *they must ever learn to dwell*. What if man's homelessness consists in this, that man does still not think of the *real* plight of dwelling as *the* plight. (Heidegger, 1971, p. 161)

We may note first of all that for Heidegger, homelessness extends to 'thinking': our very thinking is 'homeless'. The fact, and the seriousness of this homelessness, may be obscured by the intricacy and cleverness of our thinking, and by the ingeniousness of its products. But the thinking which is ingenious and which produces 'results' need not by any means be a thinking which dwells; on the contrary it is precisely this thinking which becomes bewitched with its own successes and rushes on. In this rushing, what it is 'to think' is considered no more worthy of thought than what it is 'to dwell', since everywhere we see the evidence which assures us that we already know. Heidegger invites us to ponder over the possibility that we may not; and inevitably, therefore, his thinking of dwelling proceeds in a fashion which may not be familiar.

Heidegger refers to the 'plight of dwelling'. Yet he makes it clear that this plight is not the same as the housing shortage, and that the construction of houses, however valuable a work this may be, carries with it no assurance that this 'plight of dwelling' will be any way lessened.

In today's housing shortage even this much is reassuring and to the good; residential buildings do indeed provide shelter; today's houses may even be well planned, easy to keep, attractively cheap, open to air, light, and sun, but – do the houses in themselves hold and guarantee that *dwelling* occurs in them? (p. 146)

Heidegger suggests that we may in some respects fail to realize what it means 'to dwell', since the provision of all the seeming requirements is not sufficient to ensure that 'dwelling' in fact takes place. Thus it is that man's plight – man's plight of dwelling – consists in his ever having 'to search anew' for the nature of dwelling. Ever searching anew is a restlessness. It is not content with what it has hitherto found, or perhaps what is found is simultaneously lost. If man is always searching anew for his dwelling, he has forgotten, or perhaps, precisely by virtue of having the nature of a being who dwells, *forgets* – what it means to dwell. The plight of dwelling may be a form of forgetfulness. Man dwells forgetfully. Accordingly, learning to dwell may not consist at all in acquiring further skills or competence, but rather will take the form of recollection.

How will this recollection come about? How do we recall what it is, to dwell? If we are to give thought to dwelling, we must think in a fashion which befits dwelling or belongs with dwelling. Such a thinking *stays with* that which calls upon us to think, or moves us to think; it is a meditative thinking rather than a calculative thinking which, with eyes fixed upon results, strays and wanders from its source. Such a thinking may itself already be a dwelling, for 'dwelling itself is always a staying with things'.

But staying with is not merely a matter of being around things, reducible to the objective co-ordinates of space and time, any more than dwelling is the topological relation of being within a habitation. Nor must we assume that the 'staying with' of dwelling is primarily something that we do, that is, an activity. According to Heidegger, it is rather because man's dwelling is a staying that he is 'free' to come and go, stay or leave, do this or that. Staying or leaving will in either case be included within the 'stay' of dwelling. If dwelling *were* something that we do, then perhaps the situation might not arise where dwelling, despite everything, remains in such a plight, continues to be associated with such restlessness; for could not procedures be worked out, especially with all the resources – skills, materials information – available to us, such that we might finally be able to dwell better.

Our dwelling is not of our doing – it is of our being. Heidegger turns to the Old English and High German word *buan*, to dwell, noting that the word survives as *bin* in *ich bin*. *Ich bin*, I am, says Heidegger, also means *I dwell*. Here, dwelling is not inhabitation. *Dasein*, that 'being' whose essential being resides in its comportment towards being and towards the question of what it is, to be, is now in later Heidegger characterized as a being who dwells; whose way of being is a dwelling of being. And we may now return to the question which was raised earlier, which Heidegger refers to as the 'plight' of dwelling, a plight which is shown in man's restlessness, his ever having to learn to dwell. Now it seems he must learn 'to be', or learn what it is, to be, whilst all the time he already is. It is indeed a plight – not amenable to solution by any course of action – because of the 'already'.

If we already dwell, and yet are required to learn in some fashion about the nature of dwelling, then we must turn, perhaps, to what we already know, and to what is closest. What is most close, and therefore at risk of becoming most closed, is the ordinary, the everyday, the commonplace. In being led to the commonplace we may arrive at what is most familiar; what, precisely by virtue of its familiarity, yet awaits recognition.

> The coursing can lead us into what belongs to us, into the domain where we already dwell. Then why, one may ask, must we first travel a course towards it? Answer: because we are there, where we already are, in such a way that we are at the same time not there, in so far as we still have not properly appropriated what belongs to our essence . . . We still do not sufficiently dwell where we really (*eigentlich*) already are. (Heidegger, in Fell, 1979, p. 258)

LINGERING

The word 'dwell' comes from the Old English *dwellan*, meaning to linger, to wander. It provides a good example of the antithetical senses of a primal word. *Dwellan* is akin to 'OE *dwalian*, OFris *dwalia*, to wander, to be in error, OE *dwalia*, error, OFris *dwalinge*, OE *dwolung*, doubt, ON *dvelja*, to linger, delay, tarry, retard . . . '

The *Oxford English Dictionary* traces 'dwell' to *dwellan*, meaning to lead astray, hinder or delay; also, intransitively, to go astray, err, be delayed or tarry. It lists seven principal meanings of the word:

1 Lead into error (obsolete).
2 Hinder, delay.
3 To tarry, delay.
4 To abide or continue for a while in a place, state or condition.
5 To spend time upon, linger over.
6 To continue in existence, to last, to persist, to remain.
7 To have one's abode, to reside, 'live'.

These meanings may quite conveniently be approached under the two main headings of lingering and wandering.

Lingering has the same root as 'long'. It is to stretch out, prolong, to stay, to tarry, to put off . . . Dwelling is in the first instance a staying, and a staying with. We recall Heidegger: dwelling itself is always a staying with things. We may think of where we stay, amongst other things, as where we *stand*; for the attitudinal and ethical connotations of stance are fairly clear. Stance speaks, too, both of our 'rootedness' and of the sense in which the notion of rootedness does not quite apply to humans. We stand on the earth, which sustains us and provides us with our daily bread. But at the same time we stand out, or apart from the world; we ex-ist. We exist 'understandingly', stand in the *world*.

Thinking of dwelling as a staying, a tarrying, abiding (for the temporality of 'stance' compare Italian *stanza*, a pause, hence a verse) brings to mind Heidegger's repeated utterance that it is *mortals* who dwell. His poetic discussions of dwelling are resonant with the echoes of earlier discussions of *Dasein* and temporality, being-towards-death, time and authenticity in *Being and Time*. Whilst his discussion of *space* and dwelling is most important, it is the emphasis upon the temporality of dwelling which is likely, first, to strike Heidegger's reader.

> Mortals dwell in that they initiate their own nature – their being capable of death as death – into the use and practice of this capacity, so that they may have a good death. To initiate mortals into the nature of death in no way means to make death, as empty Nothing, the goal. Nor does it mean to darken dwelling by blindly staring towards the end. (Heidegger, 1971, p. 151)

> They (human beings) are called mortals because they can die. To die means to be capable of death *as* death. Only man dies, and indeed continually, so long as he remains upon earth. (p. 150)

'All people that on earth do dwell' – so goes the hymn. Dwelling-lingering evokes (for me) a sense of sojourn, of passage. We may choose an image from the Icelandic sagas of the momentary flight of a bird through the flickering lights of a banqueting hall; a moment of appearance bounded by the darkness of the whence and the whether. Heidegger finds in the word 'dwelling' a particular interrogative power; for it is *our own* dwelling which is called into question. Dwelling-lingering sharpens the edge of this question; for the darkness does not simply *surround* the banqueting hall, framing it, on the outside, but is always there with the very essence of the light.

> The presently occurring does not lie like a cut-off piece between the absent. When the presently occurring once stands in view, everything occurs together, one brings the other along with itself, one lets the other go its way. (Heidegger, in Fell, 1979, p. 234)

To say that *Dasein* is 'towards death' or that 'mortals dwell' is to speak of that temporal relation whereby human beings may be said to 'have time'. Only *because* man's life is a staying and a passing, because man *is* as a mortal, can he linger and have time for. His dwelling *is* the mattering of time. Man's dwelling does not occur 'in' time, so much as it is an advent of time. Having time for is not grounded in objective time, and is not some allocation of time's segments, but is a freeing or opening up of time's fullness, a possibility which is granted to man and which is expressed in his standing so close to time that the nature of his being is – dwelling.

We might now flesh out this discussion a little by pointing out that the word lingering is etymologically rather close to *longing* and *belonging*. Abiding, we are *held* by the threads of belonging. This is not a possessive belonging, in the sense that my goods belong to me, or the slave belongs to his master. Neither is it a categorial belonging, in the sense that I might be said to belong to a statistical sample, or to a 'set' of the population. It refers rather to an existential belonging, a belonging in which one's very singularity is grounded, a belonging which is most profoundly interpersonal.

This familiar sense of belonging is brought out when we speak of two people belonging to one another, or children belonging with their parents. When a person speaks of belonging, in the context of his friends or family, his neighbourhood or his people, he indicates a world to which he is drawn, where he feels familiar and at home.

Belonging can also suggest a 'fitting', rather like being in one's element. It is not, of course, a matter of an activity or a doing. I cannot simply decide to belong somewhere, or with someone. However devotedly T.E. Lawrence surrendered himself to its customs, he could never, finally, belong to the Arab world. My sense of belonging to or with others can be articulated in terms of what they mean to me, what I mean to them. The infant's sense of belonging, and consequent world, opens and unfolds according to what he means to his parents, what they mean to one another, and what they come to mean to him. If finally they mean 'nothing' to one another what sense can he make of his own origins? Where does he come from? Where does he belong?

We will of course see the world differently according to the sense of belonging that we have. It is very clear, for example, that the child who has very little sense of belonging, or who does not feel at home with or know where he stands with his family, may find himself unable to assume the world as his birthright; the world does not open for him as it might for a happy and secure child.

The psychiatric patient is – in different ways, with different degrees of severity or chronicity – disarticulated from interpersonal belonging. The madman – the *unheimlich* – belongs to no one; and hence his vulnerability to institutional predatoriness. For some people this sort of disarticulation may simply take the form of a chronic loneliness, a life of quiet desperation. Others may find their desperation less containable and may show, for example, 'psychiatric symptoms' of one sort or another, which may merely invoke the model of a broken thing to be repaired. Such individuals may find their way to therapeutic communities; and where they do, the question of whether or not they come to feel in the course of time less lonely, depressed and disarticulated must depend to a very great extent upon the degree to which they have been able to articulate into a structure of belonging. And it is here that the prevailing psychologistic epistemologies can be quite misleading. For openings between people are not created by psychological techniques, but by what one might call *manners*: gestures, actions, words (which may of course be more or less honest, more or less contrived). These gestures do not arise out of nowhere, but out of a living context, or intentional matrix. The intentional matrix

37

which is of interest here is that of a community of people living together.

WANDERING

Precisely because man dwells, is mortal (that is, has time for), his staying is at the same time a leaving. It is a leaving because dwelling is only a stay and because in time everything occurs together: we are always on our way. Leaving is an allowing, a letting the other go its way; yet letting is also hindering ('without let or hindrance'). It is in this simultaneity of hindering and allowing, loving and leaving, that we can see the essential *postponement*, and errancy, of staying. The prolonging of staying, whereby staying tends to become staid, is a forgetting of the time; and a forgetting of the time of our staying, which is dwelling. But this prolonging or putting off is also *in keeping with* dwelling. To stay is at the same time to stray; lingering leads in to error, or wanders.

Wander comes from the same word as 'wind'. To wander is: to take a winding course; to turn, to turn about; to change, to bend; to err, to be in error; to wend (past participle 'wended', went). Wandering is a 'going on one's way', which is a wending, a going on one's way of indirection. The movement of wandering includes that of a turning, or winding, and a turning upon oneself. The flexibility and suppleness suggested by the word is brought out in the noun 'wand', a slender, pliant stick used, for example, in basket-making, wattled buildings, and weaving. The verb *wand* (Scottish and dialect) means to wattle, interweave, plait. Wanding is weaving. At the same time, the 'pointedness' of wand is brought out in its meaning as a 'straight, slender stick', a light walking-stick, a stick used as a pointer. A wand was also a rod or staff borne as a sign of office; a sceptre. All of these various inflections of meaning, and at the same time the magical properties of the wand, are very nicely brought together in the image of the Hermetic staff, or caduceus.

The movement of wandering may be exquisitely paradoxical in the fashion in which it is both aimless and pointed, free and unfree. The wanderer turns upon his vertiginous spirallings and re-turns. It is a theme within countless mythologies for the treasure to be arrived at only in the course of extended wanderings.

38

What is perhaps the best-known poem in the English language begins with the words 'I wandered . . .'. To put this down to poetic licence is to beg the question: why does this 'showing', this 'wealth' of which the poet speaks *belong with* wandering? Wordsworth's 'recollection in tranquillity', in 'vacant or in pensive mood' is itself a wandering, a wondering. *Reverie* is a wandering. (See, for example, Bachelard, 1958, 1969.)

The importance of wandering is very well brought out in Freud's discussion of free-association. One of Freud's most important and far-reaching 'discoveries', it was from the beginning referred to as the 'technique' of free-association. A technique suggests an instrument supplied by the analyst. This notion of free-association as an instrument for investigating the mind has been criticized by Heaton:

> Let us turn back to Freud's practice and see if he actually used free association in the way he thought he did when he was writing his theoretical works. In the famous 'Aliquis' case at the beginning of his *Psychopathology of Everyday Life*, he tells his friends, 'I must ask you to tell me, candidly and uncritically, whatever comes into your mind if you direct your attention to the forgotten word without any definite aim.' To be asked to be candid and uncritical is not to be asked to undergo a technical process but to take some moral stance towards what one says. Similarly to do something with no definite aim is hardly a technical matter – it is nearer play.
>
> Furthermore, Freud makes comments, well-aimed questions and shrewd observations to the person free-associating: again this is not the innocent application of a blind technique which produces knowledge but requires insight and knowledge of people on Freud's part. Also, Freud reported many cases of people who forgot names, who made slips of the tongue and themselves free-associated without having heard of this particular technique. (Heaton, 1982a, p. 134)

Freud's decision to abandon hypnosis as a means of 'access' to the patient was largely a consequence of his patients' insistence upon following their own way, letting their speaking take its own course.

His account of how he adopted the technique of free association, for example, is touching in its simplicity. A patient appears to have stoutly resisted Freud's interference with the flow of the clinical material. 'I now saw that I had gained nothing from this interruption and that I cannot evade listening to her stories in every detail to the very end.' At another point the same patient 'said in a definitely grumbling tone that I was not to keep on asking her where this or that came from, but to let her tell me what she had to say'. As Freud quietly put it, 'I fell in with this . . . ' Freud found that he had to be more patient in his therapy, and instead of starting out from the pressing symptoms and aiming to clear them up he left it to the patient to choose the subject of the day's work. The couch was a useful remnant from Freud's use of hypnosis, however, since it permitted both analyst and patient to relax and free-associate . . . (Roazen, 1976, p. 99)

Freud writes that his earlier methods of 'pressing and encouraging'

gave place to another method which was in one sense its opposite. Instead of urging the patient to say something upon some particular subject, I now asked him to abandon himself to a process of *free association*, i.e. to say whatever came into his head, while ceasing to give any conscious direction to his thoughts. (Freud, 1936, pp. 71–2)

Freud now encourages his patients to let their thoughts *wander*, and he proposes in effect to *accompany* his patients in their wanderings. The particular wanderings to which he addressed himself were strayings and errings; for his work was with people who had lost their way. But Freud did not propose to his patients that they 'abandon' their wandering, in favour of some 'better way of life'. On the contrary, he proposed that they stay with their wandering, linger upon it and follow its movement, in that very situation of their being together. Freud writes that 'we must bear in mind that free association is not really free'.

The patient remains under the influence of the analytic situation even though he is not directing his mental activities on to a particular subject. We shall be justified in assuming that

40

nothing will not occur to him that has not some reference to that situation. (1936, pp. 72–3)

What is binding about that situation is for example the commitment to say everything which comes to mind. But the patient's being 'bound' in meeting the requirements of the situation is precisely a staying. This staying does not place limits upon freedom, but, as staying, grants leave to wander.

I have referred to Heidegger in making the claim that to be is to dwell – and have opened up something of the meaning of what it is to dwell by referring to the etymology of the word, which speaks of dwelling as a lingering and a wandering. What is important is the manner in which these two belong together.

Lingering, or staying, is an opening, or holding open. Staying is a spatio-temporal opening, clearing, or keeping – a freeing and preserving, a gathering together of what is already belonging or perhaps fitting. We 'understand' the world in staying; we stay, for example, in language, which tells us, according to the manner of our staying, of the nature of things.

Wandering, too, opens and holds open. Wandering extends the stay, leads it out, outstays and stays out, over-reaches, takes leave, takes liberties. Wandering takes funny turns, arrives with, or at, the unexpected, and the unspeakable. Wandering finally brings it all back home.

Dwelling is both lingering and wandering: lingering and wandering belong within the unitariness of dwelling. Staying stays, wandering changes – in each case, the same. Lingering has time for wandering, staying safeguards wandering's extravagancies. Lingering protects wandering, wandering nourishes lingering. Lingering stays with the wandering, wandering prolongs the lingering, as Scheherazade in *The Thousand and One Nights* prolongs her life each night, for yet one more day, by telling her story. Wandering spins a yarn which staying remains to hear, to gather the threads.

It is in our nature to stay, to stand, to stand out, to remain where we are, to take a place, to hold our ground, to inhere, rest and shelter. It is in our nature at the same time to fall and fall out, to wander and stumble, to err, to lose the thread, become distracted, to surrender, let go, turn and return. Dwelling is the between of lingering and wandering, turning and returning, gathering and

41

dispersing, coming and going, loving and leaving; that between from which the world is born.

HOMELESSNESS

How, then, do these reflections on dwelling inform us as to the practice or discipline which most befits a therapeutic community? We may indicate, first of all, some senses in which their claim to be informative may be misunderstood. By proposing that human beings dwell I am not, for example, making an empirical claim which is proved to be false by the existence of nomads, hoboes, hunter-gatherers or people who sail round the world in small yachts. I do not propose to set therapeutic-community practice on a revived course by claiming to have discovered a 'new model of man'. Neither do I propose to embellish or augment existing therapeutic-community practices in some fashion, by reminding the reader through invocation, through rhetoric, of the importance of 'home comforts' in our life, or of considerations to do with the aesthetics of the institution. Nor, it must be emphasized, is 'dwelling' to be thought of as providing either the first brick or the final keystone of an alternative theoretical framework, whose elaboration culminates in a new 'household' model of therapeutic-community treatment. On the contrary, a step towards some recollection of dwelling may set us on our way towards a radical departure precisely from this structure of alternative treatments.

'Dwelling' reminds us of the question of *being*. Here, however, I choose to bring into view what might be termed an *epistemology* of dwelling. By this, I refer to a *way* of being with one another and knowing one's way in the world which is *being at home*. The relevance of this I hope is evident; for it seems that individuals who find their way to therapeutic communities do so precisely because they do *not* enjoy that sure-footedness in being, that freedom to move and be moved, that 'knowing one's way about', that sense of orientation which is of the essence of being at home. I propose that the various alienated, disarticulated spaces and places in the world at which individuals may arrive, existential *positions* whose negotiation may prove sufficiently problematic as to occasion the seeking of therapeutic help in the form of a supportive community, may quite instructively be embraced within the notion of 'homelessness'. This term helps substantialize, and open up, in more concreteness what was earlier referred to as interpersonal disarticulation.

Thus, the meaning of 'homelessness' has come to extend far beyond the position of not having a roof over one's head. Our ordinary language itself suggests that the domain of home reaches beyond the third skin which shelters us. We refer, first of all, to being at home *in the world*. We refer, furthermore, to a person being at home in what he is doing, being at home in language; to being at home with oneself, and being at home with another. Something of what we may have in mind when we use these terms is suggested by the notion of being 'untogether' or again, lacking that sureness in the world which is ontological security. Again, something of the disorientedness of homelessness may be articulated through such inflections as 'being out of touch', 'beside oneself', 'not knowing which way to turn', and so on. Many of these common idioms are strikingly spatial: homelessness, we might say, is being 'spaced out' as distinct from being 'homed in'. When we speak of being 'at home' we suggest a domain where we belong, and which is in some way our own. Here, the notion of *inhabitation* is useful. Writing of the human subject's enfoldment within the stuff of the world, Merleau-Ponty speaks of the 'flesh of the world'. Inhabitation very much implies such an enwovenness within the fabric of things. The obsolete verb 'habit' meant to wear and to dwell; the first huts were made of skin, or hides. To inhabit is to have and to hold; to be-have and to be held.

According to the degree and manner in which I am 'at home' where I find myself, in what I am doing, my mode of inhabitation of space will vary enormously. Thus will space itself open or close, expand or contract. Space is not some ether which surrounds and envelops us, but a field of openings and depths held or subtended by vectors of intentionality. The example of a sportsman upon his field of play, or a dancer upon the floor, may illustrate quite well that lived spatiality, that freedom of movement, which belongs with 'being at home'. The way in which we may 'be at home' and move in the world of our desire, where we are able equally to move and speak in sureness of our ground, and where we stand with one another, may contrast very vividly with the way in which we tend to move when we are not sure of our ground, when we do not know where we stand with others, where we do not feel at home.

Some situations quite clearly do not lend themselves to that free inhabitation which is symbolized by the player upon the field of play. Space now becomes 'occupied' instead of lived, taken up instead of opened up. Institutional spaces of one sort or another provide examples of inhabited spaces which do not invite people to come out of themselves.

What I am here calling 'homelessness' has more traditionally been alluded to within psychiatric discourse as 'alienation'; until comparatively recent times, indeed, psychiatrists were termed 'alienists'. But how far do therapeutic communities succeed in evoking a world in which a person might come to 'understand' or recognize himself as other than alien? How far do they succeed in evoking or recalling an ordinary or familiar world, or a world of intimacy, within which alienation might come to recognize its own strangeness? A person who moves towards a therapeutic community typically does not feel ordinary – for he has lost his way. That is his alienation – but it is an alienation which, we might say, is essentially human, since it is by straying that we find our way. Must we not say, however, that a *community* has lost its way when the most ordinary or commonplace things have become forgotten – ordinariness which is the very stuff of our finding our way in the world.

If a person turns from the loneliness and despair of his alienation towards a community of fellow beings, turns in his estrangement towards the possibility of some re-articulation into the generative matrix of community life – does this turning not suggest the notion of a *homecoming* rather than that of a cure? It is not through the neo-medicalism of 'community as doctor' nor through some carefully contrived anti-psychiatric posturing, but through the opening of dwelling, as hospitality, that the epistemology of psychological treatment becomes transcended, showing itself as one articulation of its own impoverished groundedness, its *own* homelessness.

ORDER AND THE ORDINARY

It is my argument that these considerations have important bearing upon the manner in which a therapeutic community might more creatively be thought of, set up, and guided. My thinking here departs quite radically for example from that of Crocket, for whom the concept of the therapeutic community is 'fairly clear cut':

> We bring a group of people together, first by organizing suitable accommodation, then persuading (or compelling) them to come there, after which we make use of the ensuing internal transactions for therapeutic purposes. (Crocket, 1979, p. 138)

It departs likewise from that of Kirk and Millard, who, in an article entitled 'Personal growth in the therapeutic community', write:

> The authors view the residential institution as an open system exchanging materials with its environment and having a human throughput. They suggest that what makes the institution is the interplay between resources and throughput (that is, the activities through which an intake is required, processed and transformed into an output). The stage of residence or throughput is broken up into 'conversion factors' which require the provision of both human and physical resources. The task of the institution as a whole is understood in terms of the relationship of the activities of the three systems of intake, throughput to each other, and to the environment. (Kirk and Millard, 1979, p. 115)

Here we see how therapeutic communities respond by techniques and tinkerings. Their inhabitants, typically, are referred to as 'consumers'. They 'partake as residents in the therapeutic process'. The community is a 'treatment modality', it approximates to the ideal of a 'twenty-four-hour treatment environment'. These forms of therapeutic concern are examples (and may remain more stubbornly so the more psychologically sophisticated and forward thinking they become) of de-based concern, to the extent that they wander from the commonplace, from a human sheltering whose threshold is immediate and recognizable, from the sureness of home ground. By placing my emphasis upon dwelling, and proposing as a theoretical practice the opening up of dwelling, rather than the implementing of formal methods and techniques in which it is presupposed, I propose no more than the putting of first things first. I argue for a reversal of that movement whereby we arrive at the absurdity of the tail wagging the dog.

My emphasis is upon the therapeutic community as a place where people dwell; where they unpack and get on with it. The household provides the foremost illustration of a place of dwelling. It is made up of the people who live there, with one another, where living is the way we 'go on being'. The members of a household get up, go to bed, go to work or stay at home, enjoy life's pleasures, endure its drudgeries, meet its challenges, and so on. And in this there is no difference between a therapeutic-community household and any other household in the street. In each case, the people who live there do what they want to do, as they want to, they pursue whatsoever they are drawn to in whatever fashion they like, with whomsoever they want, according to their tastes and circumstances. They generally get on with their own business as well as they are able, according to the various constraints, demands and obligations which govern their lives.

Where we might want to make a distinction between such a *therapeutic* household and any other in the street, this will not be spelled out in terms of the methods and techniques which it employs, but in terms of its style, its way, its openness to the issues which arise in the course of its members living together and coming to acknowledge what they mean to one another. According to its ambience and spirit, its concerns and the textures within which they are interwoven, different facilitating conditions may be generated, more or less conducive or enabling of its members to find themselves at home with one another. What I now wish to suggest is that these facilitating conditions are not by any means orderable, or amenable to being made to order. Here I question for example whether the distinctions one finds being made between different organizational structures, different methods of imposing order upon a therapeutic community, are not of less importance than another distinction we might make between different sorts of order, different orders.

There is, for example, the sort of order that one can institute by following a plan. It might be termed an administrative or organizational ordering. Tidying my desk might be a very simple example. I have in mind an idea or picture of what constitutes a sufficiently tidied desk, and then I simply arrange or move the objects on it until the top of the desk corresponds to the required state. A social administrator provides a more complex example, or any organizer or bureaucrat who takes his patch or area to be 'in order' when his desk is clear. The notion of 'law and order' understands order in roughly this same fashion: implementation of the law is the means to remove disorder and thereby maintain 'order'.

It seems to be widely assumed that the sort of order which pertains mostly to the successful running of a therapeutic community is of an administrative or organizational nature. Structure, therefore, is imposed, procedures instituted, programmes implemented. Rules and organizational structures, therefore, assumed to be only a more precise articulation or formal elaboration of the sorts of rules which govern life in the community at large, come to be taken for granted in therapeutic communities, providing as they do a 'reality oriented' preparation for life outside. The alternative, it is assumed, is that the (therapeutically harmful) situation will arise which is an 'absence of structure'.

It is hard to imagine what this 'absence of structure' might be in the context of a community, which is precisely structured according, for example, to its habits and rituals, the bonds of communality, the features of a common ground. At any rate, we need to be reminded, surely, that order which is brought about by formal structuring, ordering or arranging is by no means the only sort of order which may be recognized in human affairs. There is, for example, that order ('organic' possibly, as distinct from 'organizational') which *takes shape* in the course of people going about their business, or finding their own way with one another.

Some of these orders of everyday life are well illustrated by the notion of the *ordinary*; and certainly ordinariness resists being imposed by order. It is surely one of the deep ironies of neurotic life that the attempt to achieve ordinariness must be self-defeating. It is precisely its ordinariness which we might have in mind when we speak of a household being in order. We refer to the manner in which it goes about its daily business, and the ordinary things about which this going is contextualized. The structure of the house is not so much *imposed* as shaped or opened according to the abiding concerns and priorities which its members have. Like an individual, a household evolves a way, a style; and in the opening up and maintaining of this way we may think, for example, of its rhythms, its rituals and traditions, and the momentum of its

47

habits. In some senses it might be instructive to see a household being structured in a manner akin to music; for within any household will be found themes and variations, harmonies and disharmonies, points and counterpoints, accords and discords, phased in and out of rhythm. According to his response or responsiveness to the phasings of this music, a person who belongs to the household will be articulated or geared into, or attuned to, what is going on.

Let us see if something of this organic-organizational distinction can be made more clear by referring to different orders of *time*. When therapeutic communities proceed on the assumption that disturbing people are particularly in need of firm organization, then statements like this are to be expected:

> One of the crucial issues that therapeutic communities have to deal with is the problem of structuring the day. (Grunberg, 1979, p. 249)

One way of coping with this problem is to break the day down into such a 'daily round of organized activities' as the following:

7.30–8.30	Breakfast
8.30–9.45	Community meetings
9.45–10.15	Tea
10.15–11.15	Doctors' groups
11.15–12.00	Workshops
12.00–12.30	Lunch
12.30–13.00	Ward meetings
13.00–16.00	Workshops or therapeutic interviews
16.00–16.30	Tea
16.30–18.30	Free time
18.30–20.30	Unit social
20.30–21.00	Prepare for bed
21.00–07.00	Sleep (Rapoport, 1960, p. 80)

This list is commented upon as follows:

> Treatment potentialities are seen in every aspect of this pattern . . . treatment is meant to be all-pervasive, and the rehabilitation effect of treatment is meant to be enhanced by creating a pattern of activities that is like that of the average person outside. (p. 80)

It is of course true that most people in Western cultures are quite familiar with the presses and demands of timetables, appointments to be kept, and so on; they articulate their lives quite readily into the structures of conventional time. But conventional time (serial time, chronological time) is not the last word in time. It differs, surely, from *my* time, that is, the time which I live. Chronological time is usually thought of in terms of its seriality of units, everywhere the same, and the constant rate at which they pass. We tend to characterize lived time, on the other hand, by reference to its openings and closings, cycles and phases, flowerings and fruitions. The time 'to every purpose' can be right or wrong, ready or not yet ready, premature or too late. Lived time is characterized first of all by its rhythms, its ebbings and flowings (the etymology brings together the words time and tide), its arisings and unfoldings, upwellings and advents. Where we might be said to be living, either temporally or chronically, in a modality of 'chronological time' we might typically be found 'watching the clock', 'clocking in and out', 'filling time', 'killing time', going through the motions. 'Biding' our time is rather different; it is a staying with, an abiding, rather than a mere enduring. Notions which we might more readily associate with lived time are those such as spontaneity, readiness, and possibility.

We are sometimes inclined to think of lived time as simply being the 'subjective experience' of real, or objective time. Careful reflection makes this a position difficult to justify. Many philosophers have pointed out the unsatisfactoriness of the notion of a 'pure time' which flows like a stream, indicating for example that this metaphor itself presupposes time. We have seen that in Heidegger man is so essentially 'temporal' that his being is a dwelling. In Merleau-Ponty, we ourselves are 'the upsurge of time'. Perhaps the extraordinarily intimate relation between human being and time shows itself nowhere more clearly than in the particular temporalities of people who are 'mentally ill'. How could it be otherwise, for a being who dwells, than that to be 'homeless' is also to be out of time? What psychiatric disorders are not closures and enclosures of time? Typical neurotic complaints are to do with repetition, hopelessness, with the inability to be spontaneous, and with various forms of inaccessibility to one another of past,

49

present and future. We recognize typical features of lived time, such as are associated with the manic, the depressed, the obsessive, and so on. Freud, of course, drew attention to the relationship between sexuality and time, and to the timelessness of the unconscious; indeed his greatest insights are very much to do with the temporal structures of emotional suffering.

How is a therapist – or a community – able to help someone *remember* time – remember his own future, awaken to that time which is his own advent or upsurge into the world? How can a community help someone who is 'out of time', who has lost track of his time, whom time passes over, or whose time is the unending hell of eternal repetition? We might say that such a person 'needs' time, or that a community must 'have time for' its members, if time is to be opened up.

This calls for an entirely different conception of time from that which is accounted for by the activities of the house timetable. To be sure, every moment of the day there is structured as a 'having time for' the patient. Not a single second is wasted. But by no means does having time for refer to chronological time which is meted out. We can have a lot of time for someone we hardly ever see, and we can spend all day with someone for whom we have very little time. Having time for does not just mean putting in the hours and minutes. Rather than indicating that members of a community have time for one another, the timetable which I have illustrated suggests that here there is *no* time for one another's *own* time. Such a structuring forecloses the possibility of authentic time, because all time is contained within the parameters of an overall directive or plan, all time is used as efficiently as could be, in the service of a pre-ordained project, expressly designed for the patient's good. Every moment of the day is accounted for, free time being just another house activity.

The day has been divided into units, and into activities accorded to each unit, and time is narrowed or constricted to a seriality of events. There is no temporal ground for time to take seed, since all time has been used up. These slicings of the day into purposive activities cut across or disarticulate what might be called the 'temporal wholeness' of a community, and ensure that the potency of its time, its power or capacity to open time's backwaters,

50

remember time, will not be realized. A wholeness is not a uniform-ity. People may need time to remember, or 'get it together', but different times may have different fecundities for different people. Some people may need nothing so much as the reassurance of the sureness of the ordinary, the coming and going, the openings and closings of the everyday. Some people may want to do everything at once, others may need to do nothing, or to lie fallow. Some people may need time to 'give', others to take, some to work, others to refrain from working; to everything there is indeed a season. Some people may wish to stay up all night and sleep all day, or stay up day and night, or sleep day and night.

If a community can open itself to, and have the time for, all these times, and include them within its own rhythms of comings and goings, gatherings and dispersings as people go about their busi-ness, then it might find itself freed from the absurdities of 'struc-tured versus unstructured' time, and having found itself on its way towards a living of that time which is of the essence.

RICHARD

Richard was a young man of twenty-three when he first found his way to a Philadelphia Association household. He had been in and out of mental hospital since leaving school, having on different occasions been diagnosed as schizophrenic, or suffering from a severe and chronic depressive illness. Outside hospital he had lived for periods on his own; and succeeded in holding on to short-term and casual jobs; he had also stayed for a period in a therapeutic community run by a large voluntary organization. He displayed many of the features of the classic 'revolving door' syndrome. He had undergone intensive and extensive treatments of ECT and heavy medication, without any lasting signs of improvement. He had now come to feel that these treatments had damaged his brain, and his capacity to think, and that any further treatment was without question going to be the last straw. There is some reason to believe that he was in line for psychosurgery.

He had found his way to the house through the help of a social worker who had taken some interest in him over the years. Follow-ing an invitation to visit, he arrived from hospital one evening, by ambulance. The two nurses who accompanied him declined to come in: not for them the epistemological shift. The company inside consisted in the ten or so people who were living in the house at the time, the house psychotherapist, and one other visitor. The gathering took place around the large kitchen table, upon which was a fair amount of day's clutter, and upon which also would be served a regular supply of cups of tea.

Richard looked quite wretched. He had very little to say for himself beyond saying that he wanted to 'withdraw', to 'think'. He maintained that he had been trying one way or another to withdraw over the past few years, but never had been allowed to go through with this. Rather unusually, Richard was accepted into the house on the basis of this one meeting, and moved in a few days later. He pottered about the house for a couple of days, but gradually retreated to his attic bedroom.

He was to spend the next two years in bed, virtually without moving. He would have been described in hospitalese in the following sort of terms: withdrawn, negativistic, bodily obsessed, incontinent of urine and faeces, lacking in affect . . .

There were occasions during these two years, particularly towards the end, when he would speak with whomever engaged him in conversation. From these brief conversations, and from the jottings which he would from time to time leave beside his bed, others in the house managed to glean some rudimentary idea as to what he was on about. It all seemed to pivot upon his wish to withdraw. He wanted to be left utterly alone and uninterrupted, so as to be in a position to find his 'self'. Throughout his life, he felt, he had been little more than what others had expected of him. Now he felt himself to be engaged in some last-ditch attempt to retrieve, from the silent depths of his solitude, that which there might just be left of his *own* self.

He claimed that his life was utterly in balance, on the edge, and that, in order to survive, he had to remain absolutely still. He insisted on being left completely alone. He required absolute silence while he 'thought'. Every sound represented an agonizing distraction. Every move he made was agonizingly critical. Every word that he spoke was at risk of his life.

In his more articulate writings he described something of the delicate balance he was trying to maintain:

I desperately need to put all my energy into facing my anxieties full in the face and battling against any retreats into distractions such as 'displaced anxieties' which prevent me from coping with my real activities, make me lose my grip on reality and put me in a state of panic. Noise is a particular threat to me as it is an external distraction I cannot fight, preventing me from thinking and furthering my moments of panic. A loud bang in the night shatters my vision leaving me in a terrifying darkness for about two hours while I work my way back to clear vision.

How could this house help Richard? Not, at any rate by 'helping' – having to be seen to be engaged in some sort of proprietary activity such that the possibilities of attentive non-intervention are unquestioningly pre-empted. Rather, the response of the house is to gesture the opening of a conversation. It is to open or extend a conversation which is abiding, going on, being lived. It gestures the hospitality of dwelling.

But there is already a complexity to this particular situation. The position which Richard takes up within the house is somewhat ironic. He proposes to withdraw from the very community towards which, in his helplessness, he is drawn. He asks for nothing so much as to be left alone. It is at least a paradoxical request. Does the house acquiesce to it by ignoring him? It is difficult to ignore someone whose presence is so palpable. Do people tiptoe past his bedroom door out of consideration for his rather extraordinary sensitivity to noise? Or is this merely playing in to some grandiosity? At what point might others find it appropriate to step in? Do they wait until the smell from his room becomes no longer bearable? Should the house let him starve to death? At one time he was down to five or six stones, wasted and emaciated, stinking, covered with bed sores, crawling with bugs. When is enough enough?

How is Richard's request to be interpreted? Such matters as this, which are far from straightforward, would (along with the more prosaic things) engender conversation around the table. Because of the intricacies and intimacies of these issues, to do with what people mean to one another, and the latencies, undercurrents and unspoken themes with which they were interwoven, the regular attendance of the house psychotherapist was crucial to the keeping open of this conversation. On the crossroads of this common place

– the dwelling – within which he is both at the centre and outside, the therapist plays the part of hermetic intermediary, through whose mediation the boundaries of relationship emerge, and through whose words, in what they show, a guidance is offered through those enigmas which arise at the limits of what may be spelled out.

There were numerous conversations where matters to do with Richard were discussed. Around the table at which he never sat, Richard occupied a rather important position, a fact of which he was doubtless aware. People showed quite different degrees of interest in having anything actively to do with him, but for the most part there was a general agreement as to the sort of approach which was best. This was to interfere as little as possible, but at the same time to assume – in the absence of any instruction to the contrary – a freedom to interpret Richard's request to be left alone rather openly, and certainly not to the letter. Two people in parti- cular made it their business to keep an eye on him; they left food by his bedside, which in minute quantities he would eat, and they kept him from becoming too filthy. They encouraged some mini- mal movement of his limbs, and also gave him periodic baths, carrying him silent, limp, and with an expression of long-suffering agony on his face, to and from the bathroom.

There would be difficult decisions to make. What, for example, does the house do in August, when almost everyone is planning to go away to the cottage in Wales? Richard is consulted; he doesn't want to go, he wants to be left alone. But the one or two people who are left behind certainly don't want to look after Richard. So he comes along, bundled into the back of the Volkswagen van with his shitty mattress and stinking blankets. The cottage is in fact no more than a large converted barn, so now there is *absolutely no* chance of Richard getting any quiet at all. One very solitary member of the house has already pitched her tent in the nearby field, and, ever on the margins, flits between field and barn. But now there is *another* tent in the field – in the opposite corner of the field – and here Richard spends his days screaming at the sheep, because now *they* are interfering with his 'thinking'.

Richard's situation was for a long time a very serious one indeed; he was probably quite right in feeling that his life was very delica- tely poised. The household, too, walked a very fine line with him.

But the fact that it finally worked out well was partly because the house didn't take it all *that* seriously: in many ways his stay in the house was a source of much amusement, of which he was well aware. It was without doubt most important to his eventual re-articulation or recovery that, despite his pleas to be left alone, he found himself in a place where life, in some degree of vitality and quirkiness and not just in the sombre earnestness of 'helping', carried on around him. Beyond what is going on, there is nothing.

3

Therapeia, play and the therapeutic household

JOSEPH FRIEDMAN

IN PHILADELPHIA ASSOCIATION households, people go to sleep when they wish. They get out of bed under their own steam and in their own time. When they are moved to, they shop, cook, eat, clean, stay in their rooms, watch television, read, and go out to work, study, or simply escape. All this takes place in every household in the land, unscheduled, though also, as in our households, articulated by many diverse factors.

What, if indeed anything, is therapeutic about this? What sort of therapy goes on in these houses? Why call them therapeutic communities at all, for they are certainly unlike many communities which are called therapeutic? In this paper, I hope to address these questions, and the context in which they arise. For it is my contention that therapy, and particularly therapy in communities, has come to be based on an understanding of community and man's place in it which is fundamentally inadequate and misjudged. This understanding is, in Heidegger's terms, technological (that is, community is seen as a variously conceived 'resource' which can be used by man for his own purposes; see pp. 69–75), and I believe that the therapeutic process takes place in spite of it, rather than because of it.

To show how this is the case, and the way in which the ground of the debate about therapy has shifted into a technical register, I will first try to illuminate the profound Greek understanding which was involved in the concept of *therapeia* (θεραπεια) through reference to the Homeric epics. For I believe that psychotherapeutic practice, and particularly its core notions of attention, interpretation and action, springs more directly from that phenomenological understanding inherent in the Homeric epics than the modern technological vision into which it has largely been subsumed.

Therapeia is a word which was used by the Greeks to name different practices, to the modern ear dissimilar and only peripherally related. The most common usage (see Liddell and Scott, 1940) denotes 'service, attendance', particularly of persons to the gods. In this respect, the word is often translated 'worship'. However, this service and attendance may also be devoted to parents, to the care and nurture of children, or to caring for and tending to animals, and plants. The second practice is more familiar to us, that of 'medical or surgical treatment or cure'.

We are immediately struck by the way in which the first practice is described by words like 'service, attendance to', and 'care', and that though the second use does not specifically speak in this way, medical treatment is often called a caring for someone. This observation, however, does not really begin to tell us how our familiar understanding of therapeutic practice, that of medical or surgical treatment, was for the Greeks an essentially religious practice involving a coherent vision of a world permeated with the gods' presence. Indeed, in our time medical and surgical treatment is usually contrasted by its practitioners with such depending on or attending to the gods.

This contrast has created much confusion about therapeutic practice, therapeutic communities, and indeed the very nature of therapy. If, as I am contending, our work in therapeutic communities has both its roots and heart in a modern understanding of the relationship between man and god which is so essential a part of the Greek vision brought to light in the Homeric epics, then a clarification of this Greek vision will help us to be clearer about its nature. (My attempt to explicate the Greek understanding of the gods, their appearance and their effect is primarily based on Walter Otto's *The Homeric Gods* (1979). Vincent Vcynas's *Earth and Gods* (1969) and E.R. Dodds's *The Greeks and the Irrational* (1951) have been other invaluable sources for this discussion.)

THE GREEK GODS

The Greek world which is described in the Homeric epics is one in which the importance of the gods cannot be doubted. Indeed, it often seems that no action of man or nature can be described

without reference to them. This is already difficult for us to com-
prehend, for the gods no longer play a part in our thinking or
perception. They no longer inhabit our world; for us, as Heidegger
put it, they have retreated. And yet to understand the place of
therapeia in the Greek world, it is critically important to see the
way in which the gods were part of the Greeks' experience. Here, I
will concentrate on exposing those aspects of the Greeks' understanding of the gods and their appearance which shed light on the
roots of our modern practice of *therapeia* in communities. These
aspects will help me to draw two different distinctions, between a
practice that is founded in *therapeia* rather than technology, and
between therapeutic and other households.

The Greek experience of the gods was inextricably bound up
with a profound understanding of the natural world. Indeed, it was
in the most natural of occurrences that the Greeks perceived the
gods' presence. We cannot begin to grasp their vision when we
assume, as is so often the case, that the Greeks 'had' gods because
they did not have adequate scientific knowledge or theory. (Rather,
we might say that the reason that we cannot give science its proper
place is because we have lost contact with that which the Greeks
called the gods.)

> The Greek deity does not operate from the beyond upon the
> inwardness of man, upon his soul, which is connected with it in
> some mysterious way. The deity is one with the world and
> approaches man out of the things in the world *if he is upon his
> way* and participates in the world's manifold life. (Otto, 1979,
> p. 174)

Here, the appearance of the gods is linked both to the natural world
and human projects. Moreover, the god's existence is said to be a
matter of experience, rather than faith. That which the Greeks
called the gods was manifest in 'the things of the world'. The
Greek understanding of the gods was thus phenomenological in
that it involved a devoted attention 'to the things themselves'. As
Heidegger saw it, linked as they were to the things of the world,
the gods and their action were a matter of knowledge and evidence
and thus could be the subject of philosophical and phenomenological analysis. (Indeed, many of his later writings make reference
to the gods and the 'fourfold' of which they were a part. This was

part of his attempt to bring more clearly a perception of the gods and that which they named into phenomenological analysis and more ordinary human experience.)

How *did* the Greeks experience the gods? What kind of evidence and knowledge were involved in their perception? Perhaps these questions are best answered by looking at several examples of the manifestation of one god, Athena. Athena, the daughter of Zeus, is often portrayed in sculpture as a maiden with a large shield, surrounded by warrior women, or giving aid and comfort to men engaged in battle or other heroic deeds. She is known by many epithets; she is of 'many counsels', the 'maid', the 'virgin', 'bright-eyed' like the owl, the 'tamer of horses'. For the Greeks, these epithets, though seemingly contradictory and disjointed, found their unity in a single vision, a vision which can be seen in the various ways her presence was known.

For example, when in the *Odyssey* Telemachus follows a dream urging him to return to the Greek mainland to do battle with his mother's suitors, 'Grey-eyed Athena sent them a favouring breeze, rushing violently through the clear sky that the ship might speedily finish her course in the salt sea' (Homer). Athena's presence and action are here seen in a natural phenomenon. She does not show her power by pushing Telemachus's vessel *against* the natural wind, in the manner of an Eastern god. Rather, she was known in a favouring breeze, something which was thus more than a wind happening to go in the direction we prefer. Indeed, in our everyday lives (when sailing?), we never experience a wind which just happens to go in the direction we prefer (as is 'scientifically correct') – such as wind is always for us . . . favouring.

In the following scene, we can see how Athena became manifest in the world of men

In the *Iliad*, Achilles begins to draw his sword, inflamed by passion, keen to kill Agamemnon for his insulting words. 'Even as he pondered and was drawing the sword from his scabbard' (*Iliad*, 1: 194), Athena touched him. Her touch *is* the coming of reason. He sheathes his sword and the situation is henceforth guided by her spirit. Does not reason still come to us in this way, as a spirit which touches and transforms us in an instant?

Here we can see how the Greeks experienced both Athena's mode of action and her nature. She was for them the 'tamer of horses', of unbridled passion. 'What she shows man, what she inspires him to, is boldness, will to victory, courage. But all this is nothing without directing reason and illuminating clarity' (Otto, p. 53). For the Greeks, Athena, her presence and her nature, all become manifest in a single moment – those moments in which good counsel, courage, boldness, practical understanding and action prevail. Athena was nowhere when that which she showed was not embodied in human action and perception. Conversely, when she was absent, so too were these qualities. Each of the Greek gods brought a different world of experience to presence. When reason prevailed, Athena was present. When people or situations were dominated by bloodthirsty rage (Ares' domain), she was not. Ares was Athena's sworn enemy. Does not this phenomenological description still apply to our world?

The Greek gods (and their interrelationships) thus define a phenomenology of presence and absence. The Greeks were devoted to understanding this phenomenology partly because they understood it as having a divine sanction. Can we not trace such a phenomenology in our own experience? Is it not true that we do not devote ourselves to this task because of our keenness to pursue a scientific causal understanding?

GODS AND COMMUNITY

Typically, as in the case of Achilles, Athena appears only for a moment, and often only to the person she touches. Her being and presence made the coming of reason a divine phenomenon. For the Greeks, the ability to keep one's head was not solely within oneself but in a unique co-presencing of one's own being and that of the god. As Diomedes says about Achilles in the *Iliad* (9: 702), 'He will fight again whenever the time comes that the heart in his body urges him to and the god drives him.'

In our therapeutic households, we witness this interplay between person and that which is larger than him (or her) as a co-presencing of community and individual. We see mental and emotional balance and imbalance as not primarily internal or external but rather as a co-presencing of individual and community. Action too finds its home and place in this co-presencing. In community therapy, my interpretative stance aims at allowing this interplay to come fully into focus, at showing the way in which all speech (whether by words, action, silence or the placing of the 'material stuff' of the house) is understandable in its terms. For in so far as it is only an abstract entity, community is nowhere. It is not the context in which all texts can be deciphered.

To the modern eye, the Greek conception of the god's appearance (for example in Achilles' action) seems to take something away from the man. It is as though credit for his cool-headedness must go to another. He is diminished by this, for us, to no good effect. Equally, when for example Helen reproaches not only herself but also the goddess Aphrodite for her unfaithfulness, we see this as an avoidance of responsibility.

For the Greeks, however, the individual was no less a hero and received no less approbation because of a general recognition of the god's part in his/her action. Similarly, though Aphrodite was seen to have moved Helen, Helen (and those associated with her) can in no way escape a remorseless punishment. This was true because for the Greeks right action came from perception and perception derived from the path one was on and one's ability to see that which encroached upon it.

Indeed, in the *Iliad* and the *Odyssey* an important phenomenology of this sort of perception is revealed. There are some individuals who are shown to move through the world unaware of, or indeed disdaining, the larger forces that prevail, the gods' presence. There are others who are able to sense that a god is near, at play in a particular action, thought or situation, and yet who cannot name or recognize the particular god, the particular spirit that reigns. And finally, there are those who are able to recognize that not only is a god near or present, but which god it is. Their ability, like that of Homer the poet, to name the god, to take into account his/her particular presence, inevitably leads to right action. Yet even this perception is a gift of the gods, and the man who is capable of it is ennobled.

Many of those who come to our households find themselves similarly unaware of the larger forces at play in communal situations. In regarding themselves as wholly separate loci of action and perception, these individuals are 'out of it' and have lost their way. This characteristic human loss can never be understood without the context of another and the community the other brings to representation.

If community is only an abstract entity for those who live, work or are otherwise involved in the therapeutic household, then the chances for these individuals to find their place are slim. For it is only in so far as community can come into play, and be seen to be in play, that individuals can come to more clearly define their relationship to it and work through those understandings of it that have kept them on their own.

This is indeed the heart of community therapy. Through our interpretations we aim to bring the presencing of community and the way it exists for those who live in it into focus and, at the same time, into question. By doing this, we enable people to take on the problematics of their own individual positions and the larger issues in which they are sited.

In the Homeric epics, the way in which individuals were able to recognize the presence of a particular god (and thus to act correctly) was through careful attention to everything that became manifest in a given situation. The Greeks understood that in any circumstance the place of the god inevitably emerged from its many aspects.

In community therapy, we understand that the concerns of the community – what it is 'for' – become manifest in its daily life. The way in which the cooking and washing-up are done or not, the way in which individuals speak to one another or not, and indeed the things that are left around (tea cups piling up in the room where the television lives) or disappear (telephone messages) are all part of the arena of the household in which the life of the community is articulated. Community therapy involves attending to these phenomena with the intention of elucidating the question, 'What is going on?' The ever-changing answers to this question make reference to the different spirits which can play through a situation, striking its participants in different ways depending on their own predilections and histories. These different spirits show themselves in different elements of the situation, and may be constantly changing or stubbornly immovable.

By attempting to answer the question, 'What is going on?' – given by naming the god and the world he presided over – not the more modern 'why' of causality, the Greeks promoted inquiry into the nature of things, rather than their causes, as it was hubris to assume to know the 'why' of the gods' ways. (Gods were clearly seen to be a different order of phenomena from rocks, animals, plants, etc. Our human 'whys' perhaps inevitably reveal more about our basic assumptions of what is important (what was 'in the beginning') than about the nature of the phenomena themselves.) In our households, we can often see the way in which the question why ('Why do I always do this?') can be a sidestepping of the unbearable present. For the Greeks, this sidestep (and the infinite regress to which 'why?' can so often lead) was foreclosed in advance by the way in which the god was part of their concrete experience of the world – in much the same way as physical causation is part of ours – as the inextricable hallmark of the world's presence and meaning.

This foreclosure meant that for the Greeks the things of the world were never 'things' in the modern sense of the word, but always something more. The wind which Athena sent to Telemachus was not essentially a movement of molecules of the air, or an internal experience of the god projected outward, but a co-presencing, a playing out of god and natural phenomena. Indeed, all life – plants, animals, parents, children, the healthy and the sick (and indeed so-called 'natural phenomena' – the wind, rain, thunder, lightning) – was part of this vision in which an entire world was sanctified and its meaning guaranteed.

It was this world in which *therapeia* was so crucial. The things of it were a constant call to a larger Being, that was manifest in it. The practice of *therapeia* was to witness this and be in accord with it, to be articulated by it and to it, with the highest form of this articulation being the naming which called the particular presence which was becoming manifest correctly. This is what we call 'interpretation'.

When the co-presencing of which the Greeks were so aware is lost, the things of the world (whether wind, feeling or even God) become mere 'objects', denuded of meaning. Our 'minds' become the locus of meaning which then becomes only a 'view' of things. The notion of 'world view' comes to dominate intercourse, and the common world and community are obscured. When the gods have retreated, the understanding of world as picture arises. Meaning in such a world is always precarious, subjective, always 'added on'. Therapy becomes something one does in special places, an 'add on' to specifically created communities and/or relationships. It is precisely this which we challenge in community therapy, a practice in which we address ourselves to the ways in which that which ultimately reigns in any situation is not the inwardly or outwardly generated will of a person. Perhaps the modern psychoanalytic concept which comes closest to this is Winnicott's notion of play. In the next section, we will consider this to see how it can further illuminate the co-presencing of community and individual.

PLAY

Winnicott's concern with play developed from his interest in the baby's experience of the 'transitional object', for example a teddy bear, a piece of blanket. For the baby, the transitional object is neither internal or external. It is the first 'not-Me' possession, and thus involves an 'abrogation of omnipotence'. This abrogation is possible because the object has a 'vitality' of its own. Winnicott believed it is crucial that the intermediate and paradoxical nature of the transitional object be respected and tolerated by those in charge of the child. If this occurs, 'its fate is to be gradually allowed to be decathected, so that in the course of the years it becomes not so much forgotten as relegated to limbo . . . It loses meaning, and this is because the transitional phenomena have become diffused . . . over the whole cultural field' (Winnicott, 1971, p. 5).

'It is not the object, of course, that is transitional' (p. 14). Rather, the object is the first manifestation of a different positioning of the infant in the world – the first appearance of an intermediate territory between and other than the internal psychic reality and the external world. This intermediate territory is the world of culture, language, creativity and the living transforming experience of the world Winnicott calls 'play'.

In play, we experience the living meeting of person and culture, a revitalizing gathering together of personal and larger-than-personal concerns. As Winnicott puts it, 'Play is immensely exciting [because of] the precariousness of the interplay of personal psychic reality and the experience of control of actual objects' (p. 47). When we play, we inhabit and are contained within a larger structure than ourselves. This structure gathers us to it and, in its space, we can witness and become participant in the healing eruption of the new. (Think of the way we are drawn into a game of football,

wherein the 'new' arises, new moves being revealed by the interplay of player and game.)

It is from his position in the game, as Winnicott emphasizes,
that his new understanding arises. Often, his interpretations are
not only playful but acknowledge their origin in his place in the
game. They are an invitation to join him in a reflective play in
which the new can arise and be seen. For example, 'I am listening
to a girl. I know perfectly well that you are a man but I am listening
to a girl, and I am talking to a girl. I am telling this girl: "You are
talking about penis envy"' (p. 73).

In play, if we are game enough, we are seized and both find
ourselves and lose ourselves in a larger whole which plays through
us if we no longer insist on being rulers of it. That which reigns
(Play) is neither inside nor underneath what goes on, but is indeed
at its very heart, the guarantor of its place and significance. It is
fully present to those who are graced with the ability in any given
moment to be open to it. The healing renewal which we experience in play is not gained by any simple human willing or
intention.

For play, like community, is not simply a human invention or
construction but something larger. As such it needs to be entered
into. For though this way of thinking may seem initially strange to
us, the healing renewal which we experience in play can be seen as
a structure of play itself. For if we examine the phenomenon of
play, we can see that play has its very existence in being played
out, or as Gadamer (1979) puts it, in its presentations. A piece of
music has its true being not in a notation of notes on paper but in
its presentations or performances. Similarly, a game of football is
not essentially a set of rules and regulations agreed by the Football
Association, but rather is that which is played out on the football
pitch. Indeed, those structures which Freud attributed to a 'psychical apparatus' (sometimes described as fictitious and at other times
more literally) were not encountered there, but in the play of the
transference. It was in living play that these structures were seen
through and moved on.

If we look further, to the way in which our language gives us
'play' with respect to the non-human, we find the play of light, the
play of waves, the play of colour. All these expressions indicate
that 'the movement which is play has no goal which brings it to an

end; rather it renews itself in constant repetition. The movement backwards and forwards is obviously so central for the definition of a game that it is not important who or what performs this movement' (Gadamer, p. 93).

This revelation is more than mere 'playing with words'. Rather, it is the issue of our attention to the way in which language plays through us. 'Language has performed in advance a work of abstraction' (p. 92). Etymological analysis can help us to see this abstraction more clearly. It is in our experience of being 'taken up' by a game that we can best see how a game draws us into its area and fills us with its spirit. It defines certain tasks for us, and gives us space to solve them. Our choices are limited once we are in a game, yet we experience no constriction of freedom. Indeed, when we play, we experience freedom from those egoic constraints by which we often feel imprisoned.

However, we are not always glad to be free of these constraints. We may be attached to them. Indeed, we may regard these constraints as our very being, and their loss as the destruction of this being. Thus, though we can say that something is always at play or being played out in any human activity, it does not follow that we are always playing. We often struggle against being taken up by that which is larger than us, by that which plays through us. We can feel we are losing ourselves in it – that it diminishes us to nothing.

One way of resisting play's claim is to 'fit in'. In this (often socially encouraged) form of resistance, the game-structure of community and intercourse is regarded as a set of externally imposed rules which cannot be escaped. (Indeed, language can be regarded in this light, as in autism.) To give our allegiance to these rules is seen as a loss of freedom, and we are bound to resist their all-pervasive claim. One way to do this is to 'fit in', to learn the rules and live as though they (are?) matter. In this often resentful and despairing manifestation of resistance, no one can complain, but no one experiences much joy or satisfaction.

Therapeutic community theorists who see a goal of such communities as the inculcation of social skills or the encouragement of social learning (for example, 'psycho-education') miss this essential distinction. They have abstracted from the fabric of community 'functions' which they then believe give rise to its therapeutic

66

potential. (The Richmond Fellowship, the biggest 'therapeutic community' organization in England, in its search for suitable 'models' for its 'residential facilities' (Jansen, 1980, p. 19) has often been subject to, and a proponent of, this confusing tendency). Such theorists see only the husk of community. For though community like play does involve an intricate structure of rules and regulations which are constantly in play, it is precisely *how* this structure exists for someone that determines their potential involvement in it. It is this 'how' that an individual plays out in his involvement (or lack of it) in the world. It is his throw into the game. Therapy involves taking up this throw as the opening throw of a game, an invitation to play. To regard this throw as a misthrow, to be corrected by training in social skills, is not only a refusal of a particular and personal invitation to play (however disguised and unconscious) but a presentation of community as mechanical. If it is indeed the resident's fantasy (the resident's 'how') that to be part of a community is to be caught in an unsympathetic machine, then the possibility of learning to 'fit in' better might be attractive, if only to avoid being crunched up. Such a resident might indeed be keen to learn social skills and to have his lack formulated in this way.

The tendency to formulate a community's generalized 'goals' in terms of variously conceived residents' 'lacks' can cement this process. Of course, in so far as this theoretical stance is put aside in the actual interaction which takes place in the community, its effect is reduced. I believe this is what happens in most therapeutic communities which are truly therapeutic. In these communities, theoretical and technological goals give way to the practice of the community as a whole, a practice which at its best is considerate and thoughtful – neighbourly. Often it is only in thinking and speaking about the therapeutic effects that result from community that its practitioners speak of 'social skills' or 'social education'.

Any thinking in such terms already makes the individual's articulation into community an essentially disjointed fitting-in of cogs into a larger organizational machine. Community is not understood here as the given it is. Neither is its relation to the individual properly understood. We cannot choose to be in a community (in the largest sense of the word) or not. We are not essentially separate entities which must in some way be joined to a larger separate entity. From our first breath (and, of course, before) we are already part of the larger play of family and community. This is a given. The only real question is how one participates in this. We can see this most clearly when someone who only knows the rules joins a game which we enjoy. They may move correctly, but are not 'in' their moves. They have not been taken up by the game's proper spirit. Their absence from play may be because they are too libidinally involved in winning, or in being seen to move correctly. For whatever reasons, the absence in their presence throws us. We find ourselves concerned with it, rather than the game. We may succeed in ignoring it. If not, we may find our sport has been spoiled.

Winnicott's famous formulation about play points to the way in which therapy is a concern with that which keeps us from being able to play, a concern with those attachments which keep us from enjoying ourselves in the healing renewal of play.

> Psychotherapy takes place in the overlap of two areas of playing, that of the patient and that of the therapist. Psychotherapy has to do with two people playing together. The corollary of this is that where playing is not possible then the work done by the therapist is directed towards bringing the patient from a state of not being able to play into a state of being able to play. (Winnicott, 1971, p. 38)

For Winnicott, therapy is a 'highly specialized form of playing in the service of communication with oneself and others' (p. 41). Here the word service reminds us of the original meaning of *therapeia*. Playing is always at the service of something larger – a piece of music or theatre, the game of tennis. It is important to distinguish this from having goals, except in so far as these are given to us by play itself.

For play does give us goals and aims as part of its structure, as does community. But in play, as in community, the achievement of these goals is part of our serving to represent play. (In kicking a goal in football, we serve to re-present an aspect of the game itself.) These goals are part of the game, not its end. If they become ends in themselves, play is no longer well served. For if 'in service of' becomes the attempt to achieve pre-defined goals, the community can no longer be an arena in which desire is freely played out. Desire is chained, however subtly, to technology and its reasoning.

THERAPEIA AND TECHNOLOGY

Technology, in Heidegger's terms, is a revelation of nature as a resource base which stands awaiting man's definition, exposure and utilization (1977). As a revelation, technology is a form of truth – in that it brings to light, or unconcealment (*a-lietheia*), some aspect of being.

In a technological mode of thought, everything that is is seen as a potential resource for our use. Thinking in terms of social skills is thus technological in that it is part of a revelation of human being as a potentially developable resource – as skills. This is technology's pre-view, imposed on being. Once nature is defined in this way, we are freed to proceed in furthering technology's way of being – that of directing our energy towards bringing into being a pre-visioned moment (for example, the existence of a dam) at which we aim, arranging the factors necessary for its appearance. Technological thinking is thus characterized by two main aspects, a revelation of nature as potentially developed resources, and a commitment to bringing into being a moment in the future which is already known.

Pre-defined therapeutic goals (if taken seriously as goals instead of as by-products of community itself) are thus technological in that (a) they pre-define community as a resource base to be developed to serve human requirements and (b) they direct our attention towards the realization of certain pre-visioned goals. Knowing these goals, and knowing community as a potentially developable set of resources, we find the only real questions we have to have revolve around defining those goals we wish to achieve, and deciding how we can best do this.

In technology's vision, the nature of the community we experience every day of our lives is subtly but radically changed. If nature is simply a certain ordering of things, any reordering we might want to undertake is not seen as a radical change. But, as Heidegger points out, the Rhine that we wish to dam to release the energy resources we see in it is not the same Rhine seen by poets

(1977, p. 20). And, indeed, the community which is seen technologically as simply 'there' to serve us is not the same community that we experience daily.

When community is defined as a resource base, the playing out of its concerns is short-circuited. This playing out centres on such (ultimately unanswerable?) questions as 'Who am I and what is my relation to the community?', 'What place can I have in it, can it have for me?', 'How do I serve it, how does it serve me?' and so on. This short-circuiting is one to which therapeutic communities are particularly vulnerable as, unlike the community at large, they are taken by most people concerned to have been founded to achieve some goal – that is, to be 'therapeutic'.

If therapeutic work is taken to be technological – specifically targeted – certain questions become important (What are the therapeutic resources? What is the most efficient way to use them? How can we achieve this efficient use?) and others recede. The literature of therapeutic communities is largely devoted to these questions. What is not usually questioned is the understanding of community as resource (in which conversation, friendship, and desire are all properties to be harnessed, developed and utilized) and the concern with pre-defined goals.

One point of difference between therapeutic and technological truth can be seen in the notion of service, one integral to both play and *therapeia*. Service has to do with attending to the goals, aims, problematics and questions raised by that which is to be served (whether that be a game, a piece of music, a friendship, and so on). It has as part of its structure a concern with boundaries (What is to be served?) rather than goals other than those given to us by what is to be served.

In therapeutic communities, for example, a major area of concern is represented by questions about what the community is and what it should be: Who decides the boundaries to the community and who maintains them? Who is inside the community and who is outside? If someone is inside, how do they stay in? If someone is outside, how are they admitted into the circle? These questions are all crucial because they help define what the community is – its boundaries – and unless one is clear about what one is serving, the nature of one's service will be hesitant, confused and sporadic. This clarity is not (just) cerebral, but must be embodied – as in the case of play, the community must be made one's own.

It is an important characteristic of games that their boundaries (not just physical) be defined clearly. There is sometimes space for playing with these boundaries, for bringing them into question, but the need for boundaries or a play-ground is clear. If the boundaries are clear, the game gives us, as part of its proper spirit, certain tasks and possible solutions to them. It is in the space for defining the tasks and the solutions that games differ and in which the new can arise. The new arises, so to speak, in service of game-given and game-defined goals. (This also applies to participation in the larger community and its politics.) It is part of the play of play that these goals and their definition change moment by moment.

Community, play, and friendship are all the sort of beast that can only come into existence when someone serves to represent them. Man is the sort of beast who can only come into being when serving to represent a larger structure. In service, both the individual and that which is served come into presence (for example, when a friendship blossoms, so do the individuals concerned). This is *therapeia*-tic truth.

In technology's vision, the situation is quite different. Nature does not need man to serve to bring it into being. It is already simply 'there', an orderable ordering of potential resources. As such, it can serve man in whatever way he wishes. Nature is at his disposal, and not vice versa.

Therapeutic communities often attempt to serve two masters, a vision of therapy and community as technological and another vision of therapy and community which we name here *therapeia*-tic. When this is the case, both masters are poorly served. If therapy is understood as a technical method of solving certain problems, this confusion is inherent in the naming of the therapeutic community. As this paper has stressed, this does not have to be the case. It only occurs when the 'therapeutic' fruit of friendship, play and community (satisfaction of needs, space for defining and solving problems, and so on) are taken to be their 'purpose'. For this way of thinking is already technological. The Greek vision, in contrast, saw this fruit as the gift of the gods, a return for the service and attention devoted to them and their world.

71

It is our understanding that attending to community – to its boundaries and problematics – produces an issue which is therapeutic. Paradoxically, the attempt by many therapeutic communities to serve technology (and thus cut out the gods) curtails this issue by changing essentially the playing out of community. The game is then fixed and the inevitable questions about originating desire and its place in the present become literal and perversely answerable. It is in the playing out of these questions and the confusion, misunderstanding, anxiety, fear, happiness and joy that they bring in their wake that community exists, re-presents itself.

The affirmation of *therapeia* is the comprehension that what is essential is always larger than any individual, beyond his attention, will, even imagination. In this understanding we take nothing away from human achievements and failures but simply see these as part of nature or community. In the Greek world, those who did not recognize this were guilty of perhaps the most important Greek 'sin', that of hubris, of not being aware of man's limited being and his place in a larger nature.

It is the *sensus communis*, that concrete generality, which founds community and gives human will its direction. The knowledge which guides *therapeia*, like the *sensus communis* (not the same as our much devalued 'common sense'), is a concrete grasp of circumstances in their infinite variety. This knowledge is outside (though not divorced from) the rational (world as picture) concept of knowledge. The community communities, we might say. It exists in its presentations. As it communities, it gathers us to a larger world. In this gathering, we are claimed, as the Greeks put it, by the gods and the worlds they bespeak.

Each of the realms of the individual Greek gods was indicated by a variety of seemingly unrelated signs. The poet's calling was to attend to these signs, to bring them together in the assembling naming. In the household too, at our meetings, in our daily life, we are confronted by a variety of seemingly unrelated signs. Our modern practice of *therapeia* involves us in attending to these signs in the attempt to name the ordering principle involved. We assume that the seemingly unrelated snatches of conversation that arise from different people around the kitchen table are related to the unwashed cups, the garden heavily laden with dog shit, the time of year. Our assumption is that all these 'signs' cohere in community. Our listening focus is not only to the signs themselves, but to how they are received. Do the signs afflict us, or those in whom they manifest? Are they fended off, changed into something different, ignored, treasured? How do individuals understand their relationship to the community which they represent in their every utterance and action? Does this frame of understanding even arise?

The Homeric vision of the relationship between gods and men established a ground which allowed men to address themselves to the ways in which in daily life they found themselves playing out and at play in larger than individual concerns. Indeed, this vision gave the often humiliating, frustrating and incomprehensible moments to which we are all subject a divine sanction. The Homeric Greeks were not the bearers of the sole responsibility for their human faults, and thus did not have to condemn themselves when their actions led them and others to pain, disappointment, disaster. Neither could they rightly overreach themselves with pride when they found themselves the beneficiaries of the god's grace and in possession of the right word, for this too was the god's gift. The notion of community is our way of addressing ourselves to the human equilibrium here evoked, the way in which we are sited, lost and found in a larger world to which we are always beholden.

Our households provide a place in which people can discover that they live *in* a community. Indeed, they are a constant meditation on the different ways in which this 'in' exists – from the fact that one cannot live truly in one's 'head', to the way in which themes and issues that play through the house are not ultimately located 'in' anyone.

One way to describe this meditation is that it is therapeutic – healing and holy in that it helps one to locate oneself in a larger (human and non-human) world which is constituted by the ever-changing meanings that play through it. As an individual increasingly abides in the community, he is less 'egoic' in that he does not place the centre of his action in himself, but no less an individual in that the responsibility for and meaning of his action is located in his being-in-the-community. This *therapeia* cannot be done to or for an individual by himself or others – but happens as a space is opened for the presence of community to manifest itself. This

73

presencing is not simply in the hands of individuals and so is not subject to human technological means.

To someone concerned with the reordering of an orderable world, the notion of community, like that of the gods, does not change anything. It has no 'cash value'. It does not help us to get on with it. And yet it is precisely this relentless drive to get on, to change, that is the death of the reflective, meditative heart of the community and the individual. This relentless drive is sanctioned by a society whose vision is increasingly technological. In therapeutic communities, it is manifest in the often heartfelt demand (from both residents and the larger community) *to do something* that we and others can call 'therapeutic', something we can point to and say '*this* is what we are doing here', something to justify our involvement in this crucible of suffering.

We can only resist this relentless drive if we are clear about its nature, and of the roots of our work in a different vision and tradition. It is because of this that the way in which nothing is difachievement. We cook, clean, eat, speak and are silent like those living in ferent in Philadelphia Association households is perhaps our proudest any household in the land. There is rivalry, competition, envy, jealousy, love, hate, tension, release, pain, joy, friendship – again, as in every other household.

We have no plan or agenda to distinguish our households from any other. Indeed, it is precisely this realization of the limitations of technological practice that distinguishes our communities from others called 'therapeutic'.

'Lightning steers the universe,' said Heraclitus. We are steered or guided by that which comes to light. Think of the way an invisible (because in darkness) country landscape comes to presence, the relationship between road and tree and house and field suddenly revealed by a flash of lightning. This lightning was traditionally wielded by Zeus, the most powerful of the gods, because it is only in his sudden lightning that any of the gods can come to presence, that the nature which they permeate can come into being. The Homeric Greeks were aware that they were not in charge of the lightning in which everything that is becomes manifest, but their understanding created a world in which this could happen and be seen to be happening.

The Latin word *templum*, derived from Greek *temenos* (Simpson, 1959), meant, literally, (a) a space in the sky or on the earth marked out by the augur for the purpose of taking auspices, (b) a consecrated piece of ground, especially a sanctuary or asylum, or (c) a place dedicated to a particular deity, a shrine or temple. It referred to a marked-out space in which omens could be read. Perhaps, in founding a therapeutic community we mark out a similar space, one in which community can become manifest. Starting a therapeutic community can thus be seen as a sacred act, an invocation of community and its healing power. This makes sense of the universal concern of therapeutic communities with establishing and preserving boundaries, these boundaries now being understood as those of the sacred space.

If establishing a therapeutic community is indeed marking out such a *templum*, in doing so and in attending to the consquences of this we are truly involved in a *therapeia* like that in the Homeric world. It might be that, as we can no longer take the Homeric vision seriously in the world at large, we must establish a limited arena (a 'small' world) which we can then regard in the same light as the Greeks, a world in which everything that happens is a co-presencing, a playing out of individual and community. When we call such a community therapeutic, are we not then involved (however unconsciously) in transmitting and re-evoking the original meaning of *therapeia*?

4

The play of difference
Lacan versus Derrida on Poe[1]

STEVEN GANS

AT THE OUTSET, I owe readers an apology for the following study, on at least three counts; first, because I am commenting on two texts by Lacan and Derrida which themselves are commentaries on a not-so-well-known Poe short story. Second, because in this study I am only able to introduce a way of thinking I call 'textual' without showing how this way works in clinical practice, which is the ultimate intention of my project; and third, because I only tell half the story, Derrida's side, without developing a possible Lacanian response. Yet, through the re-staging and replaying of critical moments of my textual encounters I set out an itinerary of considerations as something of a rite of passage if not a *sine qua non* for would-be participants in a potential dialogue between philosophers and psychoanalysts. Characteristically, philosophers scorn psychoanalysis and psychoanalysts diagnose philosophers. It is consonant with the politics of these professions to claim privilege and autonomy and to resist subordination. The philosophers' claim is often couched in a deferential 'I know, I don't know', while analysts embody their claims in a self-effacement effected to enable the Other to make the unconscious conscious.

Philosophy explicitly, and psychoanalysis implicitly, offer interpretations and 'spiritual' exercises that purport to show the way towards the fulfilment of our humanity; in a word, both disciplines constitute an ethics. Yet each regards the other with suspicion, as Other; at the best of times, as having something to offer that can be assimilated or incorporated into its own enterprise; at the worst, as antithetical, ungrounded or even as a delusional system.

Derrida and Lacan demonstrate mastery not only of their own disciplines, philosophy and psychoanalysis respectively, but with some qualification in each other's discipline as well. Each has intensively read, thought through and made major contributions, if not the major contributions, to reading the core curriculum of contemporary thought, i.e. Hegel, Husserl, Heidegger, Saussure and Freud, to mention only the highlights. So, when both address themselves to Poe's 'The Purloined Letter', we can anticipate, and are not disappointed at finding, an elaboration of major themes that characterize the state of the art of not only their own but also the other's field. Derrida's critical reading of Lacan, moreover, threatens to subvert the analytic field of theoretical practice just as Lacan's piece subverts dogmatic analytical orthodoxy. Derrida's intervention can also be read as opening new directions for psychoanalytical development, as well as legitimating psychoanalytical concerns within the discourse of philosophy.

We can preview the issue in all that is at issue between Derrida and Lacan in the following study as the question of the ultimate indivisibility or divisibility of the subject and language. Is the moral (meaning) of the story of Poe's 'The Purloined Letter' (a story about a compromising letter stolen, re-stolen and returned) that, as subjects of language, we inevitably reappropriate our own 'otherness' in our relation to others and especially in analysis, in which we are most able to hear ourselves being heard. Or is this interpretation of the letter an idealization which attempts to assimilate the multiple and multi-stable effects of writing and narrative, of subjectivity and language, into the packaging of unified meanings and identities? Is the metaphor of speaking to dominate (Lacan) or the metaphor of writing to deconstruct (Derrida)? At stake are numerous and potent questions for psychoanalytic theory and practice. For example: can any sense be made of analysis without the assumption of repetition on which repression, transference and interpretation are founded? What is the meaning of repetition without an original being repeated? What happens to the place or authority of the 'analyst supposed to know' who provides the context and occasion for an examination of one's Other relationship if the idealization of this very place is dismantled? What happens to psychoanalysis as an institution if the analyst cannot be distinguished from the non-analyst or the authorized analytic institution from the non-authorized one?

If the following study initiates readers, especially analytic practitioners, into the vortex of Derridian deconstruction (hesitation), then the way is paved for reconsideration and revitalization of psychoanalytic theoretical practice and its institutionalization. Is psychoanalysis to be understood in terms of a medical, ethical or literary metaphor, as treatment, meeting or text and what difference does this make for practice and outcome?

INTRODUCTION

I take up Derrida's reading of Lacan's seminar on Poe's short story 'The Purloined Letter' in order to illustrate Derrida's phenomenological gesture, which he has recently called 'hesitation',[2] and argue that 'hesitation' is a powerful corrective to the decontextualizing paradigms of orthodox psychoanalysis. Derrida *hesitates* at the hierarchy of presuppositions that is the history of Western metaphysics. He likens metaphysicians to knife grinders who efface the value and the head of coins which they claim, once freed from their context, acquire inestimable worth. In this manner words are removed from their context and transposed to a conceptual level. What they lose is obvious, what they gain, not clear. Derridian hesitation works by allowing the unfoundedness of the assumptions and contradictions of the conclusions of metaphysical texts to be revealed and betray themselves. The result is that metaphysical argument in general is rigorously shown to be undecidable. To the extent that metapsychology is metaphysical, psychoanalysis is vulnerable to but may be liberated by Derrida's deconstructive gesture.

Derrida reads Lacan's text as a pre-eminent instance of Western metaphysical logo-centricism. This means that Lacan's argument operates with a set of traditional assumptions, for example, the law of Identity (of signifier and signified), the hierarchy of truth (that is, symbolic, imaginary and real) and the universal design of the Oedipal configuration.[3] Derrida critiques Lacan's version of psychoanalysis in so far as it lapses into a discourse of mastery, an ontological imperialism which yokes the other, the analysand, to the same, the analyst; the other becomes supporting cast in the scenario of the analytic drama set up to preserve the privilege of the analyst and protect analysis from subversion, contamination and dissolution.

Derrida's reading of Poe's story demonstrates that this text already presupposes and stages its psychoanalytic reading in order to dismantle the possibility of such a reading in advance. Thus what Lacan intends as the paradigmatic illustration of the psychoanalytic enterprise becomes, for Derrida, a case study in the arrogance of metaphysical interpretation.

Yet Derrida's critique of Lacan, as Barbara Johnson's excellent essay on his reading suggests, enacts and replays the very crimes of which he accuses Lacan. There is an uncanny repetition of a story of revenge as restitution of an original crime that occurs not only within the Poe story but as illustrated by the story itself (repetition of the Atreus saga)[4] and in and by Lacan's and Derrida's commentaries on it.

My intention in the following is to elicit from these parallel and rival readings of Poe a pattern or protocol of conjectural reading that emerges as the inevitable staging effects of reading, in other words, as the interpretive 'frame-up', whether in the literary, philosophic or psychoanalytic fields of theoretical practice. Seeing through the 'frame-up' paves the way to elude the trap of capture within one's own analytic pretensions which Poe's story itself achieves and exemplifies.

Preliminary considerations: Derrida ends his deconstructive piece by quoting Lacan's quoting of Dupin's quote. Derrida, like Lacan, like Dupin, seems to want to have the last word but the word or letter is always set in quotes, that is, it is always subject to divisibility. Words always presuppose implied quotes or a signature, an I, you, he/she said it. Derrida argues that the quotes are a trap set by the text which at the same time conceal and reveal the retrospective illusion of a unified speaker or subject who is supposed to be speaking in terms that have univocal meanings. In fact the self-referential text is generating an illusional system into which its interpreters and analysts (Lacan–Derrida) fall. The quotes offset meaning into a chain of literary reference or difference which both enables truth to be told and betrays that truth is an ideal, dependent on the inscriptions of writing, on the fabric and lattice-work of text. Lacan, quoting Dupin's quote on the facsimile he replaced for the letter he stole from the Minister to return to the Queen, remarks that the words are fitting and oracular, and have their source in tragedy: 'A destiny so infamous, if not worthy of Atreus then of Thyestes', Atreus who served his brother's children up to him in a stew, Thyestes who impregnated his daughter with the child who would murder/depose his brother's son.

Lacan's invocation of the tragic source of writing recalls Nietzsche's inspired account of the birth of tragedy, and Derrida's argument against Lacan can be seen as a replay of Nietzsche's polemic against Socratic theoretical man, a gesture we now call post-modernist.

For Nietzsche every identity and every concept arising from identity is false. Theoretical man builds a conceptual fortress to protect himself against what Nietzsche calls the practical ethics of pessimism, whose lynx eyes (like Poe's Minister) shine only in the dark. Truth, the unveiling of the present as it is cast off, is the fetish of Socratic man who maintains the illusion that thinking can erect a fortress of light which will withstand the Dionysian onslaught. The Truth of truth, of this veil of illusion, of individuation as Nietzsche names it, enables man to act and prevents him from being engulfed by pessimism, which dictates an ethic of general slaughter out of pity. 'Individuation' is the antidote to the wisdom of Silenus, that is, best never to have been born, next best, to die quickly, the appropriate response to the terror and absurdity of existence (Nietzsche, 1976, p. 505).

Nietzsche's Prometheus, the archetypical thief, the paradigmatic theoretical and technological man, steals fire, controls it and thus acquires what is best and highest through crime. Tragedy celebrates in its dithyrambic chorus the annihilation of the veil of Maya, of individuation, as it sings of the dismemberment of the Dionysus–Prometheus–Oedipus hero or, in Derridian terms, the deconstruction of identity.

If language is the ultimate Promethean/Oedipal or technological crime, in that the word, by negating the real, reinstitutes or represents the real as framed and constant, then language creates the 'truth' of being by the fiction of the word. The word is the bond of cultural significance, the symbolic order that opens the world for the subject but chains the subject to the desire of the Other. The moment we are named we are imprisoned under the sign of Oedipus and enter the appropriative circuit of restitution and retribution, in other words, of consciousness.

If theoretical man has been hoisted on his own petard, realizing that marks of inscription are the condition for the occasion of articulation which in turn renders the self-authorization of the truth of speech suspect, what effect would this insight have on the practice of psychoanalysis? Could a deconstructive psychoanalytic practice be envisaged which did not attempt to frame analysis within the Oedipal struggle for authentic presence and truth speaking, that is, as the search for reappropriating the maternal phallus? Can we read the analytic situation as a text and through such reading occasion the deconstruction and dissemination of the analysand's pernicious and reductive hierarchical and oppositional belief in truth systems, which imprison him/her within the letter of the law of social expectations?

The letter pre-assigns the pseudo-construction of an individuality based on the model of Cartesian certitude or self-identity, underpinned by the metaphysics of presence and the authority of the phallogocentric voice.

We turn to Lacan's seminar on Poe to see the extent to which Lacan anticipates, escapes and shows the way to escape from the circuit of language's logocentric capture.

LACAN'S SEMINAR

The lesson or moral of the Poe story, for Lacan, is that it demonstrates how the pattern of an individual's experience and behaviour (the imaginary), referred to in psychoanalytic parlance as the compulsion to repeat, and re-enacted in the transference relationship in terms of foreclosure, repression, denial and displacement, is embedded in a symbolic chain that binds and orients the subject. 'It is the symbolic order which is constitutive for the subject' (Lacan, 1972, p. 40). Lacan strips the story to its, for him, essential components, that is, the enactment and re-enactment of an Oedipal or familiar story.

The site of theft of the letter is the royal *boudoir*. The Queen is caught in the act of reading a letter, just received, that could compromise her honour and safety. She manages to have it elude the King's notice by leaving the letter on her table under his nose, albeit face down. At this moment, Minister D . . . enters, his lynx eyes spot the letter and he instantly fathoms the intrigue. The Minister is 'A man who dares all things, both those unbecoming as

81

well as those becoming a man' (Lacan, 1972, p. 41) – in other
words, he is a Nietzschean Prometheus whose highest virtue is
sacrilege and robbery. Minister D . . . deftly lifts the letter, the
Queen powerless in the King's presence to stop him and thus he
puts the Queen in his power with the threat of exposure.

The second scene replays the first at the level of intersubjective
structures. Dupin, solver of enigmas, enters Minister D . . . 's
office, which has been previously searched by the Prefect of Police
at the request of the Queen, without finding the letter. His eyes
protected by green glasses, Dupin, unnoticed by the Minister, spots
the letter hanging on a rack beneath the mantlepiece. He returns
next day on the pretext of forgetting his snuff-box and, having
prepared a distraction outside the Minister's window, replaces the
letter with a facsimile. The Minister if he tries to use the letter will
find written on it in Dupin's hand the message, 'so infamous a
scheme, if not worthy of Atreus, is worthy of Thyestes'.

Lacan argues that the characters of Poe's story are subject to a
signifying chain that places and displaces them in a rotation of
roles determined by their relation to the purloined letter or signifier just as the moves of chess pieces are subject to the rules of the
game.

The signifier, word, or letter is a symbol of a pact, of an initiation
into a symbolic order of meaning and exchange which is the
foundation of intersubjectivity. It is in terms of the signifier, which
is a symbol of an absence (for Freud the infants' game of *fort-da*,
striving to master the mother's absence), that the signified, the
world of things, is organized and rendered meaningful and present.
The infant becomes capable of imagining itself as human, mortal
and sexed through language which gives the ability to recognize
and represent. The impetus to turn away from mother towards
language is the desire for mother's desire, for the other's recognition which is symbolized for the child as the father. Only by
assuming the father's place does the child become subject to the
laws of human shared significance.

Lemaire's quote and discussion of Lacan's famous phrase 'the
signifier is that which represents the subject for another signifier'
clarifies this moment in Lacan's exposition. Lemaire argues that
the human is an effect of the signifier in that the subject is
represented by a stand-in, an 'I' his/her name which introduces the

subject into the circuit of exchange by enabling the subject to assume his/her singularity. The order of the signifier, of relations with other signifiers, you, he/she, we, us, them, captures the subject. As Lemaire says, 'Insertion into the symbolic world is a mimesis, a collage. It fashions a being of "representation" for us. Mediated by language the subject is irremediably divided. The young child submits to society, to its culture, organization and language, his only alternatives being to constrain himself to it, or to fall ill' (Lemaire, 1970, p. 68). Lacan denotes the divided subject as S/.

Heidegger exercised an immense influence on Lacan's revisioning of psychoanalysis so I turn to Heidegger to interpret *logos* or language in terms of gathering. Using a wine-making metaphor he shows that the selection process of grape-picking depends on a tradition of differentiation, which enables decisions on which grapes to pick and store and which not, in order to make a proper vintage. The acquisition of the ability to differentiate in tune with a context of tradition makes intelligibility, hence recognition of self and others, possible (Heidegger, 1975, pp. 61–2).

So, the child assumes an imaginary identity to satisfy mother's demands (tradition) and is alienated or split from his/her own desire in the stereotypical forms that may become neurosis or psychosis.

Lacan appeals to the Poe story to demonstrate how the paradigmatic positions within the Oedipal configuration possess and are instanced by the characters as they fall in possession of the purloined letter. How the characters place themselves in relation to the letter bespeaks their placement in the register of what Lacan calls *truth*. The three terms, moments or places within which the characters find themselves and pass through intersubjective space are illustrated or embodied in a hierarchy of glances which determined their decisions and actions. The first glance, or the ostrich position, is occupied first by the King and then by the police: they see nothing. The second glance sees that the first sees nothing and imagines that what it hides is safe. This is the Queen, who thinks she has hidden the letter of betrayal, and later the Minister, hiding the purloined letter of blackmail. The third glance sees that the first two glances leave what they want to hide transparent and open to seizure. This is at first the position of the Minister and then Dupin. By implication it is the position of the analyst.

The first glance: The King, the royal incarnation of the legitimacy of law, and his constabulary of order are blind to betrayal, and cannot see the obvious. The illegitimate simply has no place for them in which to appear, no name, is unspeakable and thus alien. The Magisterial subject (self-presence) cannot grasp a subjectivity as other, other than compliant to or in correspondence with the order he upholds. His protection and defence is self-validation.

This is the position of the ostrich, who to protect itself from danger sticks its head in the sand. This hiding is a narcissistic denial of the Other's subjectivity, as in for example the story of the Emperor's new clothes.

The second glance: The Queen, pledged to preserve her husband's reign, hides a letter that must be kept secret. Her infidelity is high treason. She must not for fear of loss of power/life let her privacy be violated, although this privacy is a violation of her pact with the King, since she is official guardian of his law. And when the Minister holds the letter he too assumes the attributes of feminity, and shadow, by playing the role of the one who hides. The woman, Lacan claims, founds and invests her being outside the law, even though it subsumes her. Her mastery lies in inactivity, and the Minister finds that he occupies her place since the power of the letter he holds only retains its power as long as it is not used or shown. The Minister finds himself to be more and more transformed into idleness by occupying the position of holder of the letter. Ultimately he too becomes prey to surrendering the letter to a similar sort of capture as his own.

The third glance: First the Minister and then Dupin see through the naïve illusion of invisibility with which the second glance affects to cloak what it wants to hide.

Lacan invokes Heidegger's notion of Truth as *aletheia* to show that the most true discloses itself in the hidden and that the most hidden is the simplest and most obvious. As Dupin remarks to the Prefect at the outset of the story, perhaps the mystery of the disappearance of the letter is a 'little too self-evident'.

The characteristic of the third glance is that it moves in the register of interpersonal space, seeing that Truth is as much a matter of what is heard as what is said. Truth is always between us, shared or not as the case may be. What's between us or what we mean by what we say and do is always mediated by language or the symbolic order and our respective positions within this order.

The Other or the unconscious is nothing other than language. This is the site on which Freud developed the theory and practice of psychoanalysis and it is with attention to the prototypical patterns of miscommunication that his interpretations and analyses were developed. Lacan illustrates Freud's interpersonal doctrine of knowledge and truth in retelling a Jewish joke from *Jokes and Their Relation to the Unconscious* in order to situate the third glance of the Minister's and Dupin. It goes as follows: 'Why are you lying to me?' one character shouts breathlessly. 'Yes, why do you lie to me saying you're going to Cracow so I should believe you're going to Lemberg, when in reality you *are* going to Cracow?' (1960, p. 115).

Lacan redefines the Freudian unconscious in the formula, 'the unconscious is the discourse of the other'. The rupture of infantile unconsciousness and the birth of desire which wants to restore the lack of oneness with the mother by being desired by the mother is resolved by language through which the child learns the rules of identity through which to channel desire. These are the rules of discourse, the symbolic order.

Now the Minister is able to see at a glance the *folie à deux* of the King and Queen ostriches for he knows what it is to play outside the rules. The Queen's game is transparent. The letter she has turned away from the King must incriminate her as not submitting to the law of the father, as not being faithful to her pact. She has not renounced her desire to be the mother's phallus, what the mother wants, and accept herself as simply 'not having it', that is submitting to the father's – husband's law – language. The Minister identifies with her position and takes it over when he purloins the letter.

Dupin knows that the Minister knows how to play the game of identification, of odd or even – and this is how he has eluded the Prefect's search. This is a guessing game in which one player holds an odd or even number of marbles or toys and the other guesses odd or even. Dupin in explaining his methods recounts that one boy won all the marbles in his school through identification. By assuming the others' facial expressions he assessed how clever his opponent was and how he would vary what he holds after each guess, and then guessed accordingly.

Dupin knows the Minister would realize that his opponents, the police, are naïve realists. Indeed, they searched for the letter as for a hidden object in all the usual places one could imagine a letter could be hidden. They divided the entire space of the Minister's flat into numbered compartments and searched each area to one-fiftieth of an inch. The realist does not realize that only the symbolic can be missing from its place, as for example a misfiled book in a library is fully visible but virtually lost. The Minister, a poet as well as a mathematician, counts on the police to search as they do. He employs the same strategy that he has just seen through. To hide the letter he leaves it in the open. By holding the letter he occupies the Queen's initial position. Like her he imagines by turning the letter over, this time as one would turn a glove inside out, he has rendered it invisible. He knows that the police will be foiled by his camouflage, since they stop their search on the outside, the reverse side of the letter which now looks like a mere scrap, half torn and re-addressed. However, the Minister fails to appreciate that he is now vulnerable to being seen, as seeing himself not being seen, as he indeed is by Dupin. The Minister falls under the sign of woman. The woman masks and thus reveals her desire to be the phallus, the object of the mother's desire. Thus she becomes a fetish or sex object and a mystery to be penetrated. The Minister's ennui, apathy and passivity resonate with effeminacy.

Dupin is an initiate of the map game and won't miss the names of countries spelled out across the map in large letters which a beginner most likely will fail to notice, so when he enters the Minister's flat he need only undress the room as he would an immense female body, and 'with a nod to Freud', find the letter at the vaginal centre on a letter-rack hanging from a (clitoral) knob between the legs of the mantelpiece. There remains only the question for Lacan: how can we explain Dupin's rage at the Minister expressed in the horrible attribution invoked by his quotation, if not an Atreus you are a Thyestes, especially since he has successfully beaten the Minister?

Dupin now in possession of the letter also falls under its spell. His rage is 'manifestly feminine', Lacan explains. The Minister dared gamble with fortune, having stripped the Queen of her cover with the threat to expose her. He thus revealed the presence of death, which shows that every day of life is merely a reprieve, which we contrive by falling for the stories we are told. Dupin, partisan of the Queen from the outset, cannot bear to leave the Minister's assault unrevenged. However, Dupin is sure the Minister will read his hand before attempting to play his trump card and will undoubtedly avoid disgrace.

As Lacan remarks, in the end nothing happens in Poe's story although the most violent Oedipal themes are enacted. The moral of the story for Lacan is that the 'letter always arrives at its destination'. The purloined letter, the subject of the story, moves the characters along a prolonged but inevitable circuit of displacements which are the paradigmatic positions of the Oedipal knot and its psychoanalytic replay. The circuit of the letter, of the signifier, of language discloses truth as intersubjective, as ultimately tied to the laws of symbolic exchange.

It is this order of reflexivity, of retribution and reappropriation, that chains the subject to the signifier and produces the effects of repetition compulsion.

For Lacan returning to Freud the moral of the Poe story is that psychoanalysis recodifies the family scenario by restoring the contract of civilization. The gift/sacrifice of the word or pledge is the castration of natural infantile omnipotence surrendering to the order of language. Avoidance of surrender to castration, the purloining of the letter or deferring of surrender is the flight from the truth or intersubjectivity that displaces and disarticulates subjectivity into stereotypical neurotic patterns, versions of solitaire that disrupt the interpersonal field of relatedness and exchange. Nevertheless the logic of a psychoanalytic science required a principle of repetition, hence identity, for the constitution of the unconscious. Without repeatability no sense can be made of censorship and repression, the pillars of the analytic experience. The problem facing Lacan was how to preserve a dynamic unconscious without erecting Cartesian reflexivity, without making the unconscious a product of the process of which it claims to be the source, without confusing the territory with the map.

87

Lacan's Heideggerian alethetic paradigm of the unconscious raises this question for Derrida: to what extent is Lacan's paradigm, scientific, idealizing and logocentric, thus circumscribed within the closure of metaphysics?

It seems that Lacan's argument for the restoration of the intersubjective contract depends on the link between feminity, truth and the spoken word. Feminity is the truth of castration as lack. Whoever holds the letter is feminized. It must be returned to reveal that she never had it. The moment one tries to get hold of the letter, then meaning is lost. Meaning is not the whole built up through its parts but a whole that precedes its parts and emerges through them. The letter signifies the phallus or transcendental signifier which enables signifiers to be pinned to signifieds, thus making absences present, and enabling meanings to emerge.

The word becomes true, adequate and meaningful when I speak it or rather let it speak me. In speaking, the signifier becomes detached from saying. This sets in motion the intersubjective circuit which both threatens and restores the symbolic order. *Aletheia* or the unhiddenness of hiddenness, the sign of the feminine, is the structure of the true word which hides itself to reveal and conceal that of which it speaks.

To be adequate, authentic or true my speaking requires the recognition of another subject to render me identical to myself or the same. As Lacan says, 'Even if it communicates nothing, the discourse represents the existence of communication; even if it denies the obvious, it affirms that the word constitutes truth.'

Speaking presupposes the intersubjective contract or pledge, which permits the subject to become identical to itself, which amounts to the return of the letter. But is this circuit not the evidence of logocentricisms, the logos (speech) believing itself to be its own father (origin)?

As soon as truth is determined as adequation (self correspondence) albeit intersubjectively attained, and as unveiling of lack, then the word becomes idealized and effaced from its context. For Derrida, the vocal or interiority is under the spell of the metaphysical values of presence, appropriation and preservation, which is the condition of true science or the science of truth.

DERRIDA'S DECONSTRUCTION
I turn to a discussion of Derrida's reading of Lacan's seminar to illustrate Derridian *hesitation*.

The Poe text is a pretext for Lacan to stage his psychoanalytic armamentarium and show how the apparatus works in a project of exegesis or interpretation, the linchpin of his theoretical practice. In his essay on Lacan's purloined-letter seminar 'The purveyor of truth', Derrida challenges the assumptions, strategy and doctrine of truth that inform Lacan's analytical reading of Poe's text, and by means of his critique calls into question the foundations of a linguistically oriented psychoanalysis. In the following I retrace this deconstructive argument.

Derrida's strategy in his Lacanian polemic is to demonstrate negatively the reductive nature of Lacan's psychoanalytic reading of the Poe text and positively to show that this text belongs to a class of fictional texts that arc self-referential, that is, they incorporate their own interpretation. For example, Poe's text in order to undermine a reductive reading stages the analyst's search for and pronouncement on the truth only to trap and thus elude his constrictive interpretation.

Derrida's prologue is an illustration of his deconstructive strategy applied to Freud's reductive analytic reading of Hans Andersen's 'The Emperor's New Clothes'.

Freud's discovery that the narrative is a cover story or camouflage for an expression of the unconscious exhibitionist wish of castrated man fails to appreciate that this reading is already presupposed and folded into the structure of the story. The fable is about the unity of dissimulation–veiling, revelation–unveiling, about an invisible nakedness and an invisible garment, about the King, law and convention concealing shame and fear of castration and this shame and wish being revealed or seen through. Derrida asks, how can a literature (the fable) which subordinates unveiling as a theme be subordinated by the psychoanalytic reading that it has staged? In other words, the analytic scene which strips neurotic defence patterns through interpretation of resistance and transference is in play in stripping the King (ego) of his false-self system down to his unconscious drives and desires. The fable already shows what its analytic reading merely repeats.

In this prelude Derrida anticipates the conclusion of his treat ment of Lacan's Poe exposition, that contra Lacan the analytic distinctions between science and literature, between revelation and dissimulation, between individual narrative and the formulation of law are in principle untenable; these distinctions are in principle undecidable within the realm of writing, text or articulation in general.

Like Freud, Lacan will appeal to fiction to confirm the truth of his theory, so his seminar on 'The Purloined Letter' opens with a statement of the problematic relation between truth and fiction. Lacan will use the Poe text as an illustration of the law and truth of the logic of the signifier, just as a case history might be used to 2instance a general law and truth of the unconscious.

Language and its letter or signifier is founded on the Freudian *Widerholungszwang* or repetition automation (compulsion) and it is as a confirmation of this logic of the signifier that Lacan reads the Poe story. The subject is not author of the signifier but its subject, subject to its rules and laws. The circulation of the letter, its trajectory, determined the significance it acquires within the intersubjective scene. The letter insists, is unforgettable, even though it is not used, and forgotten by the Minister. But like the return of the repressed it does not forget him. It transforms him into the identity of her who surrendered it so he too surrenders it.

'We have decided to illustrate for you today the Truth that it is the symbolic order which is constitutive for the subject, by demonstrating in a story the decisive orientation which the subject receives from the itinerary of a signifier' (Lacan, 1972, p. 40). Fiction is founded on truth – it is to be deciphered to deliver the message of Freud's teaching as reconstituted by Lacan.

Derrida begins his account of Lacan's reductive turn arguing that Lacan neutralizes the narrator, thus excluding the frame and context of the Poe story which is the scene of writing. Lacan's preoccupation with the two Oedipal triangles amounts to treating the signifier as a signified, as objective content. The 'real drama' for Lacan is brought into relief by suppressing the role of the narrator, reducing this role to an idealized analytic neutrality which functions as a translucent staging event in order to bring the story into relief. This moment of exclusion ignores the fact that 'The Purloined Letter' as text feigns a narrator who feigns the purloined letter.

The narrator narrating himself has a crucial status as a fourth or other perspective within and outside the triangular relationships he recounts. It should be noted that the narrator is not to be identified with the author, Poe or the text itself. The double narrator, narrator-narrating and narrator-narrated, supplements or 'squares' the triangular set pieces that Lacan has bracketed, and his interventions and place within the text when reinstated overturn the strategy, premises and conclusions of Lacan's interpretation, according to Derrida.

By jumping into deciphering Poe's message, the narrated content, the meaning of the story becomes an object amenable to psychoanalytic schematization. The text is taken as dialogue, which is taken as the condition of the truth of the message of the text rather than realizing that it is only in terms of the fictional textual framework that the text's meaning is limned. What interests Lacan is the truth, the proper place, the proper trajectory, the destiny of the letter. The letter is read as a transcendental signifier of a transcendental signified. Derrida argues that Lacan's violence in cutting off the position of the narrator, conflating narrator, author and text occludes a central Oedipal difficulty in the scene of writing, writing as usurpation of the father's spoken word and, more radically, writing (grammar) as the pre-condition of the spoken word.

For Lacan the letter-signifier has a proper place and meaning which conditions the subjects who are subject to the significance it embodies. The origin, destination and route of circulation are encoded in the logic of the signifier which Lacan's psychoanalytic topology proposes to decode.

The letter is the lack, which opens the world – the *Da* of human being *Dasein* ('Language is the house of being' – Heidegger). The lack is an absence made present by the word. The letter circulates and returns through reappropriation, accomplished by an authentic contract. This is the proper meaning of the letter, its sense is the phallic law which links the signifier to the signified.

The proper place of the letter is woman. The lack of the penis is the truth of the phallus, the truth of truth, the meaning of meaning, the contract of truth and logos. The veiling/unveiling of a hole-lack is the truth of being as non-being. Truth is woman as veiled/unveiled castration.

91

The Queen has custody of the King's law, which she threatens to betray. The signifier-letter begins its departure in this threatened rupture and division but the Queen seeks to repair the endangered pact. She seeks to repay her debt by a reappropriation of the letter which has empowered her in the first place. Truth returns to woman, to the openness, the lack, hole or vagina, whence it originated. The place of lack embodied by woman insures that the phallus, fetish, letter, signifier returns, remains in its proper place, that is, to signify that feminity is the truth of castration. The letter substitutes for the phallus, thus it must be indivisible and indestructible. It must return to its proper place and meaning, showing that she 'never had it'. It is between the legs of the mantelpiece that the Minister hides the letter, where it is, to one who sees (Dupin, the analyst) most exposed.

For Derrida, disputing Lacan, the letter has no fixed place, or meaning, it is not found or returned. It escapes the psychoanalytic frame-up because it cannot be enclosed within the oppositional structures of the symbolic, imaginary and real. The letter stages its own frame, it does not submit to the law or norm. Moreover, it traps those who attempt to get hold of it. Dupin in the analyst's place and Lacan locate the letter in one place, the woman's opening; they map the letter as theme on to the female body, the woman as truth of castration. They do not see that the map iterates itself, it does not map a territory as a transcendental signified, a typology of being. The letter or signifier is polyvalent and multistable, hence always capable of infinite division. The symbolic system is the attempt to protect the phallus from mutilation. But the signifier, the letter, is always threatened by writing or, in Derrida's terms, dissemination. Thus the letter may not be returned, and the contract may be betrayed or breached.

Dupin and Lacan's seminar discover the letter between the woman's legs, thus the truth and meaning of the letter is revealed. 'The letter arrives at its destination.' Yet Lacan's subtext betrays his own accusation of a betrayal of the letter and the seminar itself is the site of a betrayal.

Hidden in an elliptical footnote in the seminar is a reference to the cook (Lacan, 1972, p. 67, n. 38).[5] This bitchy moment in Lacan's text shows a closet recognition that Marie Bonaparte holds Freud's letter, his endorsement of her book on Poe. Lacan has borrowed the crux of his purloined-letter interpretation, that is, that the letter means castration of women and its return means the rephallicization of the mother; and suppressed his debt to Bonaparte. Instead he attacks Bonaparte for merely handing out Freudian recipes rather than remaining faithful to the spirit of his teaching and original insights. Lacan's enterprise is to return to the letter of Freud or return it to its *proper* place out of the hands of the community of analysts who merely mouth Bonaparte's recipes without any appreciation of Freud's meaning. By challenging Bonaparte's mantle of legitimacy, and seeking to return to the letter of Freud, Lacan like Dupin remains caught in the Oedipal struggle for the maternal phallus or rather falls into all the positions within the triangle he explicates. Dupin admits that the Minister did him an evil turn in Vienna (as Bonaparte, Freud's Minister in France did to Lacan) and from the first a partisan of the Lady (the Queen) he had his eye on returning the letter.

Lacan identifies with Dupin and gives him the analyst's position outside the triangle. But Derrida argues that the more he (Dupin–Lacan) wants to be master, thinks he knows and wants the last word, the more he is caught up in the symbolic circuit, becomes feminized, rephallicized, affects superiority which betrays a foolishness.

Giving Dupin the position of the third glance, the analyst's position of seeing through the delusions of the first two glances is Lacan's way of naming himself the true heir of Freud, of putting himself in the place of self-authorization.

Dupin like the analyst in the end succeeds. He possesses the true meaning of the letter; Dupin like Lacan has the last word.

The assertion of my self-identity or the full word is only achieved within the context of intersubjectivity. In the transference the analyst holds the letter in sufferance for the patient, the patient believes the analyst has what the patient thinks he/she lacks. The analyst sees that the other cannot see or surrender to the place of castration, lack or language and awaits the patients receiving, returning, realizing the truth of their own messages: finding him/herself speaking in the context of mutual recognition. In dialogue, the patient overcomes omnipotence by receiving a reply (recognition) to his/her appeal, in Lacan's terms receiving his/her message in reverse form.

Paradoxically, the position of the analyst outside the symbolic circuit is always also in it, since Dupin, Lacan, the author, the analyst, repeat in having the last word or occupying the position of self-authorization, the King's position or Freud's who as originator of psychoanalysis has a contract with himself. Derrida demonstrates that the position of self-authorization is always in jeopardy of betrayal. The position of insight or the third glance is also the position of blindness or the first position. Taking up the position of mastery, of seeing the lack and its phallic fetish substitutions, does not free the analyst from responsibility, debt and blindness, from colluding with his patients' fantasies and believing that he does have it or is the one who knows.

The trap that traps the analyst is the trap of truth which privileges the voice or the phone and subordinates writing to the phonemic logos.

Lacan postulates an equivalence between symbolic articulation and phoneticity. Why does the law of the signifier unfold for him through voiced letters? The phallus to be kept safe requires speech. The self-presence of the voice insures the indivisibility of the letter. The signifier informed by the ideality of its message circulates, but its meaning is preserved since the symbol remains in its place out of reach of division and mutilation. The full word holds meaning; it is the phallus, the transcendental signifier, the signifier of all signifiers; it guarantees the unity of the signifier and signified. This is the monotheistic paradigm of psychoanalysis.

Derrida opposes what in effect is Lacan's resurrection of the system of Cartesian certitude. Founded on the primacy of the spoken word, albeit with a detour through intersubjectivity, the word returns and reinstitutes the metaphysics of presence. In place of this phallic erection of an ideal philosophy, which amounts to a defence against castration, Derrida proposes an original writing whose disseminating power enables speech and is the source of the letter or language. His reinterpretation of the purloined letter is intended as a demonstration of this thesis, and a call for a polytheistic approach.

In the Freudian-Lacanian unconscious, the letter insists, the symbolic meaning returns as the repressed. For theoretical man truth is the master value, truth presences and preserves. Idealizing speech brings together things with speech; truth and the power of the word go together. The subject finds itself as the other's recognition, Lacan's 'desire of the other'. The I-speak is possible because the word permits the contract which in turn founds the speaker's self-identity.

The process of analysis is accomplished in terms of enabling the other to assume his/her desire, to engage in discourse or intercourse. To speak the full word of self presence, to speak with one's voice and tell the truth – to be at one with what one is saying – presupposes authentic speaking with, or intersubjectivity. I can only take myself to be myself when I realize the other hears what I am saying as I mean it. I want to speak and be heard, I want the other to want to hear me, to want me, to desire my desire. The voice, word, phallus enables the contract between us. The privileged word is what the other, the mother wants, and the child wants to satisfy her and be it, the phallus. The woman gives what she does not have, she is the lack, the absence, the void of otherness out of which springs the desire for recognition, and the voice, the word, the symbolic or linguistic order which renders her recognition possible.

According to Derrida the phallogocentric position is the underlying assumption of Freud's sexual theory, that is, that little boys must discover castration in order to enter the symbolic order, and this position is the basis of Lacan's reading of Poe.

The signifier-phallus raises the signifiable, things, to the level of truth or meaning. The word is the mother's desire, for recognition, for the phallus. Desire can be said to be male, thus there is only one kind of libido, for Freud, male.

Derrida breaks up Lacan's metalinguistic attempt to totalize the Poe text by showing that the text has already framed the metalinguistic moment of analysis and has in fact trapped Lacan, who attempts in vain to neutralize the frame of the text. For Derrida the text begins by disseminating or dividing the letter, the characters and meanings of the positions they embody. The text stages an other – the narrator to say I, to speak, hence the text or letter does not arrive at the destination. The text never names itself – it rather reveals as it conceals its self-reference. The text unfolds in pieces, without ever being a whole, it is a fabric woven to stage or weave into itself the moment of the attempt to unravel or decode it. The game recounted in the text is the game the text constitutes. The narrator simulates Lacan's seminar by narrating himself as Dupin's analysand. He pays the price, rents Dupin, 'the society of such a man is a treasure beyond price'. But he pays for a place of writing, he pays to write and he makes Dupin the analyst speak rather than the reverse. He makes Dupin give up the letter, not only to the Queen but to him.

The divided letter gives rise to divided positions which each of the characters represents. The narrator narrates his identification with Dupin. He admires Dupin's analytic ability, Dupin can see into his persona. But he doubles Dupin's character. Dupin is creative and resolvent and thereby through identification doubles his own character. The relationships between the narrator and Dupin in and outside the triangle that Lacan circumscribes render his reduction untenable since all the characters both in and outside the so-called 'real drama' occupy all of the places or glances that Lacan isolates. The dual relationships between doubles simulate, engulf and break down any clear-cut opposition between imaginary and symbolic – between truth and reality, art and science. Hence Lacan's metaphysical hierarchy, which is his teaching on Truth, has little relevance for appreciating what is in play in the text.

Each character identifies with the position of the other, becomes divided or doubled and ultimately fragmented. The King sees only confirmation by the Queen that he has the phallus. The Queen sees she confirms the King, she is guardian of the contract; she also sees that her betrayal is hidden from him, she is castration, lack, veiling. The Minister sees the hidden betrayal out in the open, he sees that truth is unveiling of veiling, truth is the symbolic order which makes a presence of absence.

For Lacan the purloined letter detours but returns to its proper place. It grounds the structure of recognition, and ensures that circulation of the letter, of desire, remains within triangular bounds. But outside the triangle the narrator doubles Dupin and himself. Dupin occupies the King's position when he returns the letter and the Queen's position when he strikes a blow at the Minister. The Queen as betrayer is doubled; the King is doubled in his trust or pledge to the Queen and the Minister is doubled when he is feminized.

All the characters who are embodiments of the letter are doubled, hence the letter is doubled or divided. While the letter in the story is returned, the letter that is the text, the story itself, goes astray, it does not have a single meaning. The Minister and Dupin are brothers, doubles, Atreus/Thyestes. The brothers' rivalry, a central theme of the text, cannot be taken up by Lacan in terms of the triangle he outlines.

There is a labyrinth of doubles, all simulating authenticity while imitating each other, all are facsimiles without an original.

The text itself names itself as text – it pretends to name itself as an object in a story yet it itself escapes or eludes conceptualization. It mimics the work of the transcendental signifier or phallus by presenting itself as the source of itself, as origin and at the same time part of the chain of signification. It pretends to mean that a letter arrives at a destination, has a univocal meaning but even as it replays the path of arrival it divides and destroys any single meaning.

There is no analyst who can enclose the letter within an analytic situation. Writing presents all the characters as both more clever and more foolish, more powerful and more powerless than the others.

Derrida ends his essay by quoting Lacan, giving him apparently the last word, as Lacan apparently gives it to Dupin in his seminar, but by altering a letter gives Dupin's quote the meaning of harbinger of the destiny of his own message, that is, that he is heir to Freud. Following Poe's strategy Derrida by quoting Lacan puts Lacan's signature in quotes. This renders problematic precisely the point which this signature asserts, since the quotes show that the so-called primacy of the spoken word is in fact generated by the inscription of the quotes. The quotes give the illusion of a voice or speaker, a transcendental signifier, and at the same time undermine this illusion since they are the conditon for this impression.

CONCLUSION

If, as Derrida claims, the act of psychoanalysis repeats the circuit of reappropriation it seeks to analyse and subvert, as his argument with Lacanian psychoanalysis demonstrates, 'this is no objection to psychoanalysis but a profound insight to its essence' (Johnson, 1977, p. 499).

There is no neutral position or general viewpoint in analysis: the speaker/analyst/reader is always implicated in the scene/text, transference, reciprocity in which he/she is involved in the act of interpretation.

Everyone holding the letter becomes the destination of it, no one can stand back as a disinterested observer. The letter subverts the polarity of subject–object, receiver–sender, destination–arrival. The question of the origin or destination of the letter, that it arrives at its destination, is paradoxical and cannot be decided, for the repetition of the enactment of mine or the other's narcissism within the circuit of appropriation and closure returns in the act of analysis and reading. Wherever the letter is read it reads the reader so that no unequivocal, ultimate or transcendental attainment (reading) is possible. This conclusion is perhaps a basis of ultimate agreement between Derrida and Lacan within the play of their difference.

NOTES

1. An early version of this essay was given at the Irish Philosophical Society, Belfast, October 1986. See Lacan (1972) and Derrida (1975). I was unable here to take account of the rich commentary and supplementary essays in Müller and Richardson's *Purloined Poe*, which appeared after the final draft was completed.

2. Derrida used this term to characterize his reading of Heidegger, in a 1986 symposium at Essex University.

Reading Heidegger. A short stretch of phenomenology is in order: Husserl's *epoché* bracketed 'reality' to enable us to see how consciousness constructs its own domains of meaning givenness, which constitute experience. Heidegger argued that Husserl's analysis was theoretical and reflective, that it presupposed and left unanalysed the primary phenomenon of being-in-the-world, the being we are which is our relatedness to things and others prior to reflection. For Heidegger the world of relatedness is a child of language; this means that man is essentially a poet, not an animal, no matter how deficient or constricted our relatedness to language may become. If Husserl overturned common sense and saw the signified (reality) as the by-product of significance (meaning), and Heidegger radicalized this turn by showing that history (man's reality) is granted by language, then Derrida can be said to have embodied this phenomenological development in an *epoché*, bracketing or hesitation of language. Derrida demonstrates the grammatical conditions in terms of which language has been and is able yet at the same time unable to grant meaning.

3. The universal Oedipal design can be characterized as a relation of male figure (phallus) to female ground. This template structures the meta-physical grid and sets up all relationships of primacy to subordination: for example, the primacy of the spoken word (father) to the revealed truth (mother) and subordinate (children) written reproductions.

4. From the time of Tantalus and his son Pelops' treachery, the house of Atreus was accursed. Atreus' brother Thyestes seduced his wife Aerope, and stole the sign of his sovereignty, the golden ram. Atreus banished his brother but later, pretending to be reconciled, he fed Thyestes on a dish made of his children's flesh. Aigisthos was conceived in a union of Thyestes and his daughter to take revenge against Atreus by seducing Agamemnon's wife Clytemnestra and inciting her to kill her husband.

5. Bonaparte was instrumental in the decision to excommunicate Lacan from the French Institute of Psychoanalysis.

5

How can we discuss the erotic?

Plato and Freud compared

J. M. HEATON

I N HIS PREFACE to the fourth edition of *Three Essays on the Theory of Sexuality* Freud appealed to Plato to vindicate his views. He pointed out how closely the enlarged view of sexuality in psychoanalysis coincided with Plato's concept of Eros. But although Freud and Plato agreed on the ubiquity of sexuality they differed profoundly on the conclusions they drew from this insight.

Freud thought his views on sexuality were obtained by careful impartial observation and that his findings could be reported as facts free of any suggestion. According to Freud science is 'a tireless elaboration of facts from the world of perception' (Freud, 1925a). Psychoanalysis would steadily advance, brick by brick, as a grand edifice of knowledge was built. Plato on the other hand was sceptical about the steady development of knowledge for he thought that to be human meant that one is inextricably bound to the erotic and so constantly subject to persuasion and suggestion. Therefore there could not be steady progress in our knowledge of the erotic. No human being could make a perfectly true speech, only the gods could do this (*Phaedrus*, 1961, 277–8). So he created a dramatic perspective, using the dialogue as a work of art in which the personality of the speakers, the valid and fallacious arguments they use, and the circumstances under which they converse, all play a part in showing the nature of the matter under discussion.

Plato wrote two dialogues on sexuality – *Phaedrus* and *Symposium* – and in both he tried to show how writing and speech are deeply under the influence of sexuality. His way of writing had to take this into account if it was to convey the nature of sexuality accurately. In fact he did not value writing and textbooks as we moderns do, saying that acquaintance with matters such as sexuality is best obtained by a long period of attendance on the subject itself rather than reading about it.

> No serious man will ever think of writing about serious realities for the general public so as to make them a prey to envy and perplexity. In a word, it is an inevitable conclusion from this that when anyone sees anywhere the written work of anyone, whether that of a lawyer in his laws or whatever it may be in some other form, the subject treated cannot have been his most serious concern – that is, if he is himself a serious man. His most serious interests have their abode somewhere in the noblest region of the field of his activity. If however he really was seriously concerned with these matters and put them in writing 'then surely' not the gods, but mortals 'have utterly blasted his wits'. (*VII Letter*, 1961, 344c)

Clearly Plato would have had little sympathy with Freud's grievances about the resistances and splitting his writing provoked! For Plato wrote in a way that took the possibility of this into account. His writing in itself reveals the nature of Eros; in psychoanalytic terms it is insight giving working through. So there is no doctrine to resist over and above what he wrote.

THE CARNIVALESQUE TRADITION

The *Symposium* belongs to a long tradition which has been called the Carnivalesque (Bakhtin, 1984; Kristeva, 1980). A carnival is a spectacle without a stage, the participant is both actor and spectator. It is both stage and life, discourse and spectacle. In carnival, language is not used to expound theories or doctrines but rather parodies itself; it repudiates its role in representation and provokes tears and laughter. Ambiguity and heterogeneity prevail rather than linear discourse and monologue. Parody, free and familiar contact between persons – a fool can talk to a king – death and rebirth, eccentric and surprising misalliances, profanation and debasement, feasts, the drama of bodily life – copulation, eating, drinking, defecation – all emerge and disappear in the time-space of carnival. Some examples from literature are satyr plays such as Euripides' *Cyclops*, Menippean satire, Petronius' *Satyricon*, Ovid's *Metamorphoses*, and the novels of Cervantes, Rabelais, Laurence Sterne, Dostoevsky, Joyce and Beckett.

Let us turn to the *Symposium* to see how it contains many of these features. The *Symposium* was a feast held in Agathon's house to celebrate his first victory as a tragic poet. There is an ancient tie between eating and the spoken word; bread and wine disperse fear and liberate the word. It is a favourable milieu for revealing truth.

The party occurred in 416 BC. At that time Alcibiades was at the height of his influence so it was before his disastrous Sicilian expedition. It was also around the time of the desecration of the Hermae and the profanation of the Eleusinian mysteries. Three members of the *Symposium* – Phaedrus, Eryximachus and Alcibiades – were suspects. Now Plato put the date of the report of the *Symposium* around 400 BC, which was the time of the defeat of Athens by Sparta (and Socrates would die within the year). It was reported by Apollodorus, who had obtained a report of it from Aristodemus, who was actually present at the banquet. Both of them had been pupils of Socrates.

We have here the themes of tragedy, death, profanation, all of which are profoundly important in sexuality. There is the glitter of the banquet contrasted with these dark themes. There is the emphasis on indirect speech of what is memorable. The *Symposium* is a report of a report of what happened a long time ago. What is memorable is not literal but indirect; we can only approach sexuality indirectly. Plato often emphasizes this as does Freud with his notion of the unconscious.

The seating order at the banquet illustrates the heterogeneity of the participants and their erotic links. The order from left to right is Phaedrus, Pausanias, Aristophanes, Eryximachus, Agathon, Socrates (see diagram). A Greek at a party lay on a bed, turning the upper half of his body to the left, propping himself by his left elbow on cushions and taking food and drink with his right hand from a table on the left of the bed. At this party each bed was large enough for two, so they lay obliquely; each could then get at the food table.

The beds are disposed in a circle – a mandala. Note its complicated structure. Phaedrus and Eryximachus are in love, and so is Pausanias with Agathon. Aristophanes and Socrates are unattached but Socrates is ironically in love with the two most beautiful youths whom he sits between, Phaedrus and Agathon. They each give a speech on the nature of love, going round clockwise and starting with Phaedrus. However, Aristophanes is overcome by hiccups from overeating, so the physician Eryximachus gives him advice on how to overcome them and takes his turn so that Aristophanes can speak when he has recovered.

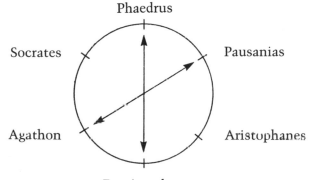

When all the invited guests have made their speeches there is a sound of flutes and revelry and an uninvited guest appears, Alcibiades, wearing an enormous wreath of ivy and violets on his head. He stands in the doorway with his enormous wreath on his head and drunkenly demands to see Agathon. He wants to crown Agathon with a wreath. They all cheer and he is invited to sit next to Agathon, Socrates having made a place for him. Agathon says they all three must make themselves comfortable. Alcibiades asks who is the third. He leaps up on seeing Socrates, and says Socrates is playing the same old game of popping up when least expected. Socrates becomes visible to Alcibiades 'instantly' – the same word which was used earlier to describe the appearance of beauty itself. Alcibiades then remarks that Socrates is sitting next to the handsomest man in the room – Agathon. Socrates replies that it is dreadful to be loved by Alcibiades as he is so jealous, and ironically asks Agathon to protect him. Alcibiades replies that he will get his own back on Socrates one day but at the moment wants to crown him because Socrates' words are for all time whereas Agathon's are ephemeral. So he crowns Socrates' head with ribbons.

There is more drunken banter until the physician Eryximachus bursts in and says they should stop behaving like a lot of thirsty savages. It is agreed that Alcibiades give an eulogy on Socrates. This eulogy is full of Carnivalesque material so is worth describing in some detail.

Alcibiades starts by saying he will use images to praise Socrates. Now images are deceptive to Plato for they only tell us what something is like. Socrates, he continues, is like the Sileni which are bought in shops; they hold pipes or flutes but when opened possess statues of gods within. Alcibiades likens himself here to Apollo as he is exposing Socrates' irony.

Second, Socrates he says is like the satyr Marsyas. Marsyas was the satyr who challenged Apollo to a contest of flute-playing and upon his defeat was flayed by the god. Socrates is like Marsyas in that he is supremely eloquent but unlike him in that his eloquence depends only on simple words from crafts such as carpentry. Alcibiades has heard many great orators, even Pericles, but none turned his soul upside-down as did Socrates. When he hears him he is smitten with a sacred rage, his heart jumps in his mouth and tears come to his eye. Socrates makes him feel that by spending his time in politics he is neglecting things crying for attention in himself, and that makes him feel ashamed. He often has to run away from Socrates. For Plato shame is the tell-tale sign of sickness of soul.

Both the image of the Sileni and of Marsyas reveal that Socrates, who is the object of Alcibiades' love, cannot be taken as he appears. For love is only revealed by a lack. The moment we love, something is lost. Love can only appear through sacrifice. The flaying of Marsyas expresses the violent disproportion by which the god attacks the human frame, which is agonized as it succumbs to the divine ecstasy. The meeting of God and man is in some sense like flaying, for the God has to strip off the bestial side of the shaggy satyr. Alcibiades goes on to describe how he once tried to seduce Socrates. He eventually got Socrates to come to dinner and spend the night with him. They slept on the same bed. Alcibiades told Socrates that he was the only lover really worthy of him. Alcibiades then took him in his arms and lay with him but in Alcibiades' words 'believe it or not, when I got up in the morning I had no more *slept* with Socrates, within the meaning of the act, than if he'd been my father or an elder brother' (Plato, *Symposium*, 1961, 219c–d).

After this Alcibiades was torn between humiliation and admiration for Socrates' manliness and self-control. This was strength of mind such as he had never hoped to meet. He was at his wit's end and in such a state of utter subjection to the man as never seen before.

The reaction of commentators to this passage is a good example of the ambivalence of European culture to the Carnivalesque. When the dialogue was first recovered in the early fifteenth century this was the only part to be translated into Latin, as it was thought to be bawdy. Later in that century Ficino, in his widely circulated commentary on the dialogue, being under the influence of Neoplatonic thought, idealized the *Symposium* and completely ignored this passage. Gould (1963) in his book on platonic love similarly idealizes love and says Socrates is depicted here as being totally without sensual desire and that he is ironic and simply pretending and playing along with others. But irony is not the same as pretending. Irony is admirable to Plato. If one were indifferent to the erotic it would not be admirable to do what Socrates did any more than one would call someone brave who was without fear, for bravery is surely the ability to face one's fears. The most recent English commentator, Sir Kenneth Dover (1980), writes that we must imagine Socrates as a healthy man who falls soundly asleep when a beautiful girl has crept naked under his blankets and put her arms round him. Plato, he says, wishes to suggest that physical relations are inimical to the pursuit of metaphysical truth. But, he adds, not everyone would regard the episode as a good advertisement for metaphysics! If Sir Kenneth is right it is difficult to see why Alcibiades responded as he did, with such admiration and humiliation; surely Sir Kenneth's imaginary girl would not respond like that even if she were so foolish as to try to seduce a metaphysician! Other commentators see it as a good example of Socratic *sophrosyne* (translated as 'temperance', better 'cool' – calmness in a situation of great passion, a supreme Greek virtue).

Lacan (1977a) points out that Socrates never claimed to know anything except Eros, that is to say desire. He is showing that not to want to desire and to desire are the same thing. For not wanting

THRESHOLDS BETWEEN PHILOSOPHY AND PSYCHOANALYSIS

to desire is *wanting* not to desire. Socrates is demonstrating the absolute authority of the desire of the Other, that 'Thy will be done'. For to fulfil Alcibiades' desire would be to deprive him – he would merely have the 'object *a*', he would possess a good. To refuse to get involved would be to cut out desire. Instead Socrates says, 'Look to your own desire', and this is something beyond good, evil, and knowledge; it is, to use a Kantian term, sublime.

During this part of his speech Alcibiades speaks to the symposists as if they were jurors – they are having a mock-trial of Socrates. He also invokes gods and goddesses. Only he and Socrates link the female with the divine in the *Symposium*. Alcibiades went on to say that after this episode he was on active service in the army with Socrates. Socrates stood up to the lack of food and the cold better than anyone. He could drink more than anyone yet never got drunk. He amazed the common soldiers as, if he had a problem, he could stand still all day lost in thought. Furthermore, in the battle Socrates saved Alcibiades' life and refused a decoration for bravery. When the army were retreating Socrates never ran but strolled along looking so unconcerned that none of the enemy dared attack him.

He concludes that Socrates is absolutely unique, there is no one like him. His speeches are in the language of craftsmen and seem plain and unadorned. But when you examine them carefully they are full of images of virtue. He has made fools of them all, for Socrates started as a lover and ends up as a beloved while Alcibiades began as a beautiful beloved and has ended up as the lover. They have exchanged sexual roles by moving from the anaclitic to the narcissistic position and vice versa. Finally he advises Agathon to learn from these experiences.

His speech is greeted with laughter at its frankness, rather than applause. Socrates says that Alcibiades is being cunning and hiding his envy and wants to separate him from Agathon. Agathon agrees and gets up to sit next to Socrates. But then a crowd of revellers enter and everyone starts drinking.

The physician Eryximachus and Phaedrus, who is a worrier about health, leave. Aristodemus falls asleep. He wakes in the early hours of the morning to find everyone asleep except Socrates, Agathon and Aristophanes. They are still drinking and Socrates is arguing that a tragic poet might be a comedian as well if he was a true master of poetry. Then Aristophanes falls asleep and finally Agathon. Socrates tucks them into bed, goes off to the Lyceum for a bath, and after spending the rest of the day as usual towards evening returns to his home to rest.

DIALOGUE

The erotic concerns people and their attachments with one another, not minds. People are embodied, have a position and attitude to one another and the situation which joins them and are in historical time. So truths about the erotic become denatured if put in a propositional form as truths about the mind; in an erotic relation we are not indifferent as to who speaks them. Who says what to whom and on what occasion is vital. Truth in the Socratic dialogue is an event which appears in the differences between the speakers, it is not a matter of the opinion of any one speaker. For example, it is notoriously difficult to state exactly what Plato's views were on anything. He questions and provokes rather than expounds his views. In the *Symposium* Socrates says very little; when he does speak it is mostly reporting, his only consistent speaking is a conversation with Agathon (Stokes, 1986). He acts mostly as a punctuation mark, a reminder, through the rest of the *Symposium*.

The *Symposium* is also misunderstood if it is taken as dialect-ical. 'Take a dialogue and remove the voices (the partitioning of voices), remove the intonations (emotional individualizing ones), carve out abstract concepts and judgements from living words and responses, cram everything into one abstract consciousness – and that's how you get dialectics' (Bakhtin, 1986).

Personality, speech and erotics interwine in the *Symposium*. Socrates is late and they start the meal without him. Half-way through he arrives and is greeted by Agathon, who asks him to sit next to him and remarks that he would like to share in the great thought that Socrates has evidently had. Socrates replies that he wished wisdom were the kind of thing that one could share by sitting next to someone, as if it flowed from the one that was full to the one that was empty. 'My own understanding is a shadowy thing at best, as equivocal as a dream, but yours Agathon glitters and dilates' (*Symposium*, 1961, 175e).

Here we have a preliminary sketch of a basic Socratic theme: the contrast between his understanding, which is dream-like and ungraspable, and Agathon's, the beautiful successful dramatist, who puts his truth across with explicit rhetorical power. We also have the theme of the container and the contained: knowledge is not a product that can be poured into another mind – a theme which Bion (1970) has elaborated.

The first speech is by Phaedrus. He is a good-looking young man who says that Eros is a great and wondrous God and a supreme benefactor of mankind. His views are of course naïve. He has lots of 'shoulds' and 'ought to's' in his speech, which indicates youthful but naïve zeal; he is a reformer. He sees love as being purely good and Eros replaces virtue: being seen and being loved are more important to him than doing or loving. He is a passive beloved. He connects virtue purely with male courage in battle. And he is beloved of Eryximachus the physician. He is one of the lighter drinkers at the banquet, which betrays his willingness to practise moderation only for the sake of physical well-being, for he follows the orders of his beloved physician Eryximachus without critical detachment, as a slave follows his master.

Pausanias the next speaker is a middle-aged pederast who is in love with Agathon. His speech is legalistic and contains many of the tricks of the Sophistic schools. He starts by criticizing Phaedrus for purely praising love. There is not one kind of love but two kinds – a good and a bad. The good love is the older and sprang from the heavens themselves and is called Uranian, while the bad love is the younger and was born of Zeus and Dione and is earthly. Actions are neither good nor bad in themselves but how they are done determines their value. Earthly love is vulgar; it is for women as well as boys and for the body rather than the soul since this love is born of male and female. It passes when the bodily bloom passes. Uranian or heavenly love is good, as it has nothing to do with the female. Those who are governed by it seek intelligence and sensibility in those they love, rather than merely lusting after beautiful bodies. He suggests there should be a law preventing men loving mere boys; after all they are unknown quantities, and they are often unfaithful. We should only be allowed to love those boys whose reason for yielding is that they believe in their lovers' virtue and hope to be improved by such an association.

Pausanias tries to establish the possibility of noble pederasty. He replaces wisdom by good taste as his concern is with the proper way of behaving. He is a conventionalist and a relativist and so a champion of law as against nature. He wants complex laws since he is less capable of arousing desire than affection and the habit of faithfulness; he needs laws to protect himself against 'wildness'. The basis of love to him is pre-Oedipal or Uranian love, which is non-genital: it comes from heaven, as opposed to Oedipal or earthly love, which is generated between Zeus and Dione.

Eryximachus the physician speaks next. His speech is pedantic and humourless; he never lays aside his professionalism and seizes every opportunity to air his medical knowledge. His speech is a good summary of the Hippocratic writings and he is obviously familiar with Empedocles – the pre-Socratic that Freud most admired. His point of view is that health is the standard by which everything should be judged; he advocates a cosmic form of selfishness. To him impiety results from failure to gratify the orderly cosmic Eros and not from disobedience to the gods. Note the similarity to Jung here. Jung justifies religion on the grounds that it is good for the psyche. In other words he reduces the source of value to a purely selfish one. Plato on the other hand indicates that obedience to the gods is primary; we should obey the gods whether it is good for our psychic health or not.

Aristophanes is seated third at table but, as we have seen, he becomes the fourth speaker because of his hiccups. He is wittier than the physician yet needs him to rescue his wit from being silenced by hiccups. He is the greatest Greek comic poet and we know that he was a personal friend of Plato. His style of speech is superior to that of the previous speakers, being an admirable piece of Attic prose. He contrasts with the puritanism of the pragmatic doctor and appears as a man of strength able to take strong drink, with a fertile imagination, wit, and hearty joviality which he uses to ridicule the science of the physician. His speech is full of imagery and myth. He starts by saying that mankind has never had a true conception of the power of Eros. Eros is a friend of man because it is he that can cure us of those ills which stand in the way of our highest happiness. He then gives an elaborate and comic myth to illustrate this. Our race was once divided into three – male, female and androgyne. These were all globular in shape, each globule having four arms, four legs, two heads and two lots of sex organs. In their arrogance they tried to scale heaven so Zeus decided as punishment to cut them all in half. Apollo then turned their heads round as the gash in their sides might frighten them, and he stitched up their wounds. Each half then yearned for the other half so Zeus then altered the position of their genitals. So each of us is a split half of an original male, female or androgyne. And the other halves we seek in love are determined accordingly. So love is the pursuit of wholeness, we all seek our original whole state, and love conducts us to our true affinities.

Now Aristophanes is distinguished from all the other speakers as he is unattached. The physician loves Phaedrus and Pausanias loves Agathon. Furthermore Phaedrus' speech and Agathon's are paired, in that the former celebrates Eros as the oldest god while the latter celebrates him as the youngest. Pausanias' and the physician's speeches are paired, as the double Eros introduced by the former is confirmed by the latter. Aristophanes' speech is distinguished as having the sharpest criticism of mankind, and he disagrees with everyone else. Human existence to him is fragmentary and in great danger of becoming more so. To bring this across he uses powerful aesthetic and mythological images, in marked contrast to the two previous speakers who used images from sociology and natural science. We must *perceive* the power of love he says.

Eros is the desire that all desires be cancelled. We were once circular and in need of nothing. Now we have holes and projections and are running around anxiously trying to find some ideal being into which to thrust one of our projections or have someone's projection thrust into us. Aristophanes uses images of the Carnivalesque body – grotesque distortions of the body emphasizing excess as in Rabelais – to emphasize the process of pleasure in exchange and to mark out the sites around which desire is created. His myth of the circular people shows how spirituality in men depends on sexuality. Man is castrated in a total sense – not merely genitally – and is perpetually restrained by the self-contradictory dimensions of desire and satisfaction. The conclusion of his speech is tragedy and not comedy.

Lacan's (1977a) interpretation is interesting. He points out that Aristophanes' fable is comic and absurd (compare *A Midsummer*

110

Night's Dream). It is a practical joke. It depicts love as a search for the 'object *a*' (the breast); that part of ourselves which we lose at birth and weaning. So the subject in the fable is the subject in the field of the drive and not the subject as he appears in the field of the Other. The subject in the field of the Other only emerges in so far as we can laugh at the fable. And we only laugh when we realize that the 'object *a*' is lost for ever and that we are only mortal. The lure of the 'object *a*' induces us into sexual relations but this drive is at root a death drive and represents the portion of death in the sexed living being. I should also point out that Lacan regarded the *Symposium* as the most profound of all works on the transference.

Freud mentioned this myth (Freud, 1920) and thought its importance lay in tracing the origin of an instinct to a need to restore an earlier state of things. He also used it to account for sexual perversions by invoking Fliess's theory of human bisexuality (Freud, 1896). However, he thought that what was important was to put the right projection into the right hole. To do otherwise is perverse and immature. He does not say what law tells us this is so other than instinct, which is a theoretical construct. Socrates on the other hand is concerned with clarity about desire.

After a little banter between Agathon and Socrates, Agathon speaks. Agathon is a key figure. He is the host; Socrates sits next to him and he is the only person besides Aristophanes and Alcibiades with whom Socrates has any conversation. He is a very beautiful and intelligent young man who has just won the much coveted prize for his tragedy. He is the effeminate beloved of the soft but clever Pausanias. His speech is that of a tragic poet – high-flown and full of rhetorical devices, and he often bursts into verse; his speech is the most seductive of all. He starts by emphasizing method; his predecessors only talked about the works of love but he will praise the god himself and then his works; he will praise the god first for what he is and second for what he gives – a premonition of Socrates' view. Agathon's speech brings down the house in admiration. Socrates says that its eloquence leaves him in despair, he could not hope to emulate it.

Agathon praises youth instead of tradition. He is optimistic in contrast to the pessimism of Aristophanes. He praises innovation and recommends that each erotic man become his own chief. The autonomy of innovation leads to asserting the superiority of one's own innovations. Agathon is narcissistic and his lovely speech matches his lovely body. But eloquence alone is like a body without a soul as it is not grounded in truth. The empty eloquence of the beloved needs the lover's truth to educate him. Socrates politely points out that the recognition of wisdom depends on the rooting of communication in the community but narcissism dissolves the community and so has no basis for praising anyone but itself. Agathon has thirty thousand lovers in the theatre audience. He has only to say 'I want' and this links ego, will, method and technical innovations.

Instead of participating in Ideas which requires an understanding of rules and law, Agathon makes us share in the song that charms our thoughts away; Eros is a master sophist and operates by necessity. Agathon says poetry can even persuade us we are free. He wants to be known and seen rather than concern himself with what knowing is. The touch of Eros is a kind of giving rather than teaching: should one give what one possesses or teach what one knows?

Socrates starts by saying he cannot possibly compete with Agathon in praising love; he personally delights in the 'magic' of speeches but then ironically drops the word 'truth'. If his listeners are interested he could tell the truth about love. They all tell him to go ahead. First Socrates has a brief conversation with Agathon which is noticeably dry compared to all the previous rhetoric. He implies that Agathon's idea of love is incestuous. Agathon says that love is the desire of like for like. So why do not beautiful parents sexually desire their offspring? Why do we not remain self-enclosed in incest? He goes on to show that desire is directed to what it does not possess. Eros brings man out beyond himself, it stretches him.

Then we move onto the main part of Socrates' speech in which he reports on a conversation he had with a woman called Diotima when he was a young man. There has been much scholarly research on who this lady was. Nobody knows for certain, but she was probably a temple prostitute, as in those days, when wives were confined to their homes, courtesans were better educated. This speech is a memory by Apollodorus of what Aristodemus remembered Socrates remembered of what Diotima told him when

he was a young man. Plato once again is underlining the importance of memory in love.

As a young man Socrates did not understand Eros. Especially he
could not understand the relation between the beauty of Ideas, the
mathematical order of the physical cosmos and the ugliness of this
world. So he took lessons from Diotima. She taught him that love
is 'the between'. It is not a god at all but a daimon which is half-
way between god and man, beauty and ugliness, good and evil,
wise and foolish. Eros does not possess but desires. He is a great
daimon but not a god to whom perfection is assigned. He mediates
between the divine and the human to create community.

This conception is made more concrete by a typically Carnivalesque myth. On the day Aphrodite was born the gods were making
merry with nectar. One of the gods was Resource who, when
drunk, had intercourse with Need. Their child was Eros. Now
Poros is the Greek for 'Resource' and *Penia* for Need. The usual
antonym for *Penia* is *ploutos* (wealth), so we must look more
carefully at *Poros*. It is cognate with *peirein* ('to pierce') and was
applied to a path or ferry, that is, a means of getting across land or
water; then it came to mean any means of coping with a difficulty
(as our 'ways and means'). In Alcman (Fragment 5.2.11) *Poros*
meant way or track in the primeval void. Also, *aporos* meant
being-at-a-loss or being in difficulties – a common and important
experience in philosophy and psychoanalysis. Note the complete
contrast with Aristophanes in which love is a completion of oneself. To Plato Eros is concerned with a way through emptiness, it is
ascetic. Since Eros had such parents his nature was to be always
needy, harsh, avid, homeless but also gallant, energetic, a mighty
hunter and master of devices, full of wisdom and an adept in
sorcery, enchantment and seduction. He is neither mortal nor
immortal, perpetually being born and dying. He stands midway
between ignorance and wisdom; for the gods, being wise, do not
seek after it, while the ignorant are satisfied with what they are
and do not long for virtues they have never missed. So Eros is a
lover of wisdom. He vacillates between cleverness which resusci-
tates him and need which vitiates, his cleverness brings him close
to the gods, his needs close to the animals; wisdom is awareness of
moving through this dialectic.

It has been suggested that lovers are people who are looking for their other halves. But this is false for it implies that Eros is a desire for a part (a part object). Similarly Eros as sole desire for the beautiful is false, for although amidst all the changing appearances of things it is the beautiful that brings Eros to the fore most readily yet beauty is captivating as well as being liberating. Any striving towards self-perfection is wrong because looked at closely it is at the same time a striving for self-destruction. For can we who are mortal and imperfect know for certain what perfection is?

The good is not some*thing* that is possessed. It is in passion, rather than in the possession of knowledge, that Plato finds promise of 'surcease of travail of soul' that stems from inner conflict. So 'good' is not equivalent to the moral, for Eros is 'greatest and all deceitful'. The good is 'beyond good and evil'. Similarly Eros longs not for the beautiful itself but for the conception and generation that the beautiful effects.

But all this is only the elementary mysteries of Eros: we are at the bottom of the true scale of perfection. To climb this scale we must start by devoting ourselves to the beauty of one individual body, next see how this is related to the beauty of other bodies. Then grasp that the beauties of bodies are as nothing to the beauties of the soul. Then contemplate the beauty of laws and institutions and then the beauties of the sciences. Having contemplated these there may burst upon us the soul of beauty itself.

It is this vision that makes man's life worth living and having seen it he will never be seduced by the charm of gold or beautiful boys; he would happily deny himself the grosser necessities of meat and drink. And it is only when a man has had this vision of beauty that he will be quickened with the true, rather than the seeming, virtue: and when this virtue is born in him and reared by him, then he can be called the friend of god and possibly attain immortality.

Plato here turns Freud upside-down. Instead of explaining the desire for philosophy as a sublimation of sexuality, Socrates understands sexual desire as a blind groping for the wisdom of philosophy. Sexual desire, rightly understood, leads to philosophy. The world as understood by the lover is reality and that which limits this insight is irrational. Right love and reason are the same thing:

114

Plato did not have the romantic notion of reason as being heartless calculation.

Finally, as we said earlier, Alcibiades bursts in. He was a distinguished Athenian aristocrat and leading general and statesman. He was, at the time of the *Symposium*, the most brilliant party leader in Athens, a man of great intellectual ability and of remarkable personal beauty, of which he was not a little vain. He was a strange mixture of great powers and great vices. He was a licentious bisexual but his loves were not so much motivated by lust as by the love of conquest and of being first. He was infatuated with Socrates. His pride is defined by Socrates as a perpetual desire 'to have more'. He was a master of hunting and dissimulation and had a chameleon-like way of assimilating himself to others. He hunted the many or simulated their behaviour in order to dominate them. Plutarch tells us that the night before he was murdered he dreamed he was dressed in woman's clothes and a courtesan was holding his head and painting his face with make-up. No wonder Socrates said, 'I shudder at his madness and passion for love' (213D6). His whole life was a self-destructive combination of daring and insolence. He is a superb example of the defects of Athenian political life and was probably the most suitable man to understand Socrates (Nussbaum, 1986).

CONCLUSION

I want to conclude by raising once again the question as to how we can discuss the erotic if we see that to be human is to be constantly subject to it. Let me quote Freud:

> Up till now we have left it to the creative writer to depict for us the 'necessary conditions for loving' which govern people's choice of an object, and the way in which they bring the demands of their imagination into harmony with reality. The writer can indeed draw on certain qualities which fit him to carry out the task: above all, on a sensitivity that enables him to perceive the hidden impulses in the minds of other people, and the courage to let his own unconscious speak. But there is one circumstance which lessens the evidential value of what he has to say. Writers are under the necessity to produce intellectual and aesthetic pleasure, as well as certain emotional effects. For

115

this reason they cannot reproduce the stuff of reality unchanged, but must isolate portions of it, remove disturbing associations, tone down the whole and fill in what is missing. These are the privileges of what is known as 'poetic licence' . . . science should concern herself with the same materials . . . though her touch must be clumsier and the yield of pleasure less . . . Science is, after all, the most complete renunciation of the pleasure principle of which our mental activity is capable. (Freud, 1910a, p. 165)

I wonder! In one of the most important scientific papers in this century in the most prestigious scientific journal – Einstein's 1916 paper on general relativity in the Berlin Archives of Physics – he wrote that although the theory may not be true it deserved scientific consideration because it was so beautiful. A sentiment echoed by many mathematicians and physicists then and since, not only about relativity but about many other scientific theories especially in mathematics and physics. Freud had no sense of the importance of beauty or of mathematics in science, he thought observation and induction were enough. Plato thought that mathematics played a crucial role in developing knowledge of the soul, Freud had nothing to say on this.

Throughout his life Einstein deplored piecemeal, fact-piled-upon-fact approaches to science such as Freud's and insisted upon the place of imagination and beauty in science and the importance of nurturing them. Einstein, like Plato, saw that beauty is not just a lot of pleasure and its effect need not be merely suggestive; for it can enable a person to master the erotic and see beyond his own ideas and experience. It is this insight that enabled him to criticize Freud. When late in life he was asked his opinion about Freud he wrote: 'The old one had . . . a sharp vision; no illusion lulled him asleep except for an often exaggerated faith in his own ideas' (Pais, 1982). Did not Einstein see a crucial and unanalysed manifestation of Freud's eros here?

Freud wanted to make discussion on the erotic a monologue – his own. He (1926a) complained that philosophers and writers made up their own psychology for themselves: 'everyone has a mental life so everyone regards himself as a psychologist', 'it runs wild', there is no 'technical knowledge' amongst such people. He

116

saw psychoanalysis as a way of ironing out the ambiguities and ironies of literature and philosophy and so creating the sure foundations of a science. This would provide techniques for a professional élite who would use them to help those in need and who would advise on the correct way to bring up children, the best way to educate them and be the repositories of the essential knowledge that a culture requires.

Freud saw himself as a scientist, a knower. He informs us directly of his knowledge of desire and sexuality in his books and papers. For example he tells us (1905) that the normal sexual aim is a satisfaction analogous to the sating of hunger and is obtained by 'the appropriate stimulation of an erotogenic zone (the genital zone itself, in the glans penis) by the appropriate object (the mucous membrane of the vagina) and that the consequent discharge of the semen brings about the pleasure of satisfaction which is the highest in intensity'.

Besides telling us in jargon what most of us already know he brings in assumptions and suggestions. But he never tells us their 'evidential value'. Does making love always have an aim? On what grounds does he say that maximum intensity of pleasure is the normal aim of sexuality? What about joy? Is joy the same as pleasure and can one measure it on a scale of intensity? Do we always want the maximum? Are there not other just as illuminating analogies of love besides the sating of hunger?

As there is no evidence for most of Freud's statements how did he obtain certainty? Freud observed that the analyst is seen by the patient as the locus of meaning and knowledge, especially in sexual matters. So as Freud wanted certain knowledge he took up the position of the analyst, the one who is presumed to know, and the patient became an 'object' who produced material which had to be interpreted. In Hegel's terms there was a 'fight for recognition' whose outcome is the sole recognition of the master – of the truth of the analyst's knowledge and the power and authority of his method and school. The function of the patient, like that of the slave, is to serve the desire of the analyst – his desire for recognition and his desire to have his knowledge recognized as being certain. So, through his experience of analysis, Freud could claim that his theories of sexuality were certain knowledge. After all, his patients repeatedly confirmed that he knew. For others to obtain this certainty he could rightly claim that it was necessary they undergo an analysis either by himself or by someone certified by him as well as analyse patients themselves. So Freud or one of his pupils certified that the analyst knew and the analyst's patients would confirm it, of course. Needless to say the problem of authority – who certifies and what are the correct experiences – arose almost immediately.

Plato wrote for aristocrats, and not for slaves wanting certainty through a dogma. He was aware that experience on its own does not yield truth and that the erotic is 'the between' and is present in all speech and writing including scientific writing. Knowledge of it cannot be captured by a method and possessed like a fact but rather it possesses us.

When, a few hours before his death, Socrates was discussing the nature of the soul, he warned his friends and pupils to scrutinize his arguments particularly carefully (*Phaedo*, 1961, 90e–91c). For he might be acting like 'uneducated lovers of victory' who discuss with eagerness not for the truth but to persuade their listeners. He warned them that as he was near to death he would be particularly likely to make his opinions appear true above all to himself to calm his anxiety. He must distance himself from the motive of self-persuasion to allow truth to appear. So his authority depended on the ring of truth in his words and deeds rather than on the experiences obtained by applying a method or the certificates issued by a school.

When Plato wanted to open our eyes to the nature of the erotic he wrote the *Symposium*. This is a drama in which philosophical reflection is interwoven with the desires and jealousies of its participants. Even Apollodorus who did not witness it is involved in its telling by his own love for Socrates. And Socrates is involved in desire for he loved Agathon and is beloved by Alcibiades. It is a drama which unfolds; medicinal lies and truths, different erotic personalities, speech and silence are interwoven, so the reader is forced to engage in interpretations and so become aware of his own Eros in reading. He may then be led to wonder, think and remember rather than absorb facts and theories. For dialogue is a game to teach man the nature of his own psyche. It is not a tasteful framework for conveying theories about people. (Compare Brenkman, 1982.)

The *Symposium* is ironical. Irony is both seductive and repellent. It questions the knowable by showing rather than saying and stating. Who can practise it? If one tries to copy it one makes a fool of oneself. Theory and information on the other hand can be directly spoken or written and can be copied and applied by fools as well as by the wise. The *Symposium* suggests that we cannot be in a position to know desire and that there is not a technical method such as psychoanalysis to which one must submit in order to know it. For in love we are irrevocably involved with others so to every position a counter position occurs. Some of these occurring in the *Symposium* are: man/woman, lover/beloved, earthly love/heavenly love, old/young, good/bad, permanent/transitory, one/many, excess/temperance, body/soul, completeness/lack, harmony/discord, truth/rhetoric, life/death, sexuality/death, beautiful/ugly, comedy/tragedy. The *Symposium* is a carnival which embraces the opposites and reveals the dynamics of desire. No one in it can occupy a position from which he can survey and describe the erotic objectively. It is, as the Greeks were later to call it, a sceptical way.

6
Otherwise than integrity

CHRIS OAKLEY

If psychoanalysts of such different tendencies as
Edith Jacobson or René Spitz, Winnicott or Guntrip have
included 'the self' in their conceptualization they did it to
find an answer to the problems posed by the analysis of some
of the patients and not to demonstrate the insufficiencies or
deficiencies of Freudian metapsychology.
–Pontalis, The Frontiers of Psychoanalysis

INTRODUCTION

IN HIS INTRODUCTION to *Through Paediatrics to Psycho-Analysis* Masud Khan describes Winnicott as 'one such the like of whom I shall not meet again' (Winnicott, 1975). One's immediate inclination is to understand this as an endorsement of Winnicott as a particular sort of being, in this case one unlike any other, set within the context of an implicit comparison with all other beings (an objective realm). It is hoped that this is equally immediately followed by the realization that the very mode of expression gestures towards the liking that Masud Khan extended towards Winnicott and it is that which is being singled out as extraordinary (a subjective realm), rather than Winnicott's identity. I am using this to open out a discussion around the subject of the self; how we appear to be inexorably drawn to reify this notion either as the totality of our being or as a partial aspect of it rather than explore the phenomenon of the experience itself. One only has to wander into the basement of Karnacs, London's premier psychoanalytic bookshop, and to peruse the titles on the shelves to witness the contemporary interest in the problematics of 'the self'. (For example: *The Analysis of the Self*, *The Search for the Self* and *The*

120

Restoration of the Self, all by Heinz Kohut; *The Privacy of the Self* and *Hidden Selves*, both by Masud Khan; and *Schizoid Phenomena, Object Relations and the Self*, by Harry Guntrip – to name but a handful.) Indeed this is set within the broader context of attempts to distil certain essential features of our times, epitomized by Tom Wolfe's 'the me generation' and Christopher Lasch's 'the culture of narcissism'.

What I want to outline are the various problematics that concern the two predominant countervalencies concerning the self within the 'world' of psychoanalysis: that which, for numerous reasons, is linked particularly with 'American psychoanalysis', namely 'ego psychology', which is informed by the work of Heinz Hartmann, and that of a more European persuasion, centring around the controversial figure of Jacques Lacan. It would need an altogether different study to review all the varying uses of the term 'self' in Western thought or even the different ways that are employed within psychoanalysis.

By focusing on the ego-psychology–Lacan debate there is inevitably something of an omission in not giving more attention to the Object Relations school, in whose tradition R. D. Laing's *Self and Others* (1961) appeared. However, I should like to draw attention, briefly, to some of the difficulties inherent in their approach, without in any way wanting to appear dismissive in relation to the enormous contribution made by such writers as Fairbairn, Bion, Khan, Milner and Winnicott amongst others. Exemplary in Winnicott's work, for example, is the 'Good enough' mother–infant dyad, whilst in Laing's we have the Jack and Jill knotted interaction, but this leaves us with the problems of the co-presencing of two human beings, a two-person psychology which has now taken up the position of a virtual centre with all the attendant difficulties fundamental to the logic of centring, of making the centre the point of view from which to evaluate ourselves. Although the I/ thou, self/other relationship is seen as basic, it should not be reduced to two centres exchanging signals with each, whether they contribute to the other's fulfilment or annihilation. The acknowledgement that our relations are structured by language disrupts an idea of the dual binary system of an uninterrupted circle drawn around and so binding the two figures together.

But I am getting ahead of myself. Let us begin by exploring certain distinctions between the self and the ego. Freud had a tendency to play on certain ambiguities by utilizing the term *das Ich*. He appeared to allow for two potentially separate conceptions which would become protaganists in a struggle for superiority within psychoanalytic theory, and if one gives him the benefit of the doubt he did so quite deliberately. The first position is that the self refers to a personal self and the second is that it refers to a specific element within the psyche, which is usually taken to be the ego.

Heinz Hartmann was particularly concerned that in psychoanalytic terminology there is no adequate term for the total person. He wanted to find a way of describing the synthesis between the id, ego and super-ego, as a unified entity. As it happens there was of course very good reason for this lack, as without it one would arrive at precisely the position that Freud had been at great pains to avoid. Freud had no desire to render ourselves as 'king of the castle' by proposing the category of a 'total person'. So Hartmann wanted to differentiate between the self and the ego in that he took the ego to be the centre of perception, an autonomous agency of consciousness, from which we can give meaning to the world, or equally from which we can fail to recognize that which is external to us. Once one has taken up this position it follows quite naturally that the ego is in a position to adapt to reality. According to Hartmann our ego is hereditarily prepared for adaptation to a probable environment but also to deal with the vicissitudes of our drives. He thought that there were two fundamental ego functions: (1) to organize our relationships with the environment and (2) to deal with conflict with the id and super-ego, both with the basic aim of arriving at a 'conflict-free zone'. For Hartmann man is a being of adaptation as distinct from a subject of unconscious desires: 'We call a man well adapted if his productivity, his ability to enjoy life, and his mental equilibrium are undisturbed, and we ascribe failure to a lack of adaptation' (Hartmann, 1964, p. 23). For many Hartmann may be hardly a familiar figure, but he has a particular historical significance in that it was his work that pioneered much of contemporary 'American psychoanalysis'. A more recent author who would appear to be following in a similar vein is Roy Schafer, who writes of a 'unitary, fully responsible agent' (1983, p. 247), and of transforming narrative into that which would be 'more complete, coherent, convincing, and *adaptively useful'* (p. 240).

Now one thing that is certain in all this is that we are at the site of a radical departure from anything in Freud. For Freud it was the id that was the constituting agency and the ego was an object of consciousness inevitably linked to narcissism and always outside in the world, other to the subject. Therefore, it would be misleading to see the ego as either an element of consciousness or the centre of consciousness itself. Depending on one's viewpoint this will be seen as an advance or a pernicious betrayal. For Jacques Lacan, who proudly and somewhat ambiguously claimed to fly under the banner of a 'return to Freud', there was no equivocation. He saw Hartmann and the persistence of ego-psychology as an attempt to purify the ego of any narcissistic elements. He was virulent in his criticism of any endeavour to strengthen the ego, or to give someone a consistent identity. For Lacan the ego (or the self, for he blurs the two) is always an object of consciousness and is primarily made up of an identification with one's self-image. It is always an imaginary construct. To take the ego as an agent of integration and adaptation ('the monarch of the self') was seen by Lacan as a monstrous confusion that would transform psychoanalysis into an enterprise primarily concerned with conformity and thereby away from its subversive edge. He took to be a fundamental principle of the psychoanalytic enterprise the endeavour to undermine any possible notion of a monadic subject, in other words, a self that could be completely sure of itself.

Lacan, whilst favouring notions of a subject as radically distinct from the ego or the self, did become somewhat ambiguous and allowed a certain enigmatic nuancing of 'I'. Sometimes this would appear to refer to the ego whilst at others to the subject of desire. At other times he would distinguish between 'I' and 'me', and so, as did Freud, allow the complexities to play across each other. However, he consistently emphasized that it is not the ego that constitutes the subject but the other way around. As we are about to see the ego, but not necessarily the self, is always a reified product of imaginary identifications, whilst the subject is no thing at all.

I. ANYTHING THAT ONE TAKES ONESELF TO BE ONE IS NOT

It would appear that we are inclined, compelled even, to represent ourselves to ourselves in the form of an image. In fact for Lacan this is a crucial founding moment in which I am established in a place from which meaning can unfold. Merleau-Ponty (1962) emphasizes the 'primacy of perception . . . the experience of perception is our presence at the moment when things, truths, values are constituted for us . . . perception summons us to the tasks of knowledge and action'. The world that is given in perception is 'the concrete, intersubjectively constituted life world of immediate experience . . . a world of familiar, natural and cultured objects, of other people, the world in which I act'. He speaks of different levels of experience: the imaginary realm, the ideological realm, the impact of language and culture and the 'many ways for consciousness to be conscious' but says we can never completely escape from the realm of perceptual reality. Even the seemingly independent structure of categorical thought is ultimately founded in perception. 'We never cease living in the world of perception but we go beyond it in critical thought, almost forgetting the contribution of perception to our idea of truth.'

Lacan in his elaboration of the notion of the subject is hardly forgetful of the significance of the perceptual, particularly in what he terms 'the mirror phase' of development. At the heart of the resolution of the Oedipus complex is our gradually developing capacity to use symbolization. In the pre-Oedipal phase meaning is lodged within the immediate, dual, barely differentiated relationship between mother and child. Lacan speaks of the '*hommelette*', the little one, the infant spreading or being driven in all directions. Inevitably we come up against the constraints of the prevailing socio-cultural order as exemplified by our family, and these drives meet limitation: this opens up a sense of distinction, of edge and of margin. The drives are located in erotogenic zones, openings of the body surface (for example, the lips of the mouth, the anus, the vagina, the penis, and so on) and there is a gradual distinguishing of the pleasurable and the exciting from the merely functional (ultimately expressed in the colloquialism, 'it's not just for pissing with'). What is important is their position on the surface, for they do not represent the outside but are more the 'stuff, or rather the lining . . . of the very subject that one takes to be the subject of consciousness' (Lacan, 1966, p. 818).

Based on our primordial longing for the maternal body we try to coincide, to fuse with all that is pleasurable, so initially we take in, incorporate 'good objects' in the sense that they are capable of filling the lack, the missing link, and project the 'bad' so that the site of displeasure is outside the subject. (By using the word 'in' (in 'take in') it would appear that I am reinstating an interiority of our self-experience. Images will displace and replace bodily experience but their provenance will always be of the body: if we begin with a basic feeling, the surface of the skin, it is difficult not to move along an inevitable trajectory: skin as covering, skin as container, from container to sphere. 'A sphere, this envelope . . . supposes a cord which knots it, and all centring presupposes the logic of the sack and the cord' (Lacan, *Ornicar*, 1977b). So initially we are taken in, and continue to be, by this idea of interiority.) The child is subject to the complexity of tracing connections and differences through the attribution of states of pleasure and displeasure to gradually disclose a differentiated world of self and other.

For Lacan, as for Merleau-Ponty in his *The Child and His Relations to Others*, the I is always constructed rather than pre-existent as in traditional psychology, and this construction occurs through identification.

The immediate 'introceptive' consciousness of one's own body is fundamentally correlated with the perception of the other (that is, progress in one domain shifts the totality in such a way that the other domain is inevitably affected . . . the idea being of a form that is informed by the totality of my body and that of another). This will gradually give way to the alienation of representation. The word alienation is used advisedly in that here is the beginning of the unified sense of self, the occasioning of an image of myself, the original site of the fiction. Whereas previously my body experience was fragmented, uncoordinated, it now begins to synthesize, to become whole through an identification with the 'mirror image', as well as with (m)other(s) bodies. The transformation is occasioned for the subject when I assume the image, the move from the introceptive to the specular self, when I see that I can be seen, when I see that others can take a viewpoint on one. I am subjected to this, I am forced to situate my identity in separation. I enter the world of 'objects', separate and thus signifiable, and this

125

is coexistent with the threshold of the acquisition of language.

This is the realm of the onset of narcissism. What Lacan terms 'the imaginary order' is thus the basically narcissistic relation of the subject to his ego. I am caught up by, fascinated by, amused by my specular image. There is the 'real' me, a lived, immediate reality, and an 'imaginary' me, potentially ideal, a constructed, fictitious me; and thus begins via the confiscation of the former for the benefit of the latter the alienation from myself and others. The I continues to spring up in primordial form 'before objectifying itself in the dialectic of identification with the other' (Lacan, 1949, p. 449).

This is for Lacan the site of a fundamental *méconnaissance*, both a misrecognition and a misapprehending, the onset of the fiction of the ideal ego. It involves an imaginary identification of the corporeal image as a unified one, which opens up the possibility of self-control. I am confronted by this image of myself and this occasions the possibility of myself as another other, the onset of my being in relation to otherness. This falsehood of the ideal totality is dismantled via the entry into 'the symbolic order' of language, where we come to experience the otherness of the unconscious, but after that entry we endeavour to cling to the fiction of an image of unity via the ego ideal, for in order to maintain psychic equilibrium a form of stability may be achieved by vestiges of representation . . . back to the hegemony of perception!

WEANING ALWAYS COMES TOO SOON

According to Lacan the subject is constituted by a separation, a splitting, the *Spaltung*, so as to establish a 'signifying place' from which to represent himself ('. . . even if only by means of a stand-in') and thus take up a position with regard to meaning. Fundamental for this achievement is first the mirror phase, outlined above, and second, the stage of the 'castration complex'. In order for there to be acquisition of sociality there has to be difference; the resolution of the Oedipus complex is our developing detachment from the founding other, that is, one's mother, on whom there is an inevitable and appropriate dependency (we are all born prematurely!) and thus we gradually locate a 'signifying place', which is ultimately a place within the symbolic order. The field of the symbolic is that which structures, which organizes our relations, in other words, human law, the family, archaic resonances of the Church, the State and so on, and within this my desire will unfold with reference to the constraints imposed by such formations. As Lévi-Strauss wrote: '. . . without kinship nominations no power is capable of instituting the order of preferences and taboos which bind and weave the yarn of lineage' (Lévi-Strauss, 1949).

IN ORDER TO BE TOGETHER WE MUST FIRST BE SEPARATE
At this point we would do well to consider some of the ideological considerations that are folded into any form of representation. In the elaboration of the subject inevitably we find our sexed subjecthood, and the subject of sexuality. Lacan in particular and psychoanalysis in general has been accused of phallocentricism and of normalizing as if universal a particular historical and political condition set within a specific discursive order. Indeed, there has been considerable protest against Lacan, who appears almost as colluding with or as an apologist for phallocentricity, whereas in many ways he was more involved with an uncovering of that system. Despite his controversial position feminist reaction, in all its multiplicity, has been less concerned with a dismissal or decentring of Lacan. Rather he appears to be at the very least coexistent with, if not an inspiration for, an impetus towards a redefinition of the images and associations linked to the figure of women. Juliet Mitchell and Jacqueline Rose's introduction to *Female Sexuality* emphasizes his rereading of women so that there is a reversal of signs: what appears superficially as negative becomes a plus, a comparative freedom from some of the impasses by which the phallic male is constrained. The difficulty is that by appearing to end up mastering the issue of sexual difference, indeed one could say that he makes a point of it, Lacan seems to re-establish the feminine as secondary.

One of his chief critics, Luce Irigaray (1977) attacks the privilege of the phallus in that women are designated as the 'negative', 'the lack'. Whilst in Freud what was taken to be missing was anatomical (that is, the penis, which as every schoolboy knows is quite distinct from the phallus, although simultaneously the two can never be quite so easily divorced). In Lacan it is a lack in language in that women make a negative entry, as far as representation is concerned, into the symbolic order (that is, the hole). Irigaray speaks of the privilege that is given to a predominantly male discourse in that what is glorified is the supposed ideal of unity (of the subject, of discourse, of the unity of presence as exemplified by the fundamental form of subject–verb–object) which is endorsed by the production of a unified form of representation of masculinity: the phallus and the almost explicit endorsement of objectivity. Whilst the discourse is male, that sex is both put in and simultaneously represents that position of privilege, of preeminence, as visible and representable, particularly through the 'becoming in a particular form': the erection.

Quite appropriately Irigaray draws our attention to the fact there is no correspondence within the realm of female sexuality. However, her attempt at representation involving 'two lips in a continuous embrace' (shades of Judy Chicago) with the emphasis on there being always two, continuously interchanging, and so endeavouring to move away from the dominant criteria of the visible or of the fixed form, still appears to be indelibly lodged within just those considerations. It is merely another erection. The feminine, if it is to move beyond phallocentricism, should not 'be universalized, not faithful, not constant to an identity' (Gallop, 1982). However, at this moment I become wary of having reduced Irigaray's contribution to a singular thrust, despite wanting to endorse her disruptive function.

Following Lacan, sexuality and language are inexorably interwoven and so via a shift from anatomy to morphology (the shape or form that something takes) Irigaray shows that whilst the masculine can look at itself, speculate about itself and imagine itself (that is, can have a meta-language), this is not possible for the feminine, lodged in the tactile, which is inevitably beyond simple description and certainly not from the outside. What she and Michèle Montreley, for example, with her distillation of the essentially feminine in terms of the olfactory ('l'odeur de feminité'), are striving towards is the underscoring of the significance of plurality, particularly as expressed in language. Thus we move beyond any notion of hierarchy of meaning for at each and every moment there will be the possibility of a multiplicity of meaning, that is, not one on top and one beneath, one conscious and one repressed, or one central and one peripheral, so that the notion of unity, of objective truth, of the proper meaning of words is dismantled.

However, this would seem fairly and squarely lodged within what might be termed the Lacanian teaching and his elaboration of the heterogeneity of the subject and its avoidance of the implicit idealism, masculine or otherwise, in any such notion as 'identity'. His emphasis is consistently that our nature is linguistic and that meaning can only be established through positionality within the symbolic or discursive order (it is our insertion within this that indeed occasions our subjecthood and our subjection to that which we are not yet aware of: the unconscious). This subject is a subject in process and the entrance fee, the price of admission to the world of self and other, the world of togetherness or at least the potentialities for it, is the *Spaltung*, the disruptive relation with consciousness. From here on it seems completely out of the question to maintain any attachment to the idea of a unified, unifying self, however much we are unquestionably drawn to represent ourselves to ourselves as such. The unconscious, just like the concept of 'the self', is bedevilled by a multiplicity of confusions and contradictions. Is it a space, a container that can be characterized by various structures (Freudian metapsychology)? A limit, a coming up against the unspeakable (Roustang, 1983)? An experience with language (Heaton, 1982a)? Can we settle on it ultimately being seen as devious, contradictory, erratic, so that any idea of a fully finished consistent subject (the fiction of the completely analysed analyst) is in error, as would any idea be of the unity of the phenomenon of consciousness itself? No doubt Lacan deserves the description as 'a phallocentric prick' (Gallop) who engaged in the imposition of his own authority not merely by the expulsion of Irigaray from the École Freudienne, for example, but also by the imposition of authority via the glossary of terms.

Lacan's formative years were linked with French Surrealism and a fellow collaborator on the magazine *Minotaure* called Michel Leiris had a certain notoriety for his 'glossalogical games . . . the glossary . . . where I air my glosses', and ultimately Lacan appears to have followed his example for there is a simultaneous disclaimer of any exhaustion of the definition of concepts and an indelible whiff of the unequivocal about his work. However, what cannot be levelled against him is any waivering in his vigilant refutation of the given, of the unity in traditional psychology and the 'Americanization' of concerns with their emphasis on know-how and adaptation.

EVERYTHING COMES FROM INTERCOURSE

(NB: Not all intercourse is sexual intercourse but all intercourse is sexual.)

Whenever and wherever there is speech there is always 'the other'. This plays on the idea that I must take into account the response of whoever I am addressing if I am to arrive at the sense of my own speech, but simultaneously goes beyond merely designating the existence of the other with a small 'o', another self, another subject, another equal. For Lacan 'the Other' is a place rather than a subject and is characterized by the trickery of the trickster . . . in psychoanalysis it is the place that is taken up by the one who is supposed to know, the psychoanalyst. For Lacan the unconscious is 'the discourse of the Other'.

Whilst the psychoanalyst takes up this position of the 'one who is supposed to know' (Freud being the one who really did know apparently!), it can be assumed that he or she will lack something and so will have desire and it is precisely because of this that my speech will address itself to, amongst other things, what the nature of this desire is, what is required of me, what is called for. At the same time my very submission to language was in order to overcome the issue of my dependency, to negotiate my pre-maturity, was in order to say what I want. Here we come up against the problematic of establishing a separation between what I want and what is wanted of me, and it is with this in mind that Lacan sees the ego 'as a locus of mistrust' because it is so difficult to know whether I am merely complying with what I take to be the other's desire (a mere 'fitting in with') or whether I dare assume my own desire. This is inevitably complicated in that for Lacan our primordial desire is to reunite with the maternal body (a 'fitting in with'?) although through the paternal metaphor we both 'name' our desire and renounce it . . . this is the primal regression which determines accession to language (Coward and Ellis, 1977, p. 130). I can only signify following my arrival or my construction as a subject positioned in relation to the signifier . . . no signifier, no subject . . . 'It

130

is not possible to speak of a subject, it speaks to him and it is necessary that he apprehends himself in language' (p. 108). In other words I am constituted as a result of that which occasions our essential humanity, our linguistic nature in eccentricity to myself, in subjection to the structure and stricture of language.

So the trouble with the so-called 'pre-Freudian position' epitomized by 'ego-psychology' is its inherent essentialism in that, as distinct from Lacan, it appears to perpetuate the traditional belief that our alienation is a secondary transformation which takes place within an essentially unified self, thus perverting it. For both Freud and Lacan the emphasis is placed on the self as primordially alienated (and we are not speaking here of R. D. Laing's 'divided self'): any refusal of this is the refusal of the Freudian initiative.

II. Self-doubt

Pontalis, probably more widely known for his *The Language of Psycho-Analysis*, in collaboration with Laplanche, cites Merleau-Ponty in the *Frontiers of Psychoanalysis* as having always been 'very reticent about all the conceptual apparatus of psychoanalysis' (Pontalis, 1981, p. 66) whilst emphasizing that phenomenology and psychoanalysis are concerned with the 'same latencies'. This should be a lesson to us all. Perhaps we should recall what Freud himself said about his metapsychology, for whilst the Freudian subject may be defined as a series of places with specific functions (first topography: unconscious, pre-conscious, conscious systems; second topography: id, ego and super-ego) Freud was only too careful to emphasize *the fictitious nature* of the 'psychic apparatus'. Unfortunately many psychoanalytic theorists appear to stumble into all sorts of difficulties in attempting to improve, purify or transform this 'fiction'. The original purpose was 'to make the complications of mental functioning intelligible by dissecting the function and assigning its different constituents to different component parts of the apparatus' (Pontalis, 1981, p. 132).

For example Masud Khan in *The Privacy of the Self* cannot resist proposing the introduction of the idea of the 'self system', which in his view can be 'as prone to sickness as the egoic, the id or super-egoic system' (1974, p. 304), but somehow admits that he is really begging the question by this manoeuvre.

So what are we to make of it all? Masud Khan rather forlornly admits that he has 'failed to define what I mean by self-experience' (p. 303) but consoles himself with the knowledge that 'no one else has succeeded in doing so either' (p. 303). In a later work, *Hidden Selves*, he responds rather pompously to a patient who asks if he has read 'all the books' (on his shelves) by saying that one does not read books but lives with them (1984), and given his editorship of the International Psychoanalytical Library and the suffusion of erudition and scholarship that informs his writing, it would appear safe to take his word for it. Winnicott too acknowledges difficulties in any attempt to clarify the distinction between the ego and the self – tentatively he suggests that 'he who uses the word "self" does not situate himself on the same plane as he who uses the word "ego". The first plane directly concerns life, the facts of living' (Pontalis, 1981, p. 144). Pontalis similarly admits that his hypothesizing within the whole domain also unfolds in an 'unquestionably confused way' (p. 132).

He wishes to move beyond conceptualization and firmly lodge the subject of 'the self' in the realm of subjectivity, 'a living reality'. He sees the self, particularly in the clinical setting, as 'a subjective phenomenon that either emerges or is lacking rather than as a structure of the person, or the person himself' (p. 132). The question that Pontalis, following Winnicott, raises in relation to this issue of 'a subjective phenomenon' is as follows: under what circumstances is the world an alive and meaningful place for us? A possible answer would be, when we have a place in the world, which begins with the recognition of the otherness of others. This place in the world would be the place of intercourse, of exchange. Now this enables us to understand Winnicott's concept of the true and false self as quite other than inherent qualities within any individual, but rather as moments within this exchange that transforms that place. Now a sense of having a place in the world may largely involve what nothing prevents me from saying is commonplace, common sense being merely a sense of what is common and may well be distinct from the true. Experience cannot be a criterion for true knowledge. What is commonplace is the idea of having a body enclosed by our skin with an inside and an outside, and we have a similar model for the mind.

We assume that we begin at conception and end, at least physically, with our death. We assume that we exist within time and space and that a certain continuity is there from one place to another and from one moment to the next.

Ordinarily we do not find ourselves thinking about this very much, we just assume it to be the case. This is what R. D. Laing in his important work *The Divided Self* (1960) termed 'ontological security', but of course from time to time we come across individuals for whom this is deeply problematic. For them it appears that there is no basic sense of being an agent of their own actions, for identity and autonomy are so fundamentally in question in that their own sense of existence is persistently under threat. Indeed, for a marvellous account of the forms of anxiety involved in 'ontological insecurity' one could do no better than to return to Laing's first book. Quite clearly what is at stake is this place, the self, for relatedness to others, the site of intercourse, is profoundly called into question in such instances.

ONE HAS TO DO IT FOR ONESELF
BUT ONE CANNOT DO IT BY ONESELF

Certainly in psychoanalysis or psychoanalytic psychotherapy it is undeniable that in many cases people come in order to undergo a particular experience that lends itself to the metaphor of birth, a coming into the world. Obviously, this is predicated on the recognition that in all sorts of varying ways one has not as yet found oneself in the world. Indeed, the therapy will turn around one finding oneself for oneself, but clearly one cannot do this single handed.

When Masud Khan (1974) speaks of 'self-experience' (equally this informs, for example, the work of Michael Balint (1968) who terms it 'the new beginning', an unfolding, a somersault even, with particular emphasis given to 'adequate holding'), it would appear that he is addressing himself to this coming into the world. In so many instances this can be a profoundly precarious enterprise suffused with anxieties of annihilation and of the expropriation of desire. Inherent in this is the negotiation of the 'castration complex', a recognition of one's inescapable separateness, or as one of my own patients put it, thus emphasizing our difference: 'Separateness . . . that's your language, I would put it "I'm here!" "You're here" . . . ' It is an opening up of a frontier or horizon, a threshold which delivers one from anonymity and indifference towards others. In one of the Philadelphia Association's community households a recent arrival spoke of just this: he wished to retain his 'anonymity . . . otherwise I am a marked man'. Allowing for the inevitable over-determination, one aspect of this is to wish to retreat into a realm of primary narcissism, to be unscathed, to be unmarked by the presence of the other(s).

In the clinical setting this meeting can only occur in moments of regression and its correlate, the provision of a holding environment, for it is essential that this experience of separateness is recognized, that there is someone there to meet it and to put it into language, and lodge it within that particular person's history (Winnicott, 1958, 1965). Interpretation is unlikely in itself to evoke or provoke such 'self-experience' but is essential if this experience is to be incorporated, to be taken in but not as an intellectual understanding. It is radically distinct from knowing that Paris is the capital of France, for example, but is knowledge none the less, for the patient comes to know that he or she is 'there, alive, real' and desiring. Masud Khan distinguishes two distinct forms of relating to patients: (1) listening to and deciphering meaning with reference to transference, what is going on between us and the patient: and (2) environmental holding, 'a psychic holding of the person in the therapeutic situation' which enables a certain experience to occur . . . 'unexpected, unprogrammed' (1974). Clearly the former will inform the latter. The patient will come to feel, presumably through my listening to and deciphering (how else?), that I am there, alive and real, and can then disregard this, take it for granted, in order to arrive at an experience of self. It is crucial at this point to emphasize that we are not talking here of any provision of a 'corrective emotional experience' (see Masud Khan's *Trauma and Reconstruction*, 1978). An interesting aspect of this is how notoriously difficult it is to illustrate such occasions, perhaps not dissimilar to the difficulties of describing the birth of one's children, for one is continually in danger of sliding into sentimentality or banality.

However, in order for this 'self-experience', or anxieties in relation to it, to come into being there must first be a 'constituted ego'. As we saw previously, the ego is 'ultimately derived from bodily

sensations . . . chiefly those springing to the surface of the body
. . . a projection of the organism into the psyche' (Freud, 1923). To
revert to Lacanian formulations there first must be the 'mirror
phase' before accession to the 'symbolic' via the 'castration complex', although the 'symbolic' was always already there . . . 'For
the self to be made conscious and experienced there must be
constituted ego, however rudimentary' (Pontalis, 1981), that is, the
ego as a representation of the organism as shape, a formal integration of the sum of identifications and the disparate set of functions. Paradoxically this must have a primacy or there could be no
problem of fragmentation, disintegration or annihilation.
Although quite distinct from any notions of identity or the
'imaginary', of taking oneself to be this rather than that, self-
experience is intimately related to body ego, and however much
we might wish to draw free from such concerns, the Tantric
hermit on the Himalayan mountainside notwithstanding, we are
all engaged to some extent in narcissistic accumulations and contributions, via affirmation or endorsement by the other, who will
be similarly implicated.

Whilst it is crucial to take up the issue of someone arriving at
the 'I am' experience, this place of the self, within the psychoanalytic relationship, it cannot be left at that. The subjective 'sense of
self', this place in the world of the movement of relationships, has
certain characteristics and I wish to turn to the work of two
Frenchmen, Roland Barthes and Emmanuel Levinas, to try to shed
some light on this terrain.

IN CAMERA

Roland Barthes has claimed to be 'a casual phenomenologist' and I
wish to employ his terms 'the studium' and 'the punctum' which
are to be found in his study of the phenomenon of photography.
The 'studium', not to be confused with studying as in homework
or the form of racehorses, is defined as 'a land of general, enthusi-
astic commitment . . . ' (Barthes, 1982, p. 49). Alan Alvarez in his
introduction to Lawrence Sterne's A Sentimental Journey endorses
the notion of a delinquent aesthetic 'where casualness and unpre-
judiced receptivity become an aesthetic procedure' (Alvarez, 1967)
and this is close to the idea of the 'studium', that of unconcerned or
'average' desire. In this place of self, in one's exchanges with

135

others, there is a body of information: feelings, sensations, thoughts, emotions, fantasies, a myriad array of different ranges of experience, all in a crucial way linked to the experience of self. Much of the time one takes only a diffuse interest in it all: taste, distaste, interest, indifference, pleasure, displeasure, all ultimately of not much consequence. This is the realm of the 'studium'.

The 'punctum' is quite other. It is a call linked to the 'burden of responsibility', one's ability to respond to the otherness of the other, and is always uncalled-for. The self that is called upon is the one embedded in the 'studium' of the one, lost in oneself. It is an occasion of disturbance, of disruption, a mark of punctuation. One cannot seek it out, for whilst in some sense one invests in the 'studium', this 'punctum' will have pierced one . . . 'an explosion makes a little star in the pane of the text' (Barthes, 1982, p. 49). It can only occur after the fact and may well involve reflections of regret and remorse. This is always a solitary experience, although possibly in the presence of others. Often attempts to try to share such moments with someone result in it all appearing trivial, it loses its sting – 'absolute subjectivity is achieved only in a state, an effort of silence' (p. 27).

Any endeavour to create concern over myself (ethical rather than ontological) will also fail. One may experience mild curiosity but will always be easily distracted because such moments must come from elsewhere, from the other, which as we recall Lacan designated as a place. One may respond by attempts to name, to categorize, to synthesize, or to re-present what takes me over – 'what I name cannot possibly prick me' (p. 31) – as one approaches the limit, the unspeakable, which simultaneously strives to be said. Superficially this may appear to have a proximity to the site of a narcissistic blow so informatively teased out by Heinz Kohut, but my claim is that this experience is rooted in a quite 'other' domain.

TO BE INCLUDED ONE MUST INCLUDE EVERYTHING:
THE ONLY GAME IN TOWN

Responsibility is the essential principle around which the occasion of the punctum will turn, and I have used the term 'burden of responsibility', which comes from the philosopher Emmanuel Levinas. This issue of responsibility, which is not reducible to a mere taking the initiative, for it is unavoidable, is in play both at that moment of vulnerability when I am faced by the other but also in retrospect – 'responsibility is set forth as the determinative structure of subjectivity' (Levinas, 1981, p. xi). It is a moment in which I am both thrown back upon myself and yet also I am thrown towards the other (it is 'the locus of signification'); it is prior to any particular dialogue, to any exchange of question and answer, to any 'thematization of the said' (p. 46). It is the structure through which truth may be revealed and this in turn involves 'sensibility' to the continuous 'vibrancies of image', a reference to the more usual term 'sensitivity' in which is incorporated the act of saying, for it is not a matter of first receiving something inwardly and then expressing it. I am called upon to respond and I proceed through nuances of identification, of naming (see for example the immediacy of gender identification and how one is thrown by an instance of ambiguity), of claiming, of pronouncement for clearly there is a distinction between the intersubjective world and the world of objects, of things.

This sensibility is the effect of what Levinas calls 'alterity' (the Otherness of others) in which I find myself appealed to, contested by, put in question by the very proximity of an other out of which the field of responsibility arises. It is a moment that comes from without. Levinas speaks of the 'facts of responsibility'; even merely to think in response to the word ('what Being gives') is a moment, a movement of responsibility, an inescapable fact that is prior to whatever my particular response might be. The locus of this imperative, of this unavoidable subjection, this ordering, this bond is 'the other who faces . . . ' (appeals, contests, and so on) and this is the site of subjectivity. When Lacan speaks of man's desire as 'desire of the other', a notoriously complex idea, included in this is the idea of recognition. Man's desire is to be recognized, not as one might recognize a particular type of engine as in train spotting, but through inclusion, the moment of the embrace, the moment of 'you are in', 'you have a place'. This will involve the responsibility of recognition: a recognition in the face of the presence or the force of the other (we speak of forceful personalities, but of course everyone has his or her own idiosyncratic 'force') that summons me to 'arise to be, to present myself'. The recognition of the other is an occasion of expressing myself and consequently of self-exposure to the other.

This recogniton of the otherness of the other extends to infinity . . . Levinas speaks of 'the elasticity, the stretch of responsibility' (p. 10). It goes far beyond the parameters of that which I initiated or committed myself to (too narrow a definition) for it certainly includes the totality of the situation in which I find myself without in any way involving structures of omnipotence. It is not inappropriate to see the horizon of my responsibility extending beyond my death which, whilst bringing to an end all my possibilities, and being the limit of my presence (force), is not the limit of my responsibility, which stretches beyond it. Implicit in this is a recognition that 'things' have a force of their own. There is no end to responsibility, for the more that I take up, the more that it increases, an unending suffusion of horizons . . . I am obliged to admit that there is still more required than what has been accomplished, there is no resting-up point. This is why there is inherent, in the process of mourning, the structure of guilt, the idea that one could have done more, for indeed one could. Perhaps to clarify Levinas in his use of the idea of infinity he neither means 'the absolution of the Idea of Truth' nor is it 'the spatial sense of the horizontal openness' but is the 'ultimate inapprehendability of the other's otherness' (p. 37). I can set forth but I shall never arrive.

What is this experience of 'alterity'? Certainly it is beyond a mere objectification or identification, and it also incorporates the recognition that the other is not my own creation, not 'a subjective object' as in the omnipotent phase (see Winnicott's distinction between the use of an object, psychoanalytic term for an other, and object relating) (Winnicott, 1971). 'Alterity' cannot be formulated as an entity, or even as a moment of being, which is equally true of the self, despite its egoic element, its endeavour to be a self-identifying source of identity. The sensibility spoken of is not merely an act of receptivity. This contains the notion of my regaining possession of myself by an act of apprehending that which affects me . . . precisely because 'alterity' is beyond issues of identification we are at the site of the unidentifiable. It is said that not to diagnose in psychiatry is to be irresponsible, but diagnosis is no response at all for we are opened up by the other, we are shaken, we are vulnerable to the immediacy of what comes next, both remote and yet simultaneously only too immediate. Of

138

course we may try to deal with the inherently unsettling impact of the other by attempting to assimilate it (see H. Oakley, 1981) or by adopting a position of terminal passivity: exposed to the other's presence I take up an implicit position of 'do what you like to me'. So this sensibility towards others is not merely an act of receptivity, that is, an apprehending of a sense, a receiving of messages, but is an occasion of vulnerability, the occasion of the 'punctum'. The true impact of 'alterity' is linked with my being shaken out of the 'studium' of my involvement with myself, of my complacency, in that I am forced up against my answerability. This simultaneously plays across my ability to answer (to respond) but also that I ultimately have to answer for my response. This exposedness to the otherness of the other is synonymous with the arrival at the place of self, the appearance, the 'birth', that which was spoken of earlier in terms of Masud Khan's 'I am status' . . . it is exposure to the exposedness of another rather than a mere putting forth, a mere 'here I am'.

However, we cannot completely dismiss the significance of identity within the field of subjectivity. We all need a viewpoint, we all are prone to clutch at, or have a stake in, that which would be stable, precise; after all, Lacan did term it 'the name of the Father'. Certainly there is singularity in the sense that I am singled out by being the one who is addressed, appealed to, or contested, neither because of any particular distinguishing marks (the given), nor because of the creation of a particular personal style. In French the self (le soi) is an accusative rather than a nominative term, and it is this note of accusation that Levinas persistently underscores as being the fundament of a sense of self. Within the unfolding of the accusation we may be drawn inexorably towards imposing a thread of coherence, a linking of an otherwise disparate succession of roles in the form of self-contemplation. Even this word contemplation is radically misleading as it inclines towards the docility of the 'studium'; perhaps interrogation would be more appropriate. We will inevitably be spurred on by the demand to be at one with ourselves. But as with all demand, gratification only occasions an opening out of an infinite seriality of demands. In order to arrive at the cessation of the distress we cannot avoid traces of trying to catch (up with) ourselves, a maddeningly elusive (ludicrous even) project – can we ever reveal ourselves to ourselves and thus arrive at self-certainty, self-possession? Is this not woven into the very heart of the psychoanalytic endeavour through a lattice-work of deviation: a greater self-possession (sense of a place) through a displacement of self-certainty with its incorrigible link with rigidity, meanwhile superimposing an endorsement of resilience via an openness to the effects of our unconscious? However, we can be sure that we are never identical with our identity; there can be no substantial coinciding of self with self; we cannot take ourselves as (id) entities however much we are driven to strive after just a representation. The self can never be equated with a fixed identity precisely because it is always subject to exchange. Lévi-Strauss put it very well in *Myth and Meaning* (1978) when he wrote the following: 'I never had, and still do not have, the perception of feeling my personal identity. I appear to myself as *the place* where something is going on, but there is no I nor me . . . each of us is a kind of crossroads where things happen.'

III. THE ROLE OF THE SELF IN THE ALIENATION OF
PSYCHOANALYTICAL DESIRE

I wish to finish by mentioning a few implications that these conceptualizations have for the work of psychoanalysis. The essence, the *sine qua non*, of psychoanalytic treatment is transference. Nothing can prevent one from saying that without transference there can be no psychoanalysis. It can also be said that someone comes into the psychoanalytic setting not so much in order to gain a particular knowledge, but rather that what is counted upon is an encounter. Of course this is not to say that transference is not based on a fundamental misconception in which the issue of knowledge plays a pivotal part. The analysand assumes that there is a subject: unconscious or repressed knowledge which is so frequently and erroneously assumed to lie behind what is said. What is to be recognized is not something which already exists somewhere, for it is in the very naming of desire that we create it . . . it unfolds, is given conscious form, is something new. At the same time there is an assumption, not only I might add by the analysand, that by turning to an expert, a subject

140

supposed to know, this unconscious knowledge will be revealed and so the analysand will come to see what it is that they want.

Of course here we come up against, at the very best, a certain ambivalence, for what is at stake is not so much knowledge as an encounter with being, which is what the analysand wants to be cured of! However it is this supposition of knowledge that gives rise to the love for the analyst – 'he whom I suppose knowing,' Lacan said, 'I love' – and of course this is a function of the position and not of the analyst's personality. The encounter that is counted upon is linked to a crucial refusal, that is, the refusal by the analyst to gratify demands of the analysand. Inevitably the analysis begins with suffering in some form or other; we can be sure that no one enters into the situation without that. This suffering will be addressed to the Other, which is where the analyst stands, standing in for the Other in the place of the Other. Eventually the analyst will respond and it is through this that the potentiality in the situation can emerge. This potentiality is for coming up against the realization that this Other does not exist. What is meant by this is that what can be revealed is that there is no final authority or knowledge (despite this being far from easy to escape), and neither is the Other complete for s/he is found lacking, in other words desires too. The Other is revealed as no object but is a symbolic locus where the subject is represented . . . absent as such and empty of any object. As this Other which is supposed to have the answer is revealed as lacking, this opens up the possibility for the analysand that they might fill the gap, that is, become the answer.

It is precisely here that the possibility of a collapse into a dual imaginary relationship occurs, underpinned by the fiction of the total person or unified self. Repeatedly we meet a persistent concern regarding identity and the recurrence of the demand for confirmation or endorsement of this. Characteristic of all neurosis is denial. Denial is absence in the sense that an absence of desire avoids the possibility of frustration and so there is an inherent impulse towards a resting-up point, a place of fixity. On occasions the strategy of the analysand can unfold like this:

I am or could become (immediate link with identity) your happiness.

141

> I want you to be happy . . . I want to be your happiness because I want you to want me (for you and my happiness are inextricably linked).
>
> I will give to you (my beloved) what will make you happy: my love.
>
> I desire that you desire me as I see you as having this love which, if you gave it to me would render me complete, without lack.

A corollary to all this is that 'without me you will be unhappy'. Undoubtedly this is an aspect of the persistent complaint of betrayal that so often accompanies an occasion of separation such as weekends or holidays. Within this strategy is the fundamental objective of avoiding castration, of sustaining an avoidance of lack despite the obvious fact that there would have to be something lacking in the other for them to be desiring.

Here one is at the threshold of a perfectly balanced exchange. One can be lured into a form of deal, and a great deal will hinge on the outcome of this. If one is engaged in fulfilling the other's desire then paradoxically one deprives the other, who would then merely be having 'a good' which is not psychoanalysis at all. However, to refuse to have anything to do with it is merely to cut off the other's desire. Of course, there is an appropriate demand for interpretation, and however silent one might be, eventually one is called upon to say something. Simply the intervention should proceed from the speech of the analysand, allowing a place for him/her to articulate what has hitherto gone unsaid.

If one allows oneself to be seduced into becoming merely the one who loves the analysand, then certain consequences will follow. There will have been an abdication from the position of the Other and one will be consigned to being merely another amongst others. Heidegger emphasized that a preoccupation with particular beings will potentially result in losing sight of the wider question of Being. Potentially one will be at the site of immense confusion in that the distinction between the function of the position that one takes up as analyst and oneself will have become blurred. It is not I who occasions the desire of the analysand . . . It does not derive from the nuances of my personality, and it can be shown that this is not what is at stake for the phenomenon of the love for the analyst has become a cliché, a truth worn out through repetition.

But of course one is involved most emphatically in the realities of a relationship of love. Freud was quite explicit about this: the reality of the passion of both love and hatred is a reality beyond contest. It is, after all, what goes on. Nor am I wanting to say that one is detached – 'we pay with our very being' (Lacan) – for if the activity goes to the very heart of the other's being, how could one remain outside of this? But there is always the analyst's supposed neutrality. Freud's famous dictum was that analysis or analytic therapy takes place through abstinence. The position that the analyst inhabits is no position in that it is a position of no: the refusal to be drawn completely into the field of intersubjectivity, the refusal of any deal involving a quid pro quo which would entail entering the circuit of the same, and the refusal to gratify demands which ultimately converge on the demand for love.

The transference position is installed on the basis of a lack. It leaves something to be desired. The analyst shifts from the possible position of lover, thus dismantling the possibility of the analyst and analysand becoming an incestuous coupling with its inherent trajectory of totalization, completion or imaginary fulfilment of essence, which cannot give us a satisfactory answer to our being or our desire. The claim is that what moves the analyst is desire for desiring, in that there is no specific objective, no specific aspiration as to outcome other than the desire for truth. Certainly there is no aim to help any other, although the enterprise is taken to be helpful; 'better is so often the enemy of the good' was a crucial axiom of Freud's. Nor is there any desire for some imaginary identification by the analysand with the analyst via a spurious substitution of the analyst's more reality-based ego for the unfortunate analysand's less healthy one.

A faint stain on the fiction of the analyst's 'pure' desire is that one may be ensnared in the rush to understand, to glimpse the truth which brings about an inversion of dependency: ironically the analyst becomes totally dependent on the analysand's words. Also whilst both are under the subjection of the signifier, there is a distinction to be drawn between the desire to be the analyst, with the egoic implications of identity, repetition and stagnation, and the desire which is the desire of enjoyment. To some extent neurosis is linked to the refusal of this desire. Lacan, in writing about female sexuality, evokes curious resonances regarding the

143

paradox of the transference, this relationship which is not a relationship (it is not a relationship because it is a meta-relationship, a relationship about relationships), resonances regarding psychoanalysis itself: 'There is an enjoyment that belongs to her and about which she doesn't know anything apart from her experiencing it. This she does know . . . she obviously knows about it when it happens . . . it does not happen to all' (Lacan, 1975).

There is an implication in Freud's proposition concerning the impenetrability of the analyst that suggests a position beyond resistance, beyond repression, the transparency of the completely analysed subject (an ideal ego). This is, of course, non-existent. The analyst is only the representation of, or the stand-in for, the function, a function that by definition cannot be embodied. The alternative is neither that this position be renounced nor that there would be a symmetrical relationship between analyst and analysand. The position of the analyst is installed via the unconscious as an unknowable and non-existent limit. This is enhanced by the place of analysis being characterized by the subjectivity of the analyst being put under the sign of negation. Therefore we can never have a simple reciprocity between the two, for what is placed under this sign is one's history, attitudes, anxieties and retaliations, all of which are not supposed to intervene. Nevertheless, are not these the very aspects which will play some implicit if not explicit part in the analysis through my conscious and unconscious reactions to what is said?

A fundamental characteristic of the analyst's position is that one asks the other for nothing, at the same time recognizing that this position is one that will bring about the other's desire. Despite the lure of narcissistic gratification there is to be a refusal to be the object of that desire. It can be said that principally what is sought is never an object anyway, for this would annihilate desire; rather what is sought is the capacity to find. Desire, whilst having objectives, is not a relation to an object for, on the contrary, it is formed via the lack of something, which has irretrievably gone. So there would be genuine grounds for disappointment if what is ultimately arrived at is an imaginary complementarity, rather than a genuine coming into the world of 'alterity'.

The dissolution of the transference that Freud set so much store by, which paradoxically would involve the dissolution of the unconscious, is precisely the coming up against the illusion of the perfect circularity of desire: the absence of any unity of presence which one must make no attempt to counterfeit. What is encountered is the emergence of the presence of the analyst: this imperfect desire. The demand is for an Other which is desired but which does not exist, and it is at the locus of the Other that the presence of the analyst as real is glimpsed. The imaginary is seen as imaginary and so the subject comes up against the lack in the Other and any idea of unified relationship between analyst and analysand is revealed as fallacy.

Clearly there is conflict in the psychoanalytic world as to whether or not it is a fundamental distortion of Freud if emphasis is placed on the ego and on adaptation to the conditions of civilization. Some would see analysis as involved in moderating narcissism, by strengthening an imaginary identification, thus bolstering the ego in the face of oppression from id drives and a persecutory super-ego. Whilst narcissism may not be idealized in this it is certainly ideological in that the other can only be more of the same in that the circuit of exchange is based on the first love object: oneself, in this instance the analyst who is taken to be the locus of truth and reality. And if not the analyst, then psychoanalysis itself is regarded as this locus rather than placing 'truth' itself in question.

Perhaps we can acknowledge that speaking the truth is beyond us, is an absolute impossibility. 'Truth shies away from language' in that it can never be contained, not just because of over-determination but also because it is always conveyed by *doxa* or opinion. Freud was clear that it is impossible not to engage in some form of illusion for we cannot get to a direct apprehension of the real; there is no ultimate or absolute liberation from imagos and no unmediated reading of any text. So if analysis is understood as a discourse leading to knowledge, a self-knowledge with this persistent demand to be unified, to be given a sealed identity, we are likely to find that interpretations informed by unequivocal meaning paradoxically may be put in the place of truth. If a problem for any self is the compulsive demand to be one, if not the one, unified with a fictitious stability or indivisibility, are we not called upon to provide a peculiar sensitivity, a place of shimmering ambiguity and ironic equivocation?

145

7

Touching and being touched

The negotiated boundaries and the 'extended' consulting room

HAYA OAKLEY

The Queen came to the King

The Queen to the King said:
'How odd;
I dreamed about you last night,
I waited for you
But you were out of sight.
Outside it was dark and cold,
Why did you come not?'
'I know nothing of this!'
said the King,
'Last night I dreamed of golden rings.'

The Queen to the King said:
'How odd
Was the dream we were in
Last night;
We sledged down the hill
The wind in our faces.
Was it not a thrill?'
'I know nothing of this!'
Said the King;
'Last night I dreamed about rivers,
I think.'

The Queen to the King said:
'How could it be,
That you are in my sleep
And yet you stay outside,
When in my dream you're being dreamed
Is there not a flutter in your heart?'

Midnight.
The Queen knocks on the King's door.
'Hello, I have come into your dream.'

'Never!' said the King, 'will another
Touch my sleep!'

'You do not understand a thing!'
Said the Queen.

(Zarchi, 1976, p. 24)

THIS IS THE STORY of Peter, who in his twenties embarked on a search for his origins and meaning. (Names and some personal details have been changed. It is by no means the whole story, which unfolded over many years, but contains selected moments chosen to illustrate the subject of this chapter.) In Peter's search he often confused 'fact' with 'fiction', a disturbing tendency that got him diagnosed as 'psychotic'. He did not take kindly to this. He left his home town and came to London where he found refuge in a Philadelphia Association house and came to see me for therapy.

When Peter and I first met, he was tangled up in the web of his dream; he brought this web to me, spread it around me and included me in it. Unlike the king in the poem (who must have been trained by an 'orthodox' school) I did not say, 'I know nothing of this.' Acknowledging Peter's dream reality I accepted the invitation and I learned to tread softly within it. I had to keep wide awake yet flow with 'the stuff dreams are made of'. I knew Peter was ready to wake up when he started to tell me his dreams.

In this paper I will describe five episodes concerning touching and being touched. I shall endeavour to explore their significance in the light of Peter's sexual and emotional way of being in the context of our relationship.

Many years ago, as a student in an out-patient clinic I apparently touched the arm of a patient while opening the door of the clinic to let her out. The secretary who 'witnessed' this told my supervisor, who that very same day gave me a serious talking to about 'the birds and the bees' of our profession. I learned a great deal that afternoon; most of all I learned what to leave out of my reports to that supervisor. For Freud, 'Touching and physical contact are the immediate aim of the aggressive as well as the loving object cathexis . . . To touch a woman has become a euphemism for using her as a sexual object. Not to touch one's genitals is the phrase employed for forbidding auto-erotic satisfaction' (Freud, 1926b).

As far as psychoanalysis is concerned its drama takes place in an 'intra-psychic' arena where 'id' and 'super-ego' fight to push each other in and out of the wretched patient's unconscious to the clanking sound of armed 'ego defences'; mere shadows of this drama are projected on to the analyst, who, if skilful enough, deflects them back to the patients who would offer 'vigorous and tenacious resistance throughout the entire course of the treatment' (Freud, 1943, p. 253).

Occasionally and with some persistence, patients will insist that their analyst is a flesh-and-blood participant in the drama; that they themselves are in the room 'in person'; they might even, as Freud found out, proceed to behave as if that was the case. In his autobiographical study (1925b) Freud recalls one such 'embarrassing' experience with a patient he had hypnotized: 'As she woke up (she) threw her arms round my neck. The unexpected entrance of a servant relieved us from a painful discussion . . . ' He quickly realized that this was not an isolated case, that patients would form 'similar affectionate attachments' to their doctors, which led him eventually to formulate his theory of the 'transference'. In it, there is no room for the 'between'; the patient simply 'transfers' feelings from the past on to the analyst; repetition is the key word and nothing new or original ever takes place. A convincing and convenient theory, provided of course one accepts the basic philosophical premise underlying it, that is, that 'there are such things as "feelings" or "affects" existing as distinct psychic formulations' and thus capable of being shifted from one person to another.

148

However, if such shiftable feelings or affects are merely mental constructions and do not actually exist . . . such psychic entities, if non-existent, can hardly be transported in the sense of Freud's transference' (Boss, 1963). Therefore, Freud's recipe for 'overcoming' the 'transference' by merely 'Pointing out to the patient that his feelings do not arise from the present situation, and do not apply to the *person* of the doctor' (Boss, 1963) but are *mere* repetition of something he (the patient) refuses to remember, cannot be wholly satisfactory. For what is one to do with the other's otherness, and are there not two persons in the room? In Freud's own words, what about '. . . the "genuine" nature of the love which makes its appearance in the course of analytic treatment' (1915, p. 388)?

Slightly more embarrassing than the patient's feelings for the analyst was the discovery that analysts themselves were capable of what they took to be 'real feelings' for their patients. Counter-transference was the term given to these by Freud. Feelings seemed to arise in the analyst as a result of the 'Patient's influence on his unconscious feelings' (1910b, pp. 144, 145). Despite great difficulties of his own Freud firmly believed it crucial to the process of psychoanalysis that one should endeavour to control these feelings. 'I am not the psycho-analytic superman . . . nor have I overcome the counter-transference,' he grieves in the famous 1910 letter to Ferenczi (Jones, 1955, p. 83); adding that maybe with time and age one might achieve that enviable state of 'blank screen' off which patients' 'projections' can bounce unhindered.

A leap forward from this rather narrow notion was taken by D. W. Winnicott. In his paper 'Hate in the counter-transference' (1947, p. 195) he classifies the phenomena into three catagories: 1. *Abnormal:* when his personal pathology colours the analyst's vision to the extent that he cannot see his patient as he appears before him and proceeds to relate to him through identification. More therapy for the therapist is Winnicott's advice. 2. *Normal:* when the analyst's way of being with his patient is influenced by his life experience and personal development, but this improves the quality of his work and helps to provide a 'positive setting'. 3. *The truly objective counter-transference:* '. . . the analyst's love and hate in reaction to the actual personality and behaviour of the patient . . . '

At last: patient and analyst have assumed earthly qualities. They are both complex personalities who can be and act in a lovable or hateful manner towards each other, in the unusual and unique situation; a therapeutic relationship. And what a strange situation it is. This is not a friendship nor a family relation; it is not a love affair yet, but for carnal knowledge, has most of the ingredients of one, most of all the passion in love and in hate. Could this be a unique form of love in its own right? 'Psychotherapeutic Eros' is the term proposed by A. Seguin (1962): where one gives all yet loses nothing; 'genuine psychotherapeutic Eros', in other words, must be 'an otherwise never practised selflessness, self-restraint and reverence before the partner's existence and uniqueness . . . ' (Boss, 1963).

F. Roustang went even further to illustrate how it is the very attitude of the 'blank screen' that would bring about the type of 'resistance' psychoanalysis claims to attempt to fight: ' . . . if the patient speaks to "no one", what support could there be for his plural transferences? He must have an interlocutor as a support for all his interlocutors past and present' (Roustang, 1983, p. 115).

THE 'EXTENDED' CONSULTING ROOM

'Il eût mieux valu revenir à la même heure,' dit le renard. 'Si tu viens, par exemple, à quatre heures de l'aprés-midi, dès trois heures je commencerai d'être heureux. Plus l'heure avancera, plus je me sentirai heureux. A quatre heures, déjá, je m'agiterai et m'inquiéterai; je découvrirai le prix du bonheur! Mais si tu viens n'importe quand, je ne saurai jamais à quelle heure m'ha-biller le coeur . . . il faut des rites.' (Saint-Exupéry, 1949, pp. 69–70)

My translation: 'It is better to arrive at the same (regular) hour,' said the fox. 'If you came, for example, at 4 o'clock in the afternoon, from 3 o'clock on I would start to be happy. The later it got, the happier I would become. By 4 I would be nervous and excited; I would discover the price of happiness; but if you come at any old time I shall never know when to *dress my heart*; rituals are necessary.'

Peter and I observed the usual rituals of Psychotherapy, we met at a regular hour twice weekly for fifty-minute sessions in my consulting room. That consulting-room relationship had 'extended' in two ways:

(1) Like the fox, Peter needed time and space to 'dress his heart'; he did that by using my living room to wait in before and 'recover' after his sessions (for as long as an hour, in the early days). My kitchen became very important, when he changed from bringing food that he placed on the floor between us, to preparing a baby's bottle before his session, and finally to making a cup of coffee. By this time, he was able to arrive on time and leave immediately after his session. I must point out that I did not suggest, encourage or prohibit any of this. (See further comments on suggestion, influence and so on, in the final section, page 163 below.) My 'job' was to interpret once we were inside the consulting room.

(2) During some of the time that Peter was in therapy, he lived in a PA house to which a colleague and I were house therapists. This meant that he would see me at house meetings, gatherings and occasional parties. For the therapy to work it was crucial not to step outside the boundaries of the 'professional' relationship but rather to 'extend' the consulting room to include my contact with Peter at the community house. Not being contained by the four walls and the analytic hour I had to 'bring them with me', as an embodiment of boundaries; a challenge that in this case proved exciting and rewarding.

EPISODE 1: ROOM, WOMB, TOMB

. . . For the neurotic the couch and warmth and comfort can be *symbolical* of the analyst's love; for the Psychotic it would be more true to say that these things *ARE* the analyst's physical expression of love, the couch *IS* the analyst's lap, a womb, and the warmth *IS* the live warmth of the analyst's body and so on. (Winnicott, 1947, p. 199)

During the first months in therapy Peter would only sit on the carpet in the corner between the couch and the wall, facing me but looking down; unable to speak he would alternate between silent sessions and the reciting by heart of pages from philosophy books.

Occasionally he would place food on the carpet between us. Much later on, when he was able to verbalize, he described how he could actually feel the floor pulsating, the walls moving towards him, and just before the end of each session a paralysing fear that he would be 'shot out of the shut door, head first'; this was accompanied by breathing difficulties and his hands protecting his penis from 'being cut off'. It was during this period that I had to go away for two weeks.

On what was our last session before the break, Peter was completely silent; at the end, looking pale and anxious, he took his clothes off, went into the bathroom and curled up in a foetal position on the floor. I had to keep an appointment elsewhere, I felt it was safe to leave Peter to recover and leave on his own but thought he needed some reassurance first; I knelt down, reached for his hand, held it and explained that I had to go but that he could stay. Peter did not respond, his hand felt strange; and I was struck by its 'humanless' feel. I thought at the time that it was like holding a fish or an internal organ; he did not seem to be quite present in this 'bodied' world. When I came back two hours later he had gone; he had got back to his house safely. Years later, in recalling that episode he said that my going away was experienced by him as 'the end of the world'. He felt me touch his hand; that perplexed him, but he felt reassured by the 'sound' of my voice. He did not recall, nor did he claim to understand, much of what I said to him in the first months; it was the physical vibrations of my voice that he felt 'soothed' and 'nourished' by; as my voice sounded secure he felt safe. Touching him that day was irrelevant; it was a social gesture that probably dealt with my anxiety, but also demonstrated to me that I had not fully comprehended Peter's way of being in the world at the time.

I would like to suggest that Peter was experiencing what F. Mott (1949) calls a 'pre-natal', 'umbilical' form of consciousness. As far as Peter was concerned, he was the foetus in my womb, that womb was my voice, my body, my room, house, and so on. The walls of that womb contracted towards him when he was about to be 'ejected . . . head first' at the end of a session; his penis, the cord, the tool of potential readmission to the mother's womb would be cut off; the food he placed on the floor was meant to seep into me, the placenta, and in turn keep him nourished. Any idea of a temporary separation was akin to suggesting to a foetus that it might be physically removed while mother was on holiday and placed back in her womb on her return.

According to Mott, 'The flow of blood out from the foetal body into the placenta and back is the first instance of our relations with our environment. This first experience of externality appears to dominate our post-natal lives; the adult social relations seem often impossible save through the mechanism of an external placenta' (p. 12). He also talks about the powerful 'Umbilical sexual feeling'. As a response to interpretations made by me on those lines, Peter produced a poem he had written at school about a chick caught in the egg unable to release itself and crying for help. He spoke of a sense of floating, his navel the centre of his balance; described body sensations of transforming from 'Fish' to 'Duck' and eventually to 'Monkey'; and spoke of not knowing 'what people do with their limbs', how you 'learn how to breathe', and so on.

Bearing all this in mind, it seemed pointless to hold his hand as a gesture of contact and comfort: he was being 'contained' by my voice, I was all around him; he was 'inside' me, an 'inside' which included the 'outside' of my body; by touching his hand I had introduced a confusion of categories. I am not proposing that Peter was re-enacting the actual 'membrane imprinted' memories of his pre-natal life that were to be 'exorcized' or turned into memories as Mott and a recent wave of humanistic 'rebirth' lobbyists would claim. I am in no position to say whether his experience correlates to his 'actual' past; however, there is no doubt in my mind that the myth he was caught up in at that point belonged to a time before breasts and penises.

'Tell me the *real* truth about babies' said one of my daughters to me. 'Not about penises and vaginas, but the real truth . . . ' Peter was looking for the 'real truth' through the myth of the womb and the cord; he had confused the metaphor of coming into the world with what he had made of the 'facts'. A note on language: in English midwives 'deliver babies'; in Hebrew they 'receive birth'. Touching was an attempt to 'deliver', I should have waited to 'receive'.

Episode 2: Water

Water is the origin and womb of all things . . . the mechanism of this cognition, which is doubtless right biologically, is distinguished from the cosmic and mythical projection of the heavenly waters and the rivers of the underworld . . . the discovery of the origin of all life in water, just because man himself had once come out of amniotic fluid. (Rank, 1973, p. 168)

For a period of three weeks, the plumbing at the community house where Peter lived was out of order. As a result there was frequently no running water and no hot water at all; Peter had complained about it and asked if he could have a bath at my house after one of his sessions. I agreed, and so, after his next session, he disappeared in the bathroom. As my next patient left I realized that Peter was still in the bath. I knocked on the door, he said he was fine, was surprised that an hour had gone by and after I specially requested it, agreed to leave. I was working again when I heard the front door and realized he was gone.

A week later Peter asked if he could have a bath again. The plumbing had been repaired by then and I said no. Peter seemed distressed and wondered why I refused this time. I explained that I had said yes to him before as I would have done to any other member of the community household at the time, because of the actual lack of facilities; not because he had a 'special' relationship to me or because having a bath in my house was 'good' or 'therapeutic' for him. Now that there was hot water in his house there was no practical reason why he should use mine. Peter was disappointed and began to feel guilty. I said that although he could not have a bath in my house, it was perfectly acceptable to me that he should want to. He was then able to talk in some detail about his experience in the bath and the meaning baths had for him.

The bath was a dangerous place where he was tempted to put his head under water, and occasionally nearly lost consciousness; it was also a place of joy and fulfilment, for losing himself in an enveloping, live, warmth; feeling timeless and full of potential. In my bath he felt that he was floating inside me; he did not wish to ever come out and was filled with anxiety when I said he had to.

The fear of a bath and the joy of it are not uncommon phenomena; Freud in his case history of Little Hans makes a connection

154

between Hans's fear of the big bath and his 'Phantasy of procreation distorted by anxiety. The big bath of water in which Hans imagined himself was his mother's womb . . . ' (Freud, 1909, p. 128). Hans is also frightened of being dropped in the bath, which is later connected with his phantasy of birth; as Freud points out, being dropped into, or getting into, water can be related to birth phantasies; he illustrates this idea in *The Interpretation of Dreams*, saying that often a person will reverse the coming out of water, that is, by dreaming of jumping into water. 'In dreams as in mythology, the delivery of the child from the uterine waters is commonly presented by distortion as the entry of the child into water; among many others, the births of Adonis, Osiris, Moses and Bacchus are well-known illustrations of this' (1900, pp. 400, 401).

It is possible that Peter's wish to get into my bath is also a desire to be 'born out of' the therapy; when he was lying in 'amniotic' fluid, enjoying an 'oceanic feeling', he was startled by my voice at the door. As he first heard it 'through water', that took him back to our early days when the room was womb, and for a moment he was panic-stricken since coming out of the bath meant birth, trauma, expulsion. However, he responded to the boundaries, and made a transition from the imaginary to the symbolic. He could then leave without resorting to a massive regressive defence and later was able to talk about my bath 'as if' it was my womb. He seemed to be moving on the cusp between our shared reality and his own phantasy world, realizing that they both have different sets of rules which do not invalidate either.

Episode 3: A place to be

. . . Take me under your wing
and be my mother and sister.
Let my head rest in your lap
Protecting my forsaken prayers.
(H. N. Bialik, 1947)

A time came when Peter, who previously had been unable to participate in the ordinary community-household activities, started to spend less time in his room and ventured more into communal space, partaking in communal meals. He still wondered most of the time 'what people had to say to each other' and how they could be concerned with 'trivialities' when he, the 'centre of the world', was 'struggling for survival with each breath'; for a while, he always dressed in a white vest, white 'long johns' and white socks, carrying a baby's bottle; the most powerful shift in therapy at that time occurred when I read out to him Maurice Sendak's children's story, *In the Night Kitchen*, and in particular Micky's chanting:

> I'm in the milk
> and the milk's in me
> God bless milk
> and God bless me!
> (Sendak, 1971, p. 31)

During this time I visited the house in my capacity as house therapist at least once or twice a week; Peter, who at first could not tolerate being with me and others simultaneously, used to avoid it by staying in his room. Gradually he started to appear when I was there for meetings or meals; he used to 'trail' around me silently, sometimes quite openly and sometimes in a sneaky way, appearing from dark corners or sliding along walls so as not to be noticed but somehow ending up next to me, right behind me or opposite me, looking at me with begging eyes. Very quickly I found that I did not like it at all; it was, although silent, a heavy demand for my total attention that I was neither willing nor able to give him in the context of my visits. I began to dislike him, I found his presence sticky and draining, I realized that this could deteriorate into a hateful retaliatory situation if I did not come clean. I felt that Peter had enough trust to be able to cope with my hate and also that I hated what he was doing and not him, in other words what Winnicott would call 'objective hate' (1947, p. 198), that is, what is directly to do with the situation in reality between patient and therapist and not springing out of the therapist's own personal problems.

I told Peter in a session how I felt: I said that it was all right for him to want my total and undivided attention; that I could understand how, from where he stood, it appeared incomprehensible that I could pay attention to others in his presence. However, it was not on . . . that is, he could feel it, we could talk about it, but when I came to the house I was there for the others. As he was one of them, I was there for him as well but not in the same capacity as in the sessions. Peter was upset: he said he understood and accepted what I *said*, but could only cope by staying in his room when I came.

That summer there was a big party at the house, many people came from other communities, the house was full of music and dancing. Peter was in his room. As the evening progressed he came downstairs and asked me if I would go up to his room. He had just moved to a new room, a big achievement for him, and had decorated it himself. He said he would very much like me to see it. Again, following the principle that had I been asked by any other resident I would have gone, I accepted his invitation. He let me into his room and invited me to sit down. I said I would, but only for five minutes. He wondered why and I said that I had come for the party; I was happy to see his room but I did not want to spend the evening there with him. I sat down, the room was very peaceful and pleasant. Peter knelt down, put his head on my lap and his arms around my waist; I felt calm and quite still, I had no desire to push him away. Time stood still for a few seconds. I was aware of the music downstairs. Peter's head started turning and a flutter of anxiety went quickly through me as I thought he might try to kiss me, but as soon as I saw his face I realized how wrong I was; it was the face of a toddler who had just been comforted by mum. He had an expression of innocence, completion and inner peace; I said the time had come for me to rejoin the party, and he slowly let go of me.

After that evening, Peter started taking part in household meetings; he stopped following me around, did not attempt to touch me and gradually the begging, longing, ever-starved look disappeared from his eyes.

A very important point that is demonstrated by this episode is the importance of the therapeutic milieu. For most people in Peter's state of mind this is often a psychiatric ward, where individual therapy may take place in the context of other ward activities. I remember feeling clearly grateful that night that I was not seeing Peter in such a milieu. H. Searles (1974), in his book *Countertransference and Related Subjects* mentions some of the problems facing the therapist who has to see his patient on the ward:

'. . . being shut out by a too confused and too noisy ward atmosphere . . . the therapist's feeling of anxious isolation heightened in
relation to those designed therapeutic milieu situations where
there is an emphasis on "total push".' No one at the house was
pushing for Peter to 'get better' or to eat, sleep or dress at a
particular time or in a particular fashion; therefore, as his therapist, I did not feel pushed to an omnipotent position vis-à-vis his
behaviour in the house. Unlike some of the problems illustrated by
Searles; I did not have to 'Report to the administrator, the nurses,
and the aides' nor was I 'deeply ashamed' to let even myself know
how much I cherished this very relatedness with 'the patient', but
even more than all of this, it was the absence of what I would call
an unreasonable sexual demand, in the milieu, that made the work
possible.

I remember a patient at the last mental hospital that I worked in,
who trusted me enough to test his hallucinations against my
'version of reality'; he often had to pop into my office to ask, 'Can
you see the chair when I see it disappear?' or the like . His frequent
visits to my office won him the title of my 'boy-friend' – in jest of
course, but coming from the nursing staff it soon scared him, it had
all the intensity of the staff's projected sexual fantasies, ones he
could not possibly fulfil in relation to me. He went back to 'seeing'
things which he could no longer tell me of for my 'own protection'.
It was very significant that Peter chose to touch me as he did at the
community household, in his room rather than mine, a private yet
'public' place, a playground that was personal and neutral where
we were alone, yet surrounded by others whose presence was
benign, where there were no tight rules about going into people's
rooms or about touching them. I did not have to look over my
shoulder in case a member of the nursing staff 'caught' me in the
patients' dormitory. Therefore what happened remained unclut-
tered, a gesture of trust and closeness, an expression of genuine
tenderness and love, made possible by the milieu and by the ability
to accept hate as an integral part of it.

EPISODE 4: HOLDING

. . . the term 'holding' is used here to denote not only the actual
physical holding of the infant, but also the total environmental

provision prior to the concept of living with . . . (Winnicott, 1965, p. 43)

The basis of the capacity to be alone is a paradox; it is the experience of being alone while someone else is present. (Winnicott, 1965, p. 30)

Peter was lying on the couch, flat on his back looking rigid and uncomfortable. He had been talking about the pain in his back and neck; a pain he had talked about many times before. In fact, it was the very pain that led him to spend many hours in bed in his late adolescence and, after doctors could find nothing physically wrong, occasioned his first encounter with psychiatry. He was turning his head to face me occasionally and that seemed to increase his discomfort, he spoke about not being able to stand up supported by his spine or to hold his head up. After a short silence I said 'It can take up to sixteen weeks for a baby to be able to hold his own head; the neck muscles can't support the head at first, that's why when holding a new-born baby, one must support the head . . . '

As I spoke, I gestured with my hands in the air, as if holding an imaginary baby, one hand under the body, the other at the back of the head; I was not especially conscious of doing so as I quite often 'talk' with my hands. There followed a long silence. Peter slowly turned from his back to his side, facing me, he drew his knees nearer his body, relaxed and closed his eyes. A thought went through my mind that he was ready to be 'tucked up in bed'. I said nothing. The rest of the session was silent. We've had silent sessions before but this felt different. Peter did not curl up in a foetal position, he was very much there, the silence was not one of withdrawal but of being with. A new experience.

When time was up, Peter got up and left. At the next session he said that when I gestured in the air, as if holding a baby, he felt physically held by me, although he knew he was not. It was, he said, an exciting and new experience. He then felt like a child being gently put to bed, alone in his room, yet knowing there were others in the house and feeling safe. What startled him was that when he got up to leave, the pain had gone. We talked about his 'not having a spine', a feeling he used to have, and his growing awareness of his spine: his confusion between physically being supported by a spine and the metaphorical notion of not being centred around one.

The holding that had taken place at the previous session was of a new and different order to Peter; and quite clearly had a dramatic effect on him. It was as if in Winnicott's terms he had come to accept his psychosomatic existence without needing an actual surface-of-the-skin contact. As a result a clearer sense of 'me' and 'not me' started to evolve. He was no longer concerned with keeping his floating balance inside my womb, nor was he expelled and devastated. He was outside of me, organizing his sense of balance around his spine, literally and metaphorically. We were not fused, there were two of us. He came to 'have an inside and outside, and a body scheme' (Winnicott, 1960, p. 45).

Peter started acknowledging an inner psychic reality. He started to tell me dreams, now clearly distinguished from his waking life.

A child in physical pain, writes Winnicott, may need carrying, as soothing words may not be enough. A patient can be held by the therapist's knowledge and understanding of his deepest anxiety, conveyed through words. What happened between me and Peter was a transition between the two. It was the gesturing in the air he was held by; as we were 'touched' by each other, there was no need to touch.

EPISODE 5: ON BECOMING A MAN

> . . . the right standard by which to judge every human being is that he really is a being who ought not to exist at all . . . Are we not all sinners condemned to death? We expiate our birth firstly by our life and secondly by our death. (Nietzsche, quoted in Rank, 1973, p. 169)

The following episode took place quite a while after the others. Peter was now able to work, assisting a professional gardener. A job far below his intellectual capacity, yet he loved it, as it enabled him to take care of 'mother nature'. He was still liable to burst into tears at the sight of a tree trunk that had been chopped, as he could identify with it and 'feel the pain' in his navel. It was at the end of a session, I stood in the doorway waiting for him to leave. As he passed me he quickly pressed his body against mine. As my back was against the door frame, I could feel his erect penis brushing against me. He left immediately.

The sessions which followed all revolved around a main issue that Peter and I came to call 'Being a man or a mouse'. Basically Peter's position was that he had no right to be. Unable to use the initial regressive defence of denying his arrival in the world, he was now engaged in trying to withhold, contain and suppress his own power, which he described as 'charging up from the base of the spine'. The power was expressed through his ability to 'get on' out there, in the world of the talking, eating, working people, and in his strong sexual feelings. He felt he was a sinner. Erection would mean the destruction of the other, which would in turn destroy him; it was now a question of having accepted his birth, assuming his 'birth rights'. Of not only being in the world but of himself as a sexual being.

The location of the episode, namely, the threshold between the consulting room and the 'outside world', signifies Peter's position vis-à-vis inside and outside separation and separateness.

The pressing of his body against mine was the transition between two modes of sexuality. In the first, Peter had replaced (in his phantasy) his penis by his whole person, and so, copulation meant the re-entry into the mother's womb with the fear of castration being the fear of separation, or, more literally, the cutting of the umbilical cord. The second mode was that of genital sexuality between separate adults. Peter is in the doorway, he is making a move similar to the one described by Freud following Ferenczi's theory of the connection between castration anxiety and copulation: 'The high degree of narcissistic value which the penis possesses can appeal to the fact that the organ is a guarantee to its owner that he can be once more united to his mother, i.e. to a substitute for her in the act of copulation' (1926b, p. 139). Most important of all was Peter's discovery that he might have strong sexual feelings without always having to act under their total influence or be punished for them. He did not magically disappear inside me, nor was he cruelly rejected or castrated.

Had I been sexually aroused by him he most likely would have been scared and forced to suppress his sexual feelings, experiencing me as making an unreasonable sexual demand. Had I been repelled or disgusted by his erection, he would have felt rejected, 'cut off', ridiculed, and punished. All of which he was subsequently able to talk about in his therapy. I did not feel 'neutral', I felt warm and loving yet did nothing. I did not welcome or reject him. What followed was his ability successfully to cross the threshold. Once again, through this 'symbolic realization' (see 'Past perfect' below), he moved from infantile sexuality to being an adult. During the years in therapy that followed, a deep and genuine fondness developed between us, but never again did Peter need physically to touch me.

It was no accident of course that I found myself waiting for him to leave, standing at that very threshold.

'PAST PERFECT'

> The theory of the instincts is, so to say, our mythology. Instincts are mythological entities, magnificent in their indefiniteness. (Freud, 1933, p. 95)

It is surprising that despite Freud's awareness of the mythological nature of his meta-psychological constructs, Freudian theory still assumes the actual existence of such psychic entities as instinctual representatives residing in an 'unconscious' and 'cheating' their way to our consciousness in various guises. One would have to believe this to accept Freud's concept of 'acting out'.

If a patient must say everything that comes to mind but *only say* it, then all else is 'acting out'. And so when Peter did anything other than speak he was supposedly 'in the grip of his unconscious wishes and phantasies, reliving these in the present with a sensation of immediacy which is heightened by his refusal to recognize their source and their repetitive character' (Laplanche and Pontalis, 1973, pp. 4, 6).

Alternatively, if we are to take Freud's 1933 statement seriously, we must see his meta-psychology for what it is, that is, as pre-scientific philosophical articles of faith, ones that Freud himself referred to as a 'speculative superstructure' (1935, p. 61). If instinctual derivatives, ideas and affects do not exist independently of our experience and do not pop in and out of an 'unconscious' (seen as a place inside the 'mind'), it follows that what happens in therapy can no longer be seen as a mere repetition of those, so far presumed 'locked up', 'repressed' and so on.

Something new and genuine may take place, be it to a greater or lesser extent influenced by our past. We are then forced to see Peter's acts not as a mere 'acting out' (and mine a 'collusion') but to see them in their meaning as it unfolds through language in the unique nature of a therapeutic relationship. His acts become 'rituals' to dispel his confusion before it is spelt out. Rather similar to Sechehaye's (1951) notion of 'symbolic realization': 'This consists in an attempt to make up for the privations the subject has suffered in his earlier years by meeting his needs on a symbolic level and thus giving him access to reality' (Laplanche and Pontalis, 1973, p. 441).

As I pointed out earlier, I never proposed, suggested, encouraged or discouraged Peter's various 'symbolic realizations'. My concern was to see and to be able to show him their meaning. However, I do not believe it possible to have a relationship with anyone without some implicit suggestion and influence. When Peter became capable of genuine concern for others he was quite aware of this. He said to me: 'You are not interested in me at all, you are just interested in babies.' I replied that it might be true (that is, my interest in babies) and why not make the most of it as long as it was not in his way. He went on to say: 'How do I know that I can trust you; that you will not mould me into something you want me to be – you might put me together again as a sort of phantasy baby of yours.' Here Peter is discovering his own desire, thereby seeing me as 'other', capable of an inner life, separate and independent of him.

Peter's recognition of others and his capacity for concern were expressed in a variety of ways: at some point he felt ready to leave the community household. It was, he said, a dark, damp, depressed place that was necessary for him, like a seed, to sprout in. Now he needed sunshine and the company of 'normal' people. However, he felt that it would be wrong to leave before he could express his gratitude and stay a bit longer, not for himself, but to be there for others.

A professor of psychiatry who met Peter at the beginning of his therapy and some years later expressed great surprise at his progress. So much so that he wondered whether Peter was a 'true schizophrenic' or was there a mistake in his diagnosis. The best reply to that sort of question is to my mind on a poster I saw in a paediatrician's waiting room. It is a picture of a smiling child with the words:

You say mongoloid
We say Down Syndrome
His mates call him David . . .

I never 'examined' nor did I diagnose Peter. It was the 'David' in him that I saw, met and worked with, even when he tried his best to deny himself and his right to exist. When Peter was relatively healthy again, able to work, love and lead a 'magically ordinary' life, when he realized that to become adult he did not have to give up the child in him, nor give in to it, he said that the most helpful experience for him in therapy was that I always said no to him.

It seems that the 'extended' consulting room offered him firm but not rigid boundaries: a playing field in which to practise a delicate balance or, in Peter's own words: 'It is like learning to balance on a bicycle, you try to think yourself into doing it, you practise various methods, you fall and hurt, and then one day you just trust yourself enough to take off . . .'

As for touching: did I collude with Peter's 'acting out' by allowing physical contact and did I do the 'right thing'? Was it 'good for him'? I think that those questions are irrelevant, they reduce what happened between us to a technique, depleting it of its meaning in the context.

I propose that we cannot do therapy if we are not 'touched' by our patients, but we are not doing therapy if we advocate physical contact, be it hand holding, hugging, back patting, and so on, as a therapeutic technique. P. Lomas points out the danger in such a move in his book *True and False Experience*. He describes the uneasiness he felt at one time holding a patient's hand: 'What am I doing holding her hand? Am I a therapist applying a technique or am I just doing this? What had started as a spontaneous response had become for me a considered procedure . . . ' (1973, pp. 144, 146). He goes on to say that touching or revealing one's weakness to one's patient is not a necessary or useful method in psychotherapy but belongs in the realm of the ordinary, which is sometimes of crucial importance in therapy.

Equally dangerous to writing off any physical contact as 'acting out' is prescribing it as a method of treatment; in taking it to its

164

ultimate conclusion, sexual intercourse, the therapist is confusing 'fact' with 'fiction' or, in Searles's terms: 'He has succumbed to the illusion that a magically creative copulation will resolve the patient's illness which tenaciously has resisted all the more sophisticated psychotherapeutic techniques learned in his adult life training and practice' (1974, p. 431).

Some psychoanalysts who have undertaken analytical work with psychotic or deeply regressed patients write about breaking with conventional boundaries; the practical difficulties involved with such changes are often used as reasons for not undertaking this work. I would like to emphasize that if we are to accept the phenomenological critique of the analytical definition of transference, boundaries, and 'the' unconscious, this chapter is not proposing a modification of technique but would like to question the very basic premises on which the theory of 'usual boundaries' is constructed. F. Roustang did not confine himself to the psychotic patient when he wrote: 'The analyst does not have directly to share his personal history, his personality, or his anxiety with which the patient has nothing to do; nevertheless, those things are precisely what enter into the analysis' (1983, p. 115).

I like to see it as 'the lunacy of mothers and lovers', a notion introduced by E. G. Howe (1965, p. 94), and add the lunacy of any therapist undertaking work with patients who are caught in the web of their dreams. That 'lunacy' is healthy and absolutely necessary in the early stages, just as it is crucial to be able to keep awake, alert and maintain a firm foothold on reality, or else it would be impossible to fall in love, care for small babies or work therapeutically with people like Peter.

When I told Peter about the book and asked if he minded, he laughed and said that he could not know until he had read it; he might like it, alternatively he might never speak to me again. Three weeks later he told me a story from his early teens that somehow 'came to him'. He was on a school outing to a big trade fair. The group decided to go on a small train through a tunnel where a display of electrical inventions was arranged. Sitting next to a girl, in the dark he remembered what a friend said to him about touching girls. He decided to try, held the girl's hand and when she did not resist, touched her knee. On the way home, crowded in a train carriage, he realized to his horror that the girl was telling the whole group loudly what had happened. He felt guilty and embarrassed and felt compelled to deny the incident. 'I never spoke to her again', he said; he went on to say that what struck him when he remembered the event was that it never occurred to him, at the time, that the girl was not accusing him at all but simply showing off! I pointed out his use of the same statement, that is, 'never spoke to her again', and 'I may never speak to you again'. Here was I sharing with the world our most intimate moments, but this time he realized that I was not exposing him or betraying our intimacy. For, as Plato so wisely said, isn't writing itself a self-promoting narcissistic activity?

8

Hazards to desire

PAUL ZEAL

*. . . and even the noticing beasts are aware
that we don't feel very securely at home
in this interpreted world.*
– Rilke, '1st Duino Elegy'

*. . . His riddle is almost completely solved,
his condition is excellent, his whole being
is altered.*
– Freud (1985), letter to Fliess, 16 April 1900,
concerning a patient, Herr E

W E ARE THE ONLY creatures on the planet who tell stories. I
want to write about what happens across the threshold
between biological nature and the symbolic structures of
our speech. And then to write about some of the issues of psychotherapy. For there is a horizon, a threshold, or a difference that
makes a difference, call it what you will, between human nature
and the rest of nature. Somehow our human nature is only insecurely natural. For instance, it is natural for us to explore the
nature of the world, an activity which the rest of nature cannot see
for what it is. Animals explore the world but not the nature of the
world, and they have no idea what we are up to. The difference has
much to do with language.

René Descartes tells a story in his *Méditations*. At the apex of
his powers, and at a time when he was 'happily disturbed by no
passions', he set about overthrowing all his former opinions by the
exercise of doubt. He set the scene for the 'aphanistic' experience
of his own body, which is to say he let it disappear. He saw no
reason to distinguish its component parts from a set of phantoms,
and sought to rescue certainty by doubting. With regard to himself

he managed the giddy conclusion that, because he could not doubt that he doubted, he existed. The implications for the development of science were considerable. He desired to establish a firm and abiding foundation for the sciences, and to do this by the withdrawal of mind from the senses. He established that sciences such as astronomy and medicine are very tenuous by the standards of the mathematical sciences, for no faith can be put in the testimony of their objects of study. It therefore comes about that the search for exact knowledge tends to invalidate what people say.

Before Descartes it could not have been thought that thought was not physically extended. Pure ideas, yes, free of any biological corporeality in themselves, but the thinking of them was felt to be extended throughout the body. The word 'Cartesian' has become the word for a split approach to things. Since the time of the Cartesian split between body and mind, there have been two main scientific currents: that which has sought to perfect the findings of dissociated rationality regardless of nature, and that which has sought to make of body and mind a whole again. We will see how Freud, for all his psychologism, sought to rescue the I from such dissociated rationality in favour of an I that would live its desire through its incarnation.

Gregory Bateson also tried to weave body and mind together, while respecting their difference. In his last book (1979), he proposed that biological evolution is a mental process. He saw in all living organisms the immanence of God, in their systems of communication, in their biological forms, and in the relation within and between these forms. Symmetry, bilateral symmetry, homology, serial homology: our left and right sides correspond in formal relationship. The bones of our arms and hands correspond to the bones of our legs and feet. Our skeletons and organs compare with those of other mammals. These forms have evolved rhythmically and repetitively with variations through time and always in an ecological space.

But the time of human culture is brief indeed compared with the ages of animal evolution, and suddenly we, pre-eminent among all creatures, find ourselves, as a hazard of our becoming, caught between the symbolic and the real. An alienation from nature has occurred, primordial to our recognitions of ourselves as human, and it is no wonder we may feel lost.

168

The *Oxford English Dictionary* defines mind as: 'The seat of consciousness, thoughts, volitions and feelings; also the incorporeal subject of the psychical faculties.' Can we define the incorporeality of mind without splitting it off as a sort of non-object object from the body? We can say that the body is mindful of itself, and of its self in its context, like any largely self-regulating, self-recuperating system. Its senses sense what they have to and as they have to. But, though 'mindful' in their own domain, they cannot know the mind. For we can say that mind is not visible, nor audible, tastable, tangible nor smellable, nor amenable to proprioception. The senses are not capable of perception or of the inference that they are organs of mind, although there is no perception without an aesthetic dimension. Only mind can infer its own existence.

The relation between body and mind, whether in the vertex of pleasure or of pain, is riddled with ambiguity. But the depth nature of mind, 'the mind of God', is a far cry from any split-off conscious fiction we may enjoy as to what mind is, and from the antithetical opinion of our modern empiricist materialism that mind is reducible to body (of which it is then but an epiphenomenon). The mind of God means at least that which is formative and elaborative of the body. 'The organs of the body are crystallizations of libido', wrote Paul Schilder (1950). That there is much at stake in this is illustrated in the way that Shakespeare (who died when Descartes was twenty), begins his will. 'First I commend my soul into the hands of God my Creator, hoping, and assuredly believing, through the only merits of Jesus Christ my Saviour, to be made partaker of life everlasting, and my body to the earth whereof it is made.' He assigns his soul and body to different destinations. He does not say what his relation to each is, nor, I think, does he say what he expects for the 'I' who is writing the will.

We know that we are going to die. We may endeavour to reduce our anticipation to a commonplace, an ontic fact of the world which we can hasten or postpone, in order that we may avoid its pathos. For whatever our phantasies of death, death defines the outer historical limit to our being here in the world in our thrownness (Heidegger, 1967). Our potential directly to participate in the unfolding and expounding of events then ends. Will we be There when we die? Our empirical anticipation of the future certainty of our death (everyone else dies, so we will have to, too) forecloses against what Heidegger calls the 'possibility' of our dying: 'That possibility which is one's ownmost, unconditional, unsupersedable, certain, and as such indeterminable.' If our death is a possibility it follows that we may miss it, not be there at the time, and so never, ontologically, surrender to dying, and die. Although as an ontic fact of others' experience we may have been found dead, we may be merely stranded in some sort of non-space, having never brought our life to closure.

Mind, soul, spirit, self. These are all words which indicate the supreme human achievement: to have established a reflective difference between the body and the incarnation. The *OED* defines incarnation as 'The action of incarnating or fact of being incarnated or "made flesh"; a becoming incarnate; investiture or embodiment in flesh; assumption of, or existence in, a bodily (especially) human form.' Thrown here in some perplexity, unless marvellously in the grip of complacency, and belonging, albeit insecurely, to the open system of nature which evolves diachronically through synchronic patterns, we may sniff the higher air of intellection, and wonder what it all means – or any of it, for that matter. 'Why are there existents at all, rather than nothing?' asks Heidegger (1959). That nature abhors a vacuum is no answer. So, in moments, we glimpse and raise the question of meaning, and we may wonder that we are able to at all.

Despite Descartes, we are existent by virtue of being in relation with others. Indeed it is inconceivable that, without some recognition of ourselves by others as human, we could have in us the freedom to survive the scrutiny of doubt.

There is a natural unfolding of the body from conception traceable epigenetically and morphologically – but what of the unfolding of desire? Given the unresolvable conflict between the real and the symbolic, it is our destiny to realize, as our inheritance, that we are divided in ourselves, and that we belong to times other than present. Our archaic flesh and our ancestors, in conflict with each other, hold sway over us, whilst we struggle to be born clear. We are born into the embrace of those who are there before us.

To even begin to be human, we need the recognition of others through our value for them, indeed through who we are for them, and this infantile quest carried us over the threshold into speech such that, as Kojève (1969) and Lacan put it, the desire we desire is the other's desire for us. It is the social nature of mind, and not its location in any one of us, that is found throughout the system. We are bound to be hazy as to the social patterns of desire in which our own are caught.

Mapping operations, as Laing (1971) calls them (redeploying a phrase employed by the mathematicians of the theory of logical types), are going on all the time. Indeed, without them 'we' would not be. We would lack any subjective dimension to our existence. One's family is the principal source of one's introjective maps, and they may be quite benign. 'She is just like her granny', a mother may say, recalling her own well-loved mother. But the arrow of love is twisted in the wound if the little girl is induced to be, has to be, her mother's mother. The final common denominator around whom these issues swirl and whom they most infiltrate is the child, the object of the gaze down the generations, handled and moulded by its possessors who lay claim to own it, and who obscure such truth as may be to its own beginnings.

The fact that each of us has one physical body tricks us into seeing each of us as a single person. But behind and within the presenting person are the hosts and ghosts of the familiar and familial others, internalized in the ways we relate, embodied in the fabric of our intentions. Each of us is a story largely told by others. Our living is its telling. We are each text in the context of others, and are context for the others. Others in the world have power to destroy our meanings, and without others we are without meaning. They hear and read us according to their own intent, but our stories are inscribed in our bodies, and through our conduct we seek to inscribe them in the world.

'Mind' does still carry forward the old Indo-European root meaning to intend, as in the phrase 'to have a mind to'. Therefore to know one's mind is to know one's intentions, which is to say, where they come from, towards whom they are directed, and under what symbols they stand. The incredible complexity of the human collective mind is due to the unfathomable interplay of intentionalities, each of them being with a mind to others.

'The body is as malleable as a dream.' It is a lucid madness to reflect upon and to search out the nature of becoming. Human nature is necessarily a madness, for it is arisen in that wound in Being called the body, and to which it is not reducible. Human nature has arisen through the body and seeks to govern it, at least 'in name'. And 'the body', death's desire, is now an insertion in the symbolic order which is both the creation and ruler of human nature.

The hazards to desire are as diverse as the natural shocks that flesh is heir to. The body is a wound in the triumph of being, a wound through which we call being into question. For that wound, dialectically unwound, discloses itself as the winding-sheet in which desire becomes quickened or buried.

INTERLUDE

Kingsley Hall, 1966. Mary Barnes was 'down', not much more than foetalized skin and bone, having to be carried to bathe and allowed to rock and suck herself for endless hours. For her the sun did not rise, it 'opened'. There was Andrew, whose room was stacked high with empty cans and other people's mail. He would not talk, but would sing in high nasal syncopation, mocking us with strange laughter and sudden grabs at knives. He was for ever running into other people's houses and standing there. A particular walk he favoured was down the Mile End Road, left at Burdett Road, and after a drink at East India Dock Road, he would zigzag back along the jagged diagonal past unreclaimed bomb sites from the last war. Surveying the devastation and desolation he would whisper, 'Lovely lovely lovely lovely lovely.'

Among the other actors on stage were: Helen, who upon awakening would put on a mask of white make-up and drift down to the kitchen trailing ghosts, who tore down Mary's paintings because they interrupted her sky. Alfred, bald from the age of five, his father a furrier; he used to hold a cigarette at the top of his skull as an aerial for the radio receiver implanted in one of his teeth. Peter, perpetually dithering, whose body was the crumbling dust of ancestors. Bernie, one with Jesus, telling his visions in rhythm and rhyme, of golden spirals through the eye which would lead us in at Heaven's door. Harry who communed with the Old Testament prophets through the mediation of his Hasidic grandfather, in the Blackwall Tunnel. Jill, who arrived at dawn clad in silks and satin *en route* for her origins in Ethiopia. Francis, who called himself a 'refugee from the sixth dimension', whose wild laughing delight at being rescued from the ECT machine and at being in the midst of such energy was that of no ordinary self at all.

Kingsley Hall was a place with madness as the core, a roving core moving from one to another, touching each of us to some degree. Only by allowing madness its way and its say was it in any way contained there. There was always conflict as to how far someone would go, into wakefulness, nakedness, intrusion upon others, withdrawal or destructiveness. The project was intended to show that madness is intelligible when given an appropriate home, and took place against the prevailing tide of compulsory hospitalizations permitted by the enlightened Mental Health Act of 1959, at a time when hospitals were being filled rather then emptied.

It could not have been otherwise, it belonged to its time, the sixties. Yet, when as research assistant to R. D. Laing, I interviewed the old psychiatrist at St Clement's, whose patience had been sorely tried by a variety of temporary hospitalizations of people staying, or trying to stay, in Kingsley Hall, he showed he too 'knew'. For he leant forward with a twinkle in his Viennese eyes, well aware of his therapeutic presence, and said, 'You know, the medication works better for me than for my registrars.'

Innumerable people, of whom Lord Perceval (1830) was a distinguished example, in the reformatories, hospitals and gaols, chained as was St John by his friends for the duration of his apocalyptic visions, revelations, on the island of Patmos, have gone through inner voyages of dismemberment and recollection, of anamnesis, without that inner reality being unduly frustrated by policing authorities. Now that strait-jackets and chains are chemically ingested, it is not the same. Madness is of many kinds and orders. Socrates in the *Phaedrus* affirms the madness of lovers, of those inspired by divinatory powers, and of those touched by the Muses. But madness distraught and disarrayed still has a heart, although triple-bound, divided within and upon itself, although it cannot function in the world of others and knows no bounds. Madness is part of our ordinary inheritance.

LANGUAGE

Language enthrals us. It is a primary tool for the acquisition of reality, but it is more and Other than a tool, for we cannot put it down. It possesses us its possessors. Being human is therefore not a technical problem, for it is by language and through the recognitions of speech that we become human. In so far as it is a tool it becomes blunt and dull through use, and there is great interest in making it blunt and dull. If it is overworked and over-used (worked over like dream wishes one kills off by distracting distortions), it can neither cut us nor reveal us, and we remain cut off and illuded. That is the reason for all chatter. By chattering we try to control language and deprive it of its power. Why should we want to do that when it is wiser than we? We envy that which makes us human. We envy our mother tongue.

Sacer, Latin, means both sacred and accursed, an example of the antithetical meaning of primary words where the same word means both its opposites. The sacrum is that in which we are first held, where we first move, and from which, to survive, we have to be born. The wiser the parenting, the more deeply it is realized that the children are held in sacred trust. Wherever they come from, they come through us, and in so doing present us with evocations of our own nameless beginnings.

Children, with all their being, are (genetically) determined to love their parents. It is their love to which their parents are not equal. A gap opens up in which the parents, tacitly given the power of creators by their children, take advantage of their young trust in the unconscious interests of making them in their own image. Children are unaware of this advantage being taken, in their own naïve desire to identify with their parents and parent surrogates in order to discover who they are, which is to say, for whom. In that sacrum of the original and originating constellation of relationships, children are incapable of transcendent reflection as to what is necessary in what is on offer, and are bound to identify with whoever is there, however spurious, irrational or unloving. In order, Freud would say, that they may take on the Oedipalization of their own being, the *sine qua non* for becoming human. In their dependency children cannot be expected to sort out the actual incestuous wishes, Oedipal loves and rivalries to which they are heir and bound, and they appeal to their parents as 'ones who are supposed to know' in order that the symbolic quest for their humanity may be neither misplaced nor transgressed. It is in the profound insecurity of the meeting between our incredibly complex genetic endowment and the sacrum of womb and family that we are found or lost.

Sooner or later, in becoming ourselves, we are bound to be disillusioned in our parents. There is no other way to get the measure of them, and no other route to ourselves. But to be disillusioned, or, to play upon an another register, disappointed, is a losing of place that makes us heir to the essential homelessness of mankind. The disillusionment involves the realization that our parents are not actually the archetypal mother and father we (unconsciously) want them to be, and which we need them to appear to be in order that we may with security enter into the symbolic discourse of humanity. The only trauma is shock to our sense of omnipotence, says Winnicott. By the same token, omnipotence in the parents has to be unmasked, and the emperor seen naked, otherwise the symbolic issues are misplaced. We are all children of Logos, whatever our generational relation to others.

'Now you know I'm your father,' says the father in Freud's wry story of the father who encourages his son to jump into his arms from higher and higher steps, but then from the jump from the highest step, steps back. Perhaps that father did not fall short of his place as father, for he taught the place of the Other, of Language, by a speaking which was divided from his gesture of receptive open arms.

A father is biologically necessary only for the act of intercourse which results in conception (not even that, now, with sperm banks); in other words his biological necessity ceases before the new life begins. No wonder there is a traditional understanding that father is essential absence. That's what the man in the story represents, as does every father but commonly in stratagems less conscious and more dangerous. Given that biologically he has nothing to do from before the new life begins, he is well placed, once historicity has begun, to be the historian and lawgiver, outside the mute realm of need. The penis rises up to become the phallus, and points from behind itself to beyond itself. The ordinary mortal male, Jane Gallop teases, has become a phallocentric prick.

175

Once weaning is over no part of either the mother's or the father's body is essential for the upbringing, yet the reception of the infant into the human world has hardly begun.

It is one of our negative potentials that the symbolic may collapse into the imaginary. The day of the royal wedding of 'Charles and Di' was remarkable for the spirit of national rejoicing in which millions engaged, regardless of the potential for envy. Was it a hype? By what are we hypnotized, when we are hypnotized? The royals still represent something sacred for the people; their ordinary passions are elevated, despite all the evidence, to the realm of sacrifice. They do it for us. Earl Spencer showed he well understood when he commented: 'The Spencers have a long tradition of dying for King and Country, and I am glad my daughter is carrying on in that tradition.' The virgin sacrifice potentiates a kingdom, and thereby a realm for the subjects.

As humans we find our being through and beyond the animal, and have established through the centuries a symbolic order whose contents we are for ever answering to. We are the creature on the planet who has heard the Word.

'May he triumph against the world, the flesh and the devil,' says the Church of England service of baptism. What does this blessing mean? What is the baby to be divided from and set against? Is it to *triumph against* the world and the flesh that we are here? He or she is set against the world and divided from their own body, and given a concept, 'the devil', by which to name that of their self they are to repress. The blessing wounds, the sacred is the curse. The blessing means to divide the baby.

By what irony or sense of sacrament have we ennobled the act of sexual intercourse, out of the round of nature's self-perpetuation? We have broken the mould of nature's basic act, and we seek it for pleasure and as symbolic of love. For enjoyment, for *jouissance*. Ruthlessly regardless of the purpose of the act itself and of the risks, over and over again we want it, that through it we may come into being. Open, naked, in atonement one with another, enraptured, whole.

That is the best of it. Or by what devil nature have we divided sexual intercourse from love? It is the human achievement, perhaps definitive of human nature, that the distinction has been seen, for then the act can symbolize and not simply express love.

The collapse of the erotic into the sexual shows our falling short of our full nature, not into our animal nature but into an imaginary caricature thereof.

We yearn to be uplifted in the release and soaring of the soul. Yet, rarely invited, she keeps her wings enfolded in our flesh. The self sleeps and shows its identikit the skin-encapsulated ego. It is the poetic understanding that, for release while yet incarnate, Love is the name of the grace which must move. The poetic vision is that Love is the power, itself of no origin, which generates the universe, and by the time its workings-out occur in our flesh it is multiply betrayed, in disarray, and yearning for itself. The living body is Love's sepulchre.

Wherever there are human beings there are language and acts of speech, and a distinction and a relation simultaneously established between body and desire, between nature's realm of signs and the human world of signifiers. Language both invents absence and stabilizes our presence in its midst, for by thought and speech we invoke what was, is not, will be. Such invocations reveal to reflection the horizonal structure of the human world (Heaton, 1982b), and, if we are equal to our lacking, will provoke us to desire.

Our dividedness from our biological nature is maintained by our self-constituting acts of speech, reflection and comment. First done in the mirror of an anthropomorphic world, as children's stories bear witness, in which animals wear clothes and talk, and from which we are never fully free, it is a dividedness maintained by the act of speech itself, that paradoxical thorn in our flesh, without which there could be no prick of conscience. It is speech that makes us, and makes our nature uncomfortable, for we have manipulated our animal nature in the pursuit of pleasure and the avoidance of death. We have heard the Word but become deaf to Nature.

Technology, in extending the powers and freedoms of the body, exists for the enjoyments of mastery, and in order to create a vehicle for desire. The technological imperative, which says 'we can do it so it must be right', is persuasive because 'doing it' provides its own justification. But it does not alter in any fundamental way the fundamental categories of Life and Death. We are still thrown here, and technology has nothing to say to that. One escape from insane technological runaways, as one *cri de coeur* would have it, is a return to our biological nature. But it is abundantly clear that we cannot do that without forsaking our human nature. And, as Bateson (1967) points out: 'The predatory action of predators and man-made mechanical predators, at the forefront of evolution, at the cutting edge, swifter and more intelligent, does not help in itself to provide any solution, in that our biological nature includes that predatory element.' It is merely predatory to try to reduce being to something technical.

It is not essentially masculine rather than feminine to be predatory but we have imposed a masculine, technological imperative upon Nature. 'We must put Nature to the rack and extort her secrets', exhorts Francis Bacon, Lord High Chancellor of England, contemporary with Descartes. To extort her secrets is to distort her secrets. We force her hand and claim God's authorization. In the Book of Genesis, God gives us the authority to name all the parts of his creation. But, as Bachelard says, 'Naming assassinates', for to name is to take power over. Parents name the child. The child accepts the gift which he cannot refuse, a name through which to live, but according to the desire of the other.

There is no biblical teaching addressed to the ecological catastrophe which our technological imperative has created and in the midst of which we live. The ultimate symbol, the Uncreated Creator, is silent on the matter; in fact the silence is deafening, as hundreds of thousands of species die out and we pollute and lay waste the earth of which our bodies are part. Homoeopaths, heirs to the tradition of Paracelsus and Samuel Hahnemann, are aware that, even despite appearances, all is not well with the human body, suspended as it is in a ghastly solution of vaccines, antibiotics, pharmaceuticals and drugs, the long-term effects of which are visible, once one's eyes are used to the darkness, in chronic diseases. The allopathic doctor, for all his compassion and gifts of healing, and although empowered by his symbolic placing, is fortunate if his gifts shine through the obfuscation of his natural powers by the drug companies and his technological education, which unwittingly he represents, whose principle, as in modern farming methods with regard to the land, is overkill. Should we wish for the day of the first body transplant?

178

Of all the creatures of the planet, only we ourselves have forsaken the Garden of Eden, and do we not in unconscious envy wreak havoc upon it? We lead a charmed life amongst the ruins.

FREUD'S DESIRE

By divining the Oedipal structure of our desire, Freud fed our appetite for symbolic existence. 'Every new arrival on this planet is faced with the task of mastering the Oedipus complex.' A universal complex to which all are subject. Here was a challenge for all to face, and the more neurotic the greater the challenge. In *The Interpretation of Dreams* he likens the unfolding of Sophocles' play to the unfolding of a psychoanalysis, and says the play is what is known as a tragedy of destiny. 'Its tragic effect is said to lie in the contrast between the supreme will of the gods and the vain attempts of mankind to escape the evil that threatens them. The lesson which, it is said, the deeply moved spectator should learn from the tragedy is submission to the divine will and realization of his own impotence' (1900).

But, he continues, it is not the contrast between destiny and the human will which gives the play its potency, 'but the particular nature of the material on which that contrast is exemplified'. The nature of the material is the revelation of the incestuous desires which hold a family spellbound, and the curse unto death, mutilation or castration concomitant upon their satisfaction, which throws it asunder. In a footnote added in 1914 he comments:

> None of the findings of psychoanalytical research has provoked such embittered denials, such fierce opposition – or such amusing contortions on the part of critics, as this indication of the childhood impulses towards incest which persist in the unconscious. An attempt has even been made recently [he writes mischievously] to make out, in the face of all experience, that the incest should only be taken as 'symbolic'. (1900, p. 263)

Mischievously because he enjoys surviving, with considerable panache and not without crisis, the threat that the cusp of difference between the categories of the real and the phantastic will dissolve, and because all the while, whether or not he knew what

179

he was doing, he was establishing a symbolic structure within which the incestuousness could be appreciated.

Witness:

Typical Example of a Disguised Oedipus Dream: A man dreamt that 'he had a secret liaison with a lady whom someone else wanted to marry. He was worried in case this other man might discover the liaison and the proposed marriage come to nothing. He therefore behaved in a very affectionate way to the man. He embraced him and kissed him.' There was only one point of contact between the content of this dream and the facts of the dreamer's life. He had a secret liaison with a married woman; and an ambiguous remark by her husband, who was a friend of his, led him to suspect that the husband might have noticed something. But in reality there was something else involved, all mention of which was avoided in the dream but which alone provided a key to its understanding. The husband's life was threatened by an organic illness. His wife was prepared for the possibility of his dying suddenly, and the dreamer was consciously occupied with an intention to marry the young widow after her husband's death. This external situation *placed the dreamer in the constellation of the Oedipus dream* . . . (1900, pp. 398–9, paper added as footnote in 1925, my italics)

He wrote, also in *The Interpretation of Dreams*:

The presence of symbols in dreams not only facilitates their interpretation but also makes it more difficult. As a rule the technique of interpreting according to the dreamer's free associations leaves us in the lurch when we come to the symbolic contents in the dream-content . . . We are thus obliged, in dealing with those elements of the dream-content which must be recognized as symbolic, to adopt a combined technique, which on the one hand rests on the dreamer's associations and on the other hand fills the gap from the interpreter's knowledge of symbols . . . The uncertainties which still attach to our activities as interpreters of dreams spring in part from our incomplete knowledge, which can be progressively improved as we advance further, but in part from certain characteristics of dream-symbols themselves. (1900, p. 353)

His argument is between the traditional method of decoding according to symbolic keys in dream-books, and the psychoanalytic recourse to the patient's own associations. His ambitious, reassuring plans for the conquest of uncertainties 'which still attach to our activities as interpreters of dreams' indicate there will be less and less recourse to the patient's associations, and more and more 'filling of gaps from the interpreter's knowledge of symbols'. The 'filling of gaps' is a metaphor which plays upon a fundamentally polymorphous perverse sexual register: the patient is full of gaps to be filled by 'the one who is supposed to know'.

A page earlier he had written:

> In a number of cases the element in common between a symbol and what it represents is obvious; in others it is concealed and the choice of the symbol seems puzzling.
>
> It is precisely these latter cases which must be able to throw light upon the ultimate meaning of the symbolic relation, and they indicate that it is of a genetic character. Things that are symbolically connected today were probably united in prehistoric times by conceptual and linguistic identity. The symbolic relation seems to be a mark and a relic of a former identity. (1900, p. 352)

Although the term 'Oedipus complex' seems to have been first used by Freud in published writings in the first of his 'Contributions to the psychology of love' (1910a), he discovered it in the course of his own self-analysis in 1897 within the same eighteen months that his last child was born and his own father died. This moves Julie Kristeva to ask:

> Could the discovery of the Oedipus complex, and thereby of infantile sexuality, and thus the beginning of the modern conception of the child, have been produced through an inverted Oedipal complex? Could the 'Oedipus complex' be the discourse of mourning for his father's death . . .? With the end of the reproductive cycle and spurred by his father's death, Freud's self-analysis led him to that telescoping of father and child, resulting in none other than Oedipus. (1981, pp. 274–5)

This suggests that Freud was well within the edge of (divinatory?)

madness, characterized by metonymy, beyond the reach of metaphor, where son is father and father is son. Kristeva discusses the heterogeneity between the libidinal-signifying organization in infancy belonging to the maternal realm, which she calls the 'semiotic disposition', and the 'symbolic' functioning of the speaker following the acquisition of language.

To bring the semiotic into the symbolic by action of the symbolic (language) upon the semiotic is the work of the poets, among whom in this instance is Freud, for his writing asserts the reverie upon impulsive wants as the source of the symbolic law which prohibits them. He sought a radical independence, freedom from the repressed infantile fixations which govern adult relationships, and it is interesting that he invoked the symbolic in order to do so, in order to lead the people out of misery. Lacking the concept of the symbolic order, it was with a marvellous, unwitting sleight of hand that Freud accomplished the shift from things as symbols to the invention or recognition of a symbolic complex, insight into which promised release from an age-old spell on the one hand, and on the other set up psychoanalysis in perpetuity. For the hidden design of the symbol, invented or spoken, is in its being brought to bear in the definition of relationships between people, which, in the 'movement', is exactly how Freud used it.

'A FAMILY IS SO CLOVEN – CLOSELY WOVEN'
This nice ellipsis, echoing myths of the cloven hoof, was spoken by a young woman who in the course of therapy was discovering that she really had been molested by her father (now deceased), about which she had for years struggled to remain amnesic. 'Whenever a penis touches me inadvertently,' she said, rather oddly, 'I feel a cold thr– well, there you are, I was going to say, "shudder".' A deathly realm had threatened to descend upon her marriage, but it opened to the recollection of obscene and forbidden pleasure. She began to recall it through the sensation of weight upon her and the memory of a whisper in her ear, 'Don't tell mummy.' The law lay with her. She heard it lie. And the law lies with the mother. For if *she* had known would she not have prevented its transgression? Yet, perhaps, presumably, she did know, obscurely. A family may indeed be cloven – split asunder by transgression yet, in self-protection, clinging to a law against knowing it.

182

Incestuous wishes are real and known to children, but not under the name of 'incest', that is, not as something forbidden, for voyagings in phantasy give perfect freedom. They know without knowing, what it is all about. One 'comes of age' in realizing that incest is natural and that it is forbidden. If it were not desired there would be no law against it.

The wishes become symbolic in the discourse between generations, where the law of language prevails in order to prevent that 'confusion of generations which, in the Bible as in all traditional laws, is accused of being the abomination of the Word and the desolation of the sinner' (Lacan, 1977c).

With the discovery of the unconscious, which has no need of memory for nothing is forgotten in that timeless realm wherein too there is no repression, we are bound to realize that incestuousness can never be entirely excluded from our sexual relations. 'The primordial Law is that which in regulating marriage ties superimposes the kingdom of culture on that of a law abandoned to the law of mating,' says Lacan. The prohibition of incest is the subjective pivot, and this is revealed clearly enough as identical with an order of language, which, in the case of my patient, was perverted by the parent.

Psychoanalytical psychotherapy for the therapist is a discipline in that non-attachment which is neither detached nor dissociated. It is a path or practice which seeks to uncover the root nature of attachment. Not for the sake of an archaeological investigation into the passionate dependencies natural to families, but in the interests of the evocation of desire, without which we are less than, or not yet, human. Psychotherapy does not deal in homilies and does not offer the comfort of a spiritual ladder. It wants to face one nakedly with one's hidden agendas and their self-constituting patterns, which is to say, with one's way of relating and mystifying one's fundamental being. It is a conversation that reaches the parts that other conversations cannot reach – there's the advertisement. In the actual relationship between patient and therapist, the transference and counter-transference mediate the realizations. In that present relationship return pasts suffered, repressed and dissociated, and possible futures emerge. When the only call is from the past we are buried.

183

A past totally past would leave no trace; it presents itself, or is represented, by trace and symptom, in the present, not in any other time. Past and future are present in that conjunction of trace and recognition, of history and prophesy (which means to expound the consequences of present events), which we call our historicity.

IN CONCLUSION AND BEYOND

In his late writings Freud (1937, 1940) appears to offer the concept of a primordial ego at one with corporeality, appropriate to the various stages of development, but which may be altered or adversely affected by contingent events, premature loss, abuse, deficiency of love, undue punishment or mystification of sexual feelings. The ego, once altered for the worse, made precarious, no longer a body-ego, cannot say 'I' of its whole being. Therapy is therefore the process through which it lays claim to its wholeness. The altered ego is one that has lost place, and strengthening that ego enables reclamation. In his discussions of this strengthening, he writes of bringing the unconscious into 'the harmony of the ego'. Harmony is a wide concept. Even on the analogy of muscle power, strength of body is not enough for a task, that strength has also to be brought to bear in relation to the task. It is all a matter of position and relation.

He wanted to deconstruct the Cartesian rational ego, to dethrone that selfish hero of the rational, in favour of a far deeper realization of the nature of the I, *das Ich*, resonant with the 'I Am that I Am' of the Old Testament. In unearthing the dynamic unconscious he invoked the past when it could not have been thought that thought was not corporeally extended throughout a whole and real being, without reservation from any cell. There was once value given to an implicate order (Bohm, 1981), which was finally wrecked on the rocks of rationality for which 'Cartesian' is the tag. But although by his formulation 'Where id was, there shall ego be' Freud asserts his intent, the I as he presents it, caught in the intra-psychic conflict between id and super-ego – fair enough, but without regard for any other person – remains bound in an interiority, which makes it a 'Darwinian' structure for survival rather than 'ecologically' sound.

Bateson points out that Darwin's error was in his perception of the unit of survival. It is not, for instance, the horse, but the horse-and-plain. Species do not survive by overrunning their life-supporting system. In our supreme pride we are now overrunning ours, and the spurious majesty of the human ego does not want to know.

The trouble with *das Ich* as presented by Freud is that, as his theory does not bring it into relation with others, it exists merely in the register of the imaginary, in other words it is non-ethical, pre-ethical, unfortunately in every sense lacks ethics. The I, founded upon *Verneinung*, denial, and being 'a mental projection of the surface of the body' (1923), is the one who, once enlightened by the encounter with the unconscious, both super-egoic and of the id, would become ethical, beyond Darwin's survival of the fittest, where the priority of the other is discovered. That is to say, recognition of the priority of the desire of the other. But it is now being discovered that although no other creature can recognize us in our specifically human nature, Nature demands priority.

We are ill-prepared to see that our purely organic waste products, from excrement to corpses (without additives), belong to the bed of life (an awareness the Egyptians emblematized in making a sacred symbol of the scarab, the dung-beetle), whereas our technological waste products are its destruction. Such may be our collective abhorring repression of the primal scene (that is, of our primitive phantasy confusion of oral, anal and genital realms), that we are destroying the bed of life and denying it. As for the drive towards death (*Todestriebe*), an animal will die for the sake of its young, that is, for the sake of the species. The death drive, as a function of the ego, can be healthy; destructive, but ethically coherent.

Freud's notion (see *An Outline of Psychoanalysis*) that the id is obscure, and has no direct communication with the external world, is itself obscure. Is not the id the realm of direct, primary communication? Of immediate non-reflective search for satisfaction of needs and instincts, according to the natural order, finally surrendering to the ultimate, folding back in upon itself in death, merged with the inorganic, all the splendid heraldry of its life extinct?

When in 'Analysis terminable and interminable' (1937) he speaks of 'the three factors which we have recognized as being

185

decisive for the success or otherwise of analytical treatment – the influence of traumas, the constitutional strength of the instincts and alterations of the ego', and goes on to say that analytical success is not in disposing of the instinct but in bringing it 'completely into the harmony of the ego', he shows himself ambivalent. He says: 'If we are asked by what methods and means this result is achieved, it is not so easy to find an answer. We can only say: "So muss denn doch die Hexe dran!" – the Witch metapsychology. Without metapsychological speculation and theorizing – I had almost said "phantasying" – we shall not get another step forward. Unfortunately, here as elsewhere, what our Witch reveals is neither very clear nor very detailed.'

Socrates' Diotima under a Cartesian hex? With thinking split between phantasy on the one hand, and metapsychologism on the other? The quote from Goethe means 'We must call the Witch to our help after all,' and is said by Faust when, in search of the secret of youth, he unwillingly seeks the Witch's help.

In *The Privacy of the Self* Masud Khan (1974) writes that 'the essential paradox of the experience of self' is that 'no one can communicate directly from his self or can be related to directly in his self. Hence the necessity of symbolic forms as Cassirer has pointed out.' He places the essential paradox at the level of a schizoid split, between self and other, which can never be directly crossed except by our symbolic representatives, whilst we remain essentially withdrawn, out of touch with each other, behind them. This schizoid split is a pale reflection of the primordial alienation the nature of which we have explored in this paper. However, he continues: 'The self is as much created by its symbols, as it is represented and expressed by them.' But it is a rather forlorn conclusion that 'The so-called "true self" of Winnicott's terminology is a conceptual ideal that is known concretely mostly by its absence.'

I am hazarding that, in so far as we are human, we are symbolic creatures. 'By thy face ye shall be known' for, being other to each other, we are founded upon recognition, and founder upon misrecognition, in the horizonal structure of the face-to-face human world. But the essential alienation (another otherness in which we are bound to participate) is not between us, but between nature and human nature, although in our own bodies they are both so mingled that they cannot be told apart. Unconsciously sharing in that primordial alienation from our biological nature by virtue of language and speech, we are directly in touch with each other, except in so far as we are isolated in regions of the imaginary or ideal. The symbolic is not our mediator, but our specifically human nature.

If, in the struggle for recognition, one has fallen prey merely to being another's symbol, one is imaginary. If, as one woman said of another, 'She is just a symbol, not a person with her own right to speak,' psychoanalysis would want to subvert 'her'. For the wish inherent in the desire to peruse the unconscious and to discover the ruses by which we disguise ourselves is that one who is imaginary, isolated, another's symbol, may come to their own *jouissance* (an English word, by the way, not only French, although neglected), which necessarily involves others. We each want, albeit ambivalently, to be called out of our imaginary fixations and splits, out of the state of the traditional child 'seen and not heard'. For we are for each other, each other's horizon, for whom we yearn beyond our own self-enclosedness, in order to find between us that emancipation of spirit which is all that can be hoped for toward the fulfilment of desire, desire being not only wish, but continuous force and insatiable.

In the Schreber case (1911) Freud comments, 'An individual's megalomania is never so vehemently suppressed as when he is in the grip of an overpowering love', and follows with a quote from Rumi:

For when the flames of love arise
Then Self, the gloomy tyrant, dies.

To apply these quotes to our gloomy genius, we may wonder at Freud's own megalomania indirectly expressed in 'The theme of the three caskets' (1913). Not for a moment does he forsake his analytic stance, the solver of riddles, and it is a paper inadvertently interesting for our theme of desire as that which yearns to go beyond the satisfactions of self-enclosedness. Confronted by a pattern of stories and myths in which, of three sisters, the third, the youngEst and fairest, is chosen by the hero, the finest, he resolves Love back into primeval unity with Death.

He begins with a discussion of the three caskets in *The Merchant of Venice* and is pleased by his interpretation that the gold,

187

the silver and the lead caskets refer to 'a man's choice between three women'. The fact that there is one woman, Portia, and, of her many suitors, three are presented in the play, does not delay him. He is taken up with Bassanio's short speech in which he says to the casket of lead: 'Thy paleness moves me more than eloquence.' Freud does not for a moment attend to the words inscribed upon each casket. Had he done so he would have been involved in ethics. Instead he follows up the stories of Cordelia, Aphrodite, Cinderella and Psyche, each the third of three sisters and each of whom he is able to link with death. Paleness is deathly, and it turns out that these third sisters tend to share in qualities of silence, dumbness, concealment. Why do heroes choose them, for their qualities of beauty and youth, or of silence and deathliness? Freud cites the Grimms' stories, 'The Twelve Brothers' and 'The Six Swans', in both of which the brothers are restored to life by their sisters' staying dumb under trial. (Do heroes favour women's silence?)

He arrives at the conclusion that the third of the sisters is the Goddess of Death and that therefore the sisters are known to us. They are the Fates, the third of whom is called Atropos, the Inexorable. Death is our final overdetermined choice, and embrace. In this paper his genius moves unconsciously towards the eventual articulation of the death instincts.

But let us turn to Shakespeare's play. Portia's dead father has decreed that he who wins his daughter will do so by choosing that one of the three caskets which contains her portrait. Says Portia: 'O me, the word "choose". I may neither choose whom I would nor refuse whom I dislike; so is the will of a living daughter curbed by the will of a dead father. Is it not hard, Nerissa, that I cannot choose one nor refuse none?'

Her waiting-maid replies: 'Your father was ever virtuous, and holy men at their death have good inspirations; therefore, the lottery that he hath devised in these chests of gold, silver and lead, whereof who chooses his [that is, the father's] meaning chooses you, will, no doubt, never be chosen by any rightly but by one who you shall rightly love.' Her father's love for her is evident, as is her anger at his death and at her own being at risk. Here we have the symbolic law of the father, exercised at the threshold, when his daughter will lose and betray his name in favour of the name of another's father.

Portia's first suitor is the Prince of Morocco. He goes for gold, whose inscription reads, 'Who chooseth me shall gain what many men desire,' and because gold best represents her value. But there is nothing going on between him and her and all he gets when he opens the casket is a Death's head with a scroll which ends, 'Fare you well your suit is cold.'

The Prince of Arragon is next. He goes for silver: 'Who chooseth me shall get as much as he deserves.' He does: the scroll says '. . . Some there be that shadows kiss/Such have but a shadow's bliss.' Nerissa comments:

> The ancient saying is no heresy
> 'Hanging and wiving go by destiny'.

But lo, Bassanio approaches, and Portia comes alive. 'I pray you, tarry: pause a day or two before you hazard.' She wants him to know, by passage of time but without her breaking her word not to tell, the choice by which to win her. But he wants to choose now, to be off the rack, he wants her so much, so she calls for music to accompany his choice. He says:

> . . . thou gaudy gold,
> Hard food for Midas, I will none of thee;
> nor none of thee, thou pale and common drudge
> 'Tween man and man: but thou, thou meagre lead,
> Which rather threatenest than dost promise aught,
> *Thy* paleness moves me more than eloquence,
> And here choose I: joy be the consequence!

The words inscribed upon the leaden casket and which add to the threat rather than the promise are: 'Who chooseth me must give and hazard all he hath.' For love, death and the symbolic, one gives one's all. If Bassanio is in flight from death in the form of the 'lost object', the mother he can never have again, yet is unconsciously impelled toward it, his love will founder. If Portia is so identified with the father's word that she belongs to him dead, she will come to have no time for her lover. Appearances present or fake their potential depth. The future holds their unfolding and their dissolution. From their own depth, appearances may be barred.

189

If Bassanio and Portia are able to allow the Other, that of which they are yet unconscious, to participate in the destiny of their love, to open out and to become known to them, they will have proven themselves capable of symbolic exchange, through the mediations, confrontations and recognitions of speech. These occur in the give and take of relationships in which the unconscious determinants of choice about who each is for the other do not rule by virtue of being unconscious, but are brought into play.

This Other to whom priority is to be given is never the egoical other (that is, a part of whole being). For that is imaginary. Ego to ego is a failure of the unconscious and of participation in the analytic. (Etymologically 'to analyse' means both 'to loosen' and 'to resolve' (Skeat).) Ego to ego is but mirror to mirror, the alienation of one's being in a visual or verbal image. Nor is the Other to be found in symbiotic fusion, for there separateness has not been established. The Other is the language of form and of difference, in which all human beings participate, however falteringly, and which holds all realizations about the relations between our existences, the changing of cultures and the forces of nature.

The hazards to desire are ubiquitous unconsciousness and the conflict of intentions. They are such that desire may never quicken, may collapse prematurely, be mad or transgressive, destructive or inaccessible, all by virtue of what is lacking. The forces of nature which we live to interrupt, claim us in the end '. . . the death drive does not possess its own energy. Its energy is libido. Or, better put, the death drive is the very soul, the constitutive principle, of libidinal circulation' (Laplanche, 1976).

This essay, this attempt, or foray, involves speculation, towards the clearing of a hidden ground. Psychoanalysis belongs not to the desire that would wrest from, but to the desire that would let be. For in allowing, or welcoming, we discover what may be properly allowed, and what must be forbidden.

NOTES ON THE CONTRIBUTORS

Robin Cooper gained his MA in psychology from the University of Edinburgh in 1968, and subsequently studied with the Philadelphia Association. He was awarded his PhD degree for work which arose out of his experience of one of the Philadelphia Association houses. He has trained with the Institute of Group Analysis, is a therapist to one of the PA households, and works in private practice.

Joseph Friedman was raised in the United States, and received an honours BA from the University of Michigan. On moving to London he trained with the Philadelphia Association. He has extensive experience in running dream groups and has taught adult education classes and lectured in a variety of psychology and philosophy-related subjects. He now works in private practice and is a house therapist in one of the PA households.

Steven Gans received his BA in philosophy from Queen's College, New York, and his MA and PhD in philosophy from Pennsylvania State University. He was Assistant Professor of Philosophy at Windham College, Putney, Vermont, for six years. He then trained in Phenomenological Psychotherapy with the Philadelphia Association and is now in private practice. He is also the Director of the University of Maryland's London programme. He has lectured and written articles on phenomenology and existential philosophy and psychotherapy.

John Heaton was trained in medicine at Cambridge University and University College Hospital. He worked as an ophthalmologist and wrote *The Eye: Phenomenology and Psychology of Function and*

Disorder (Tavistock, 1968). He has been practising psychotherapy since 1961 and joined the Philadelphia Association in 1965. He is a Vice-President of the British Society for Phenomenology and a founder member of the Guild of Psychotherapists. He has published many papers on phenomenology and psychotherapy, and is currently finishing a book on Wittgenstein and psychotherapy.

Chris Oakley was educated at Trinity College, Dublin, and the Institute of Criminology at Cambridge University. He is a full member and training committee member of the Philadelphia Association. He works as a psychotherapist in private practice and as a community therapist to one of the organization's households.

Haya Oakley was born and educated in Israel where she graduated as a psychiatric social worker from the Hebrew University of Jerusalem. She is a full member and training committee member of the PA and the Guild of Psychotherapists. She works as a psychotherapist in private practice and has worked as a community therapist with the PA. She appeared on the Channel 4 series *A Change of Mind* and BBC Radio 4's *Room to Listen, Room to Talk*.

Paul Zeal graduated from Bristol and London Universities and subsequently worked with R. D. Laing from 1966 to the late 1970s. He taught for three years (1967–70) in a school for maladjusted children, before training in psychotherapy with the Philadelphia Association. He graduated in 1974. He moved to Somerset in 1985, where he is in private practice, and is a member of the Training Committee of the Philadelphia Association and of the Severnside Institute, Bristol.

BIBLIOGRAPHY

The place of publication is London unless otherwise indicated.

Alcman (fl. 620 BC) Fragment 5.2.11, in T. Bergk, *Poetae Lyrici Graeci*, 1843.

Alvarez, A. (1967) Introduction to Laurence Sterne's *A Sentimental Journey*. Harmondsworth: Penguin.

Bachelard, G. (1958) *The Poetics of Space*. Boston, MA: Beacon.

— (1969) *The Poetics of Reverie*. Boston, MA: Beacon.

Bakhtin, M. M. (1984) *Problems of Dostoevsky's Poetics*, C. Emerson, trans. Minneapolis, MN: University of Minnesota Press.

— (1986) *Speech Genres and Other Late Essays*, V.W. McGee, trans. Austin, TX: University of Texas Press.

Balint, Michael (1968) *The Basic Fault*. Tavistock.

Barnes, Mary and Berke, Joseph (1971) *Mary Barnes: Two Accounts of a Journey through Madness*. MacGibbon & Kee. Harmondsworth: Penguin, 1972.

Barthes, Roland (1982) *Camera Lucida*. Fontana.

Bateson, G. (1967) 'Challenge seminar: ecological destruction by technology'. Dialectics of Liberation Records, no. DL 23.

— (1979) *Mind and Nature*. Wildwood.

Berke, Joseph, ed. (1969) *Counter-culture: The Creation of an Alternative Society*. Peter Owen/Fire Books.

Bialik, H. N. (1947) 'P.MA', Haya Oakley, trans. *Collected Works*. Israel: DVIR.

Bion, W. R. (1970) *Attention and Interpretation*. Tavistock.

Bohm, D. (1981) *Wholeness and the Implicate Order*. Routledge & Kegan Paul.

Boss, M. (1963) *Psychoanalysis and Daseinsanalysis*. New York: Basic.

Brenkman, J. (1982) 'The Other and the One: psychoanalysis, reading, the symposium', in S. Felman, ed. *Literature and Psychoanalysis*. Baltimore, MD: Johns Hopkins University Press, pp. 396–456.

Cooper, D. (1967) *Psychiatry and Anti-psychiatry*. Tavistock.

— (1971) *The Death of the Family*. Allen Lane.

Cooper, D., ed. (1968) *The Dialectics of Liberation*. Harmondsworth: Penguin.

Coward, Rosalind and Ellis, John (1977) *Language and Materialism*. Routledge & Kegan Paul.

Crocket, R. (1979) 'The therapeutic community and social network theory', in R. D. Hinshelwood and N. Manning, eds *Therapeutic Communities*. Routledge & Kegan Paul, pp. 128–39.

Deleuze, G., and Guattari, F. (1972) *Capitalism and Schizophrenia: The Anti-Oedipus*. Athlone.

Derrida, J. (1975) 'The purveyor of truth', W. Domingo, trans. *Yale French Studies* 52: 31–113.

— (1987) *The Postcard from Socrates and Beyond*. Chicago/London: University of Chicago Press.

Dodds, E. R. (1951) *The Greeks and the Irrational*. Berkeley, CA: University of California Press.

Dover, K. J., ed. (1980) *Plato, Symposium*. Cambridge: Cambridge University Press.

Esterson, A. (1970) *The Leaves of Spring: A Study in the Dialectics of Madness*. Tavistock.

Fell, J. P. (1979) *Heidegger and Sartre*. New York: Columbia University Press.

Flower MacCannell, J. (1986) *Figuring Lacan, Criticism and the Cultural Unconscious*. Croom Helm.

Freud, S. (1896) 'Extracts from the Fliess papers', in James Strachey, ed. *The Standard Edition of the Complete Psychological Works of Sigmund Freud*, 24 vols. Hogarth, 1953–73. vol. 1, letter 52, pp. 233–9.

— (1900) *The Interpretation of Dreams*. S.E. 4 and 5.

— (1905) *Three Essays on the Theory of Sexuality*. S.E. 7, pp. 125–245.

— (1909) 'Analysis of a phobia in a five-year-old boy'. S.E. 10, pp. 3–149.

— (1910a) 'A special type of choice of object made by men'. S.E. 11, pp. 163–75.

— (1910b) 'The future prospects of psycho-analytic therapy'. S.E. 11, pp. 139–51.

— (1911) 'Psycho-analytic notes on an autobiographical account of a case of paranoia'. S.E. 12, pp. 3–82.

— (1913) 'The theme of the three caskets'. *S.E.* 12, pp. 289–301.

— (1915) 'Observations on transference-love'. *S.E.* 12, pp. 157–73.

— (1920) *Beyond the Pleasure Principle. S.E.* 18, pp. 3–64.

— (1923) *The Ego and the Id. S.E.* 19, pp. 3–66.

— (1925a) 'The resistances to psycho-analysis'. *S.E.* 19, pp. 213–24.

— (1925b) *An Autobiographical Study. S.E.* 20, pp. 3–74.

— (1926a) 'The question of lay analysis'. *S.E.* 20, pp. 179–258.

— (1926b) *Inhibitions, Symptoms and Anxiety. S.E.* 20, pp. 77–175.

— (1933) *New Introductory Lectures on Psycho-Analysis. S.E.* 22, pp. 3–182.

— (1935) *Autobiography*, James Strachey, trans. New York: Norton.

— (1936) *An Autobiographical Study.* Hogarth/The Institute of Psycho-Analysis.

— (1937) 'Analysis terminable and interminable'. *S.E.* 23, pp. 209–53.

— (1940) *An Outline of Psycho-Analysis. S.E.* 23, pp. 141–207.

— (1943) *A General Introduction to Psycho-Analysis*, Joan Riviere, trans. New York: Liveright.

— (1960) *Jokes and Their Relation to the Unconscious.* New York: Norton.

— (1985) *The Complete Letters of Sigmund Freud to Wilhelm Fliess, 1887–1904.* J. Masson, ed. and trans. Cambridge, MA: Belknap Press of Harvard University Press, p. 409.

Gadamer, Hans-Georg (1979) *Truth and Method.* Sheed & Ward.

Gallop, Jane (1982) *Feminism and Psychoanalysis: The Daughter's Seduction.* Macmillan.

Gould, T. (1963) *Platonic Love.* Routledge & Kegan Paul.

Grunberg, S. (1979) 'Thinking and the development of structure in a community group', in R. D. Hinshelwood and N. Manning, eds *Therapeutic Communities.* Routledge & Kegan Paul, pp. 249–62.

Guattari, F. (1973) 'Mary Barnes, or Oedipus in anti-psychiatry', *Nouvel Observateur*, 28 May 1973, trans. in *Molecular Revolution: Psychiatry and Politics.* Harmondsworth: Penguin, 1984.

Hahnemann, S. (1974) *Organon of Medicine*, 6th edn. New Delhi: B. Jain.

Hartmann, H. (1964) *Ego Psychology and the Problem of Adaptation*. New York: International Universities Press.

Heaton, J. M. (1982a) 'Freud and Heidegger on the interpretation of slips of the tongue', *J. Brit. Soc. Phenomenology* 13: 129–42.

— (1982b) 'A discussion of phenomenology, psychiatry and psychotherapy', in A. J. de Koning and F. A. Jenner, eds *Phenomenology and Psychiatry*. New York: Academic Press/Grune & Stratton, pp. 11–33.

Heidegger, M. (1959) *An Introduction to Metaphysics*. New Haven, CN: Yale University Press.

— (1967) *Being and Time*, J. Macquarrie and E. Robinson, trans. Oxford: Basil Blackwell.

— (1971) *Poetry, Language, Thought*, Albert Hofstadter, trans. New York: Harper & Row.

— (1975) 'Logos (Heraclitus, Fragment B50)', D. Krell and F. Capuzzi, trans., in *Early Greek Thinking*. New York: Harper & Row, pp. 61–2.

— (1977) *The Question Concerning Technology and Other Essays*. New York: Harper/Colophon Books.

Home, H. J. (1966) 'The concept of mind', *Int. J. Psycho-Anal.* 47: 43–9.

Homer, (1950) *The Iliad*, E. V. Rieu, trans. Harmondsworth: Penguin.

— (1953) *The Odyssey*, E. V. Rieu, trans. Harmondsworth: Penguin.

Howe, E. Graham (1965) *Cure or Heal?* Allen & Unwin.

Irigaray, L. (1977) 'Interview with Irigaray', *Ideology and Consciousness* 1: 57–76.

Isaacs, S. (1952) 'The nature and function of phantasy', in M. Klein, P. Heimann, S. Isaacs and J. Riviere, eds *Developments in Psycho-Analysis*. Hogarth, pp. 67–221.

Jansen, E., ed. (1980) *The Therapeutic Community*. Croom Helm.

Jay, M. (1986) 'In the empire of the gaze: Foucault and the denigration of vision in 20th-century French thought', in Couzens Hoy, ed. *Foucault: A Critical Reader*. Oxford: Blackwell.

Johnson, B. (1977) 'The frame of reference: Poe, Lacan, Derrida', *Yale French Studies* 55, 56: 457–505.

Jones, E. (1955) *The Life and Work of Sigmund Freud*, 3 vols. New York: Basic.

Khan, M. M. R. (1974) *The Privacy of the Self*. Hogarth. (International Psycho-Analytical Library 98.)

— (1978) *Trauma and Reconstruction*. Hogarth.

— (1984) *Hidden Selves*. Hogarth.

Kirk, J. D. and Millard, D. (1979) 'Personal growth in the therapeutic community', in R. D. Hinshelwood and N. Manning, eds *Therapeutic Communities*. Routledge & Kegan Paul, pp. 113–27.

Kojève, A. (1969) *Introduction to the Reading of Hegel*. New York: Basic.

Kristeva, J. (1980) 'Word, dialogue and novel', in Kristeva (1981).

— (1981) *Desire and Language*, L. S. Roudiez, ed. Oxford: Blackwell.

Kuntz, P. G. (1967) *The Concept of Order*. Seattle, WA: University of Washington Press.

Lacan, Jacques (1949) 'Le stade du miroir comme formateur de la fonction de je', *Rev. Française de Psychanalyse* 4: 449–55.

— (1966) *Écrits*. Paris: Éditions du Seuil.

— (1972) 'The seminar on "The Purloined Letter"', J. Mehlman, trans. *Yale French Studies* 48: 39–72.

— (1975) 'Encore', *Le Séminaire*, Livre XX, *Encore, 1972–3*. Paris: Éditions du Seuil.

— (1977a) *The Four Fundamental Concepts of Psycho-Analysis*, A. Sheridan, trans. Hogarth.

— (1977b) *Ornicar*. Paris: Éditions du Seuil.

— (1977c) 'The function and field of speech and language in psychoanalysis', in *Écrits: A Selection*, A. Sheridan, trans. Tavistock, pp. 30–113.

Laing, R. D. (1960) *The Divided Self*. Tavistock.

— (1961) *The Self and Others*. Harmondsworth: Penguin.

— (1967) *The Politics of Experience and the Bird of Paradise*. Harmondsworth: Penguin.

— (1971) *The Politics of the Family*. Tavistock; Harmondsworth: Penguin, 1976.

— (1976) *The Facts of Life*. Allen Lane.

— (1985) *Wisdom, Madness and Folly*. Macmillan.

Laing, R. D. and Cooper, D. (1964) *Reason and Violence*. Tavistock.

Laing, R. D. and Esterson, A. (1964) *Sanity, Madness and the Family*, vol. 1, *Families of Schizophrenics*. Tavistock.

Laing, R. D., Phillipson, H. and Lee, A. R. (1966) *Interpersonal Perception: A Theory and a Method of Research*. Tavistock.

Laplanche, J. (1976) *Life and Death in Psychoanalysis*. Baltimore, MD: Johns Hopkins University Press.

Laplanche, J. and Pontalis, J.-B. (1973) *The Language of Psycho-Analysis*. Hogarth/Institute of Psycho-Analysis.

Lemaire, A. (1970) *Jacques Lacan*, D. Macey, trans. Routledge & Kegan Paul.

Levinas, Emmanuel (1981) *Otherwise Than Being, or Beyond Essence*. The Hague: M. Nijhoff.

Lévi-Strauss, C. (1949) *Elementary Structures of Kinship*. Eyre & Spottiswoode.

— (1978) *Myth and Meaning*. Routledge & Kegan Paul.

Liddell, H. and Scott, R. (1940) *A Greek–English Lexicon*. Oxford: Oxford University Press.

Llewellyn, J. (1983) 'The "possibility" of Heidegger's death', *J. Brit. Soc. Phenomenology* 14: 127–39.

Lomas, P. (1973) *True and False Experience*. Allen Lane.

Lyotard, J.-F. (1986) 'Complexity and the sublime', in *Postmodernism: ICA Documents*. Free Association Books, 1989, pp. 19–26.

Merleau-Ponty, M. (1962) *The Phenomenology of Perception*. Routledge & Kegan Paul.

— (1969) 'Phenomenology and psychoanalysis', in A. Fisher, ed. *Essential Writings of Merleau-Ponty*. New York: Harcourt, Brace, pp. 81–7.

— (1970) 'Phenomenology and psychoanalysis: preface to Hesnard's *L'Oeuvre de Freud*', *The Human Context*, vol. 11, pp. 476–81.

Mitchell, J. and Rose, J., eds (1982) *Feminine Sexuality*. Macmillan.

Mott, Francis (1949) *The Universal Design of the Oedipus Complex*. Edenbridge, Kent: Mark Beech. Philadelphia, PA: David McKay, 1950.

— (1959) *The Nature of the Self*. London/New York: Integration.

Nietzsche, F. (1976) 'The birth of tragedy', C. Fadiman, trans., in A. Hofstadter and R. Kuhns, eds *Philosophies of Art and Beauty*. Chicago: University of Chicago Press.

Nussbaum. M. C. (1986) 'The speech of Alcibiades: a reading of the Symposium', in *The Fragility of Goodness*. Cambridge: Cambridge University Press, pp. 165–99.

Nuttall, Jeff (1968) *Bomb Culture*. MacGibbon & Kee.

Oakley, Haya (1981) 'Diagnosis and the anxiety of the therapist', in J. Agassi, ed. *Psychiatric Diagnosis*. Philadelphia, PA: Balaban, pp. 145–8.

Otto, Walter (1979) *The Homeric Gods: The Spiritual Significance of Greek Religion*. Thames & Hudson.

Pais, A. (1982) *'Subtle is the Lord': The Science and the Life of Albert Einstein*. Oxford: Clarendon.

Perceval's Narrative (1830) *A Patient's Account of his Psychosis 1830–1832*, edited with an introduction by G. Bateson. Stanford, CA: Stanford University Press, 1961.

Plato (1961) *The Collected Dialogues of Plato*, E. Hamilton and H. Cairns, eds. New York: Bollingen Foundation.

Pontalis, J.-B. (1981) *The Frontiers of Psychoanalysis*. Hogarth.

Rank, Otto (1973) *The Trauma of Birth*. New York: Harper, Torch.

Rapoport, R. N. (1960) *Community as Doctor*. Tavistock.

Richardson, W. (1983) 'Psychoanalysis and the being question', in J. H. Smith and W. Kerrigan, eds *Interpreting Lacan*. New Haven, CT: Yale University Press, pp. 139–57.

Rilke, R. M. (1960) *Poetry*, in J. B. Leishman, trans. *Selected Works*, 2 vols Hogarth, vol 2, p 225

Roazen, P. (1976) *Freud and his Followers*. Allen Lane.

Rosen, S. (1968) *Plato's Symposium*. New Haven, CT: Yale University Press.

Roustang, François (1983) *Psychoanalysis Never Lets Go*. Baltimore, MD: Johns Hopkins University Press.

Rowbotham, Sheila (1973) *Woman's Consciousness, Man's World*. Harmondsworth: Pelican.

Rycroft, C. (1966) *Psychoanalysis Observed*. Constable.

Saint-Exupéry, A. de (1949) *Le Petit Prince*. Paris: Librairie Gallimard.

Schafer, Roy (1983) *The Analytic Attitude*. Hogarth.

Schilder, P. (1950) *The Image and Appearance of the Human Body*. New York: International Universities Press.

Searles, Harold F. (1974) *Countertransference and Related Subjects*. New York: International Universities Press.

Sechehaye, Margaret (1951) *Symbolic Realization: A New Method of Psychotherapy Applied in a Case of Schizophrenia.* New York: International Universities Press.

Sedgwick, Peter (1982) *Psycho Politics.* Pluto.

Seguin, A. (1962) 'Love and psychotherapeutic Eros', *Acta Psychotherapeutica et Psychosomatica* X.

Sendak, Maurice (1971) *In the Night Kitchen.* Puffin.

Sigal, Clancy (1976) *Zone of the Interior.* New York: Thomas Y. Crowell/Toronto: Fitzhenry & Whiteside.

Simpson, D. P. (1959) *Cassell's New Latin Dictionary.* Cassell.

Stokes, M. C. (1986) *Plato's Socratic Conversations.* Athlone.

Turkle, S. (1979) *Psychoanalytic Politics.* Burnett.

Vcynas, Vincent (1969) *Earth and Gods.* The Hague: M. Nijhoff.

Winnicott, D. W. (1947) 'Hate in the counter-transference', in Winnicott (1975), pp. 194–203.

— (1958) 'The capacity to be alone', in Winnicott (1965), pp. 29–36.

— (1960) 'The theory of the parent–infant relationship', in Winnicott (1965), pp. 37–55.

— (1965) *The Maturational Processes and the Facilitating Environment.* Hogarth.

— (1971) *Playing and Reality.* Tavistock; Harmondsworth: Penguin, 1974.

— (1975) *Through Paediatrics to Psycho-Analysis.* Hogarth/Institute of Psycho-Analysis.

Zarchi, Nurit (1976) *The Tiger under the Bed*, Haya Oakley, trans. Israel: Massada LTD.

INDEX

This first edition of
Thresholds between Philosophy and Psychoanalysis:
Papers from the Philadelphia Association
was finished in June 1989.

It was set in 10/13 Trump Mediaeval Roman
on a Linotron 202
printed on a Miller TP41
on to 80g/m$_2$ vol.18 bookwove

The book was commissioned by Robert M. Young,
edited by Ann Scott,
copy-edited by Peter Phillips,
designed by Wendy Millichap
and produced by Martin Klopstock and Selina O'Grady
for Free Association Books.